The Divine Progression of Grace is no ... grace based upon one's cultural persu ... It is indeed an informative and inspiring expository teaching on grace from Scripture supported by contextual elaboration and practical application.

This book is a refreshing departure from what is too often presented about grace—from ideas that devalue or even discredit other important Biblical teachings. Bob Santos helps us to understand grace from many different perspectives while upholding the "whole counsel of God."

—Gary E. Ham
President
The Eleventh Hour Christian Initiatives
Rochester, New York

The Divine Progression of Grace tackles the facets of grace that are often ignored or marginalized by many believers. Bob does a great job of simplifying the subject in a way that's approachable for someone at any point in his or her walk with Jesus.

—Mel Masengale
Lead Pastor
Summit Church
Indiana, PA

The Divine Progression of Grace reveals the richness of God's provision for His children to walk in His ways and touch the world with His heart. Every reader who approaches with an open heart will find a treasure trove that can transform their service to God, be it current or future, of many or few. My ministry as a missionary and homeschool mom has been forever changed by a new understanding of God's grace for my own life, as well as for my calling.

—Rose Salazar
Missionary to Mexico

God says, "My people are destroyed from lack of knowledge" (Hosea 4:6). In his book, *The Divine Progression of Grace*, Bob Santos gives us not only intellectual knowledge but revelation knowledge about the multifaceted gem called grace. This is one tool (book) you need to keep handy in your tool belt!

—Elaine Rice
Keystone Ministries
Dearing, Georgia

Bob Santos writes in a way that forces you to really think about issues and principles. He does not settle for pat answers but delves deeply into the topic of grace to discover God's fuller meaning of this important truth.

—Joe Jansen
Director of U.S. Ministries
Elim Fellowship
Lima, NY

THE
DIVINE
PROGRESSION
OF
GRACE

THE DIVINE PROGRESSION OF GRACE

BLAZING A TRAIL TO FRUITFUL LIVING

BOB SANTOS

SEARCH FOR ME MINISTRIES, INC.
INDIANA, PA

The Divine Progression of Grace: Blazing a Trail to Fruitful Living
By Bob Santos

Cover Design: Sean McGaughran
Cover Photo: Chris Zeigler
Interior Design: Sean McGaughran

Published by SfMe Media
A Division of Search for Me Ministries, Inc.
865 School Street
Indiana, PA 15701
www.sfme.org

Printed in the United States of America

Library of Congress Control Number: 2014918240

ISBN: 978-1-937956-07-3
ePub ISBN: 978-1-937956-08-0
Mobi ISBN: 978-1-937956-09-7

*To my wonderful wife Debi who has faithfully
and sacrificially supported my ministry "habit"
all these years.*

CONTENTS

PREFACE

Few things are more soul-stealing than trying really hard to do the right thing and still failing miserably. God knows that I've had more than my share of frustration seeking to live out the teachings of the New Testament. Perhaps you can relate.

I was raised with good morals, but even from an early age I found myself bent toward wrongdoing. No, Roger Brown didn't trip over his own clumsy feet in first grade as he walked toward the pencil sharpener. I, Bob Santos, tripped him. Now the entire world knows. And though I feel a tad better about finally bringing my first-grade moral failure into the light, I could fill this entire book with the sins that followed—something that would not be profitable for any of us.

It didn't help that through my high school years I made every possible effort to avoid attending church services. In addition to the mysterious illness that would overtake my body on Sunday mornings, I was put off by the vast amount of hypocrisy I saw in the lives of so many churchgoers. My secular life seemed to me no less moral than their religious ones. I finally came to admit that even though religious hypocrisy was a significant problem, the real issue was with my own rebellious heart. I was not willing to bow to anyone, including the God of the Universe, if He existed.

Everything changed during my sophomore year in college when friends challenged me with the gospel. Over time, I came to not only believe in the deity of Christ, but to fully embrace Christianity. Radically opposed to my old, self-centered lifestyle, my newfound faith promised to propel me into a brand new existence—or so I thought.

Jumping in with both feet, I committed myself to prayer, Bible reading, and Christian meetings of all sorts. Then, only a short time after graduating from college, I became a twenty-five-year-old "elder" in our church. Wishing to be the "Ultimate Christian," I joined nearly every committee possible and undertook any ministry that seemed doable. And so it was that my long list of church-related activities served as my spiritual badge of honor. On the surface, everything looked great. At the core of my being, however, I was dying.

After several years of struggle, I finally came to the honest realization that Christianity wasn't working for me. I can't begin to express how difficult—and painful—this process was. The problem, I reasoned, was either with the Christian faith and its conception of God, or with me. In the end, I came to the wise conclusion that God was doing just fine. This too, was particularly painful because it meant that not only was I a failure in the grand scheme of the Universe, I was also a failure in Christ. What remains in life for the person who has failed to live out the most meaningful lifestyle ever known to the human race?

Many of the leaders around me seemed to "have it all together" so I began to look to them for answers. In addition, I asked questions and read books. Then I asked more questions. No one seemed to offer what I needed. I'm sure that the answers were out there somewhere in our voluminous body of Christian teachings, but I couldn't find them. Eventually, I began to do what I should have done in the first place; I cried out to God for help. I wasn't just asking for help to do better or to feel better. I wanted to understand why my day-to-day existence bore only a faint resemblance to the Christianity I read about in the Bible. Slowly and mysteriously, the Holy Spirit began to open my eyes to areas of my life that were out of alignment with God's design.

Just as our bodies are nourished and grow with the right diet of healthy foods, so our spiritual lives will flourish when rightly aligned with God's intended design. My problem was that few Christian leaders seemed to be teaching about the areas that were negatively impacting my spiritual well-being. I wasn't looking for motivational speeches, nor did I want to be pressured with lists of things that a Christian man should be doing. I needed to understand how to personally experience a new life in Christ. Looking back, I now realize that bits and pieces of the puzzle were all around me. I just wasn't able to see how those pieces fit together.

As God began to teach me about His ways—and the error of mine—I made painstaking adjustments. Do you know what happened? My life began to change! I wish I could say that the transformation came without struggle, but that was rarely the case. More often than not, change took time and effort. Even so, many of the positive changes in my life were both real and lasting.

Soon, I found myself working with college students—and teaching them much of what I believed God had taught me. Once again, transformation resulted. Through the course of our sixteen-plus years of college ministry, my wife Debi and I saw real and lasting spiritual growth in the lives of many young people whom we had the honor of serving. Biblical Christianity, I discovered, really does work!

That being said, I don't profess to have cornered the market on God's truth. In seeking my heavenly Father for wisdom through my personal struggles, I have been privileged to draw upon a multitude of Christian leaders, scholars, and mystics who have gone before us. Without their valiant efforts to build on, my understanding of the Christian faith would be dead in the water. Also, I freely admit that there are aspects of human and divine behavior that are still a little foggy to me. Some of these are highlighted in various places throughout the book. All in all, though, I believe that this book will provide more answers for the person seeking to live out the Christian faith than the questions it provokes.

From the title of this book—*The Divine Progression of Grace*–it is clear that the content centers on grace. However, the tagline—*Blazing a Trail to Fruitful Living*—may seem a little odd to you. What, you might wonder, does God's grace have to do with blazing a trail? Actually, a lot! I fear that too often we adopt an incomplete view of grace that leads to passivity on our part. Certainly, learning to rest in grace is a central component of the Christian life, but those who truly abide in God's grace cannot help but live out an active faith.

Grace, by its very nature, creates radical changes in our own lives and in the lives of those we touch with God's love. The process by which it does this always begins with an inward transformation followed by a change in outward actions. Grace does a progressive work in our hearts as we journey from the point where God unconditionally accepts us as we are, to the exciting place He is trying to take us—a fully fruitful life. *Through the progressive work of grace, we are accepted, transformed, and empowered to become agents of change for God's eternal kingdom.*

And so I present to you *The Divine Progression of Grace*. Within the pages of this book, you will find the body of teaching that has captured my attention for the past twenty years. Debi and I have gone to considerable lengths to produce this book to help others break free from an ineffective existence and move toward a more fully fruitful lifestyle. As my spiritual journey connects to yours for a season, I sincerely hope and pray that the joys and struggles of my personal learning adventure somehow bless you and those you love.

Bob Santos

This book is the collective effort of many people—only a few of whom I can mention. Our reviewers—Gary Ham, Mel Masengale, Elaine Rice, and Ted Yohe—all provided valuable feedback. Our volunteer editors—Deb Croyle, Jeff Ference, Jason Hutchins, Lynda Logue, Rose Salazar, and Debi Santos—also played vital roles as they patiently helped me polish the content. Sean McGaughran did a great job with the cover, incorporating a photo by Chris Zeigler and help from David Coffey and Steve Margita. Finally, excellent editing input from Mary Campagna Findley and Sean McGaughran helped tie everything together.

CHAPTER ONE
OUR BUILDERS HAVE ERRED

If the foundations are destroyed, what can the righteous do?
Psalms 11:3

Grace is the empowering Presence of God enabling you to be who He created you to be, and to do what He has called you to do.
—James Ryle

Is there a biblical topic surrounded by more confusion than grace? I don't think so—and the problem is not a new one. While I celebrate the fact that much of the church has come to realize the extreme importance of grace, I can't help but conclude that our collective understanding of grace continues to miss the mark.

Almost twenty-five years ago I sat in a church service—on one of our sticky pews coated with cheap varnish—listening to a young pastor speak about grace. By that time, I had been a Christian for about ten years so I was quite familiar with the topic. "There is nothing you can do that will please God!" the young man boldly proclaimed. I don't recall the rest of his message, but that one statement brought me to attention—and not in a good way. It felt wrong, but I couldn't explain why. Not long after, mostly due to some disconcerting behavior, that pastor was no longer serving in ministry. He was also out of his marriage. And though he was still very much a father, his children would no longer wake up in a home where Mom and Dad were together. Crash and burn!

Can I prove that a misunderstanding of grace was the sole cause of that young man's spiritual train wreck? No. But we had enough interaction for me to know that it was a key contributing factor. Now, many years later, I can recall other messages about grace which were followed by significant spiritual breakdowns of the messengers.

No one is ever completely free from the potential for a spiritual crash, but repeated patterns of failure reveal an inherent flaw in our beliefs. It's not enough for us to simply profess Christ, or even to base our lives on the Scriptures. We must develop a working understanding of grace that aligns us with God's design, enables us to continually connect with His love, and empowers us to do all that He calls us to do.

MY DIY DRIVEWAY PROJECT

I am a *DIYer—Do It Yourselfer*. If I think I can tackle a home improvement project by myself, I probably will. It's not because I'm confident, but because I am frugal (some might say that I'm cheap). Like any brave DIYer, every once in a while I get in over my head. That was the case when I decided to replace our crumbling asphalt driveway with concrete. The driveway was difficult enough, but we also had to replace the retaining walls on either side. After some consideration, Debi and I decided to use decorative concrete blocks. A standard, full-sized block is 16" wide at the face, 6" high, and 12" deep, weighing over 80 lbs. My project required about 200 blocks; including caps and corners, the total weight was almost 20,000 lbs. This was in addition to the tons of dirt and gravel we had to move, much of it by hand.

Through this project, I came to better understand that properly preparing a base is essential to building. If the foundation isn't right, all of the other hard work will fall short of its desired end. A fantastic-looking wall loses its magnificence when the blocks are caving in toward one another.

Laying the base involved digging at least six inches below the intended bottom row of blocks. I added a layer of 2B gravel, packed that gravel tight, threw down some limestone chips, and packed those chips as well. After that, I laid my bottom row of blocks on each side. But I wasn't finished yet. I had to make sure that each block was at the exact height and that it was level in all directions. This was no easy task. Each one had to be put in place, checked for level, and then lifted back out so that the appropriate adjustments could be made. In some cases, it took only two or three tries to get it right. At other times, I needed six or seven attempts—a tedious and tiring process with 80 lb. blocks. With my back aching, my arms sore, and sweat dripping everywhere, the temptation to cut corners was almost overwhelming.

My project was especially challenging because I had to build around our front porch. That meant a lot of cutting with an obnoxious-sounding concrete saw. As soon as the spinning metal blade touched a block, a thick cloud of cement dust and gasoline exhaust enveloped me. I quickly took on a ghostly white, zombie-like appearance. Worse still, I had to build steps from the driveway to our existing sidewalk. More cutting—and lots of measuring.

I'm pretty sure the entire neighborhood wanted that project quickly put to rest, but as I laid the final blocks for the side of my new steps, I suddenly realized a critical error. One part of the wall was 3/8" too high. I know that 3/8" sounds like a trivial mistake when talking about a wall that is 32 ft. long and several courses high, but that little bit of height could not have been in a worse location—at the top of the steps where the wall meets our sidewalk. Can you say, "tripping hazard"? My heart sank to my stomach as I stood staring at my folly. All I could picture was my mother-in-law falling onto a corner block and sprawling face down on our cement driveway. In spite of the work involved, I removed that section of the wall, lowered the base, and then painstakingly replaced each block.

Looking back, I'm glad I took the time to build those walls right. Not only do they look good, I can be at peace knowing I made every available effort to ensure the safety of those who use our steps. In the short term, building the right way often feels like a waste of time, money, and energy, but time always reveals the true substance of our work.

A SURE FOUNDATION

I share my DIY story not to tell you about my driveway project, but to provide necessary context for this book. Christians—especially Christian leaders—are builders. Building human lives can be both exciting and frightening. Often we get it right, but sometimes we don't. If a ministry, family, or human life is not "constructed" wisely and skillfully, the final price paid will be steep. The importance of laying solid spiritual foundations cannot be overstated!

> *According to the grace of God which was given to me, like a wise master builder I laid a foundation, and another is building on it. But each man must be careful how he builds on it. For no man can lay a foundation other than the one which is laid, which is Jesus Christ. 1 Corinthians 3:10-11*

If we were to ask one hundred pastors if they were building their churches on the foundation of Christ, few—if any—would say they weren't. Reality disagrees. Much of the Western church is in disarray.[1] Many young people feel alienated by traditional Christianity. Confusion about sexuality abounds. Leadership scandals surface on a routine basis. Regardless of how well we think we've been building, many of our spiritual walls are collapsing around us. Clearly, we need to make adjustments.

The process of laying a firm foundation *begins* with developing an accurate understanding of biblical truth. This, my friends, is where I believe that our builders have erred. To the casual observer, the error may seem minimal, but to the trained eye, to a wise master builder like the apostle Paul, the blunder is massive. We need only watch large numbers of people stumbling spiritually to recognize that something is desperately wrong. I contend that an inaccurate—or incomplete—understanding of grace is the primary reason that we are entangled in sin and passive in the pews.

Problematically, the solidity of a young Christian's spiritual foundation is often measured by the ability to regurgitate a few simplified doctrines while using the appropriate "Christianese" lingo. In other words, *knowledge* is the foundation. This perspective fails to realize that Christ's definition of a firm foundation was quite different:

> *"Therefore everyone who hears these words of Mine and **acts** on them, may be compared to a wise man who built his house on the rock." Matthew 7:24 (emphasis added)*

---

1. Three excellent sources for objective information about the state of the U.S. church are https://www.barna.org/; http://www.lifewayresearch.com/; and http://www.pewforum.org.

We dare not miss a primary point of this passage: even though a firm foundation begins with accurate knowledge and understanding, they must be followed by *active obedience* leading to godly character. Christian growth cannot be equated with passively absorbing knowledge. Growth is active. Grace is active. The Christian life is active. Even finding spiritual rest in Christ takes effort of some sort; letting go of our self-sufficiency does not come easily.

LIVING STONES

The apostle Peter wrote of the church using the imagery of "living stones" being built into a spiritual house for the glory of God—a temple in which Jesus Christ is the cornerstone (1 Peter 2:4-8). A temple made out of people! Who besides God would ever consider such an idea? Have you ever dealt with people?

The difficulty involved with constructing a temple made with living stones appears to be insurmountable. We're dealing with human emotions, human perspectives, and human wills. It's like trying to herd cats. An inevitable lesson in futility. Only one thing can make such an ambitious project possible—love. Love is the motivation that causes people to build up rather than tear down. And love is the only "glue" that could ever hold these living stones together (Colossians 3:14). Real love requires both strength and action, not simply a passive nod of approval. All too often, genuine Christian love is in short supply.

"But," you may ask, "what does the measure of our love have to do with God's grace?" Love is the *fruit* of grace's progressive work in our lives. Those who begin with grace should end with love. What farmer would be content to plant seeds that never sprout? Or to grow plants that never bear fruit? As the Master Gardener, God plants seeds of grace in our lives with a purpose that goes beyond delivering us from eternal damnation. This is not to suggest that we could ever move beyond the need for grace, but that God's grace transforms the state of the human heart. If we don't have grace right, we won't have love right, and if we don't have love right, the church will never stand against the onslaught of wickedness that seems to come from every direction. A lack of love may be staring us in the face—or stabbing us in the back—but a misunderstanding of grace lurking beneath the surface is fueling the fires of conflict. Do you see a lack of love in our Christian expression? The roots can be traced to an incomplete understanding of grace.

THE GREAT ERROR OF OUR AGE

If we don't get grace right, Christianity simply will not work. If the foundation is not properly prepared, we will have serious problems with our spiritual walls—regardless of architecture, craftsmanship, or size. A massive, beautiful building has little value if its walls are uneven and unstable. The great error of our age is that we have expended huge amounts of time, money, and effort to build beautiful Christian edifices while failing to lay strong foundations—ones that link obedience and its fruit to a grace-filled life.

> *We give thanks to God, the Father of our Lord Jesus Christ, praying always for you, since we heard of your faith in Christ Jesus and the love which you have for all the saints; because of the hope laid up for you in heaven, of which you previously heard in the word of truth, the gospel which has come to you, just as in all the world also it is constantly bearing fruit and increasing, even as it has been doing in you also since the day you heard of it and **understood the grace of God in truth** . . . Colossians 1:3-6 (emphasis added)*

Do you see it? The gospel—the eternal message of God's grace—produces spiritual fruit by transforming human lives! If we aren't seeing genuine change, we aren't grasping a full understanding of grace. It's as simple as that. These types of things are virtually impossible to quantify, but more than twenty years of practical ministry experience have confirmed my observations.

While serving as a campus minister, I saw dynamic spiritual growth in the lives of young people who grasped the message of grace, but that is by no means the sum-total of my experience. Since leaving college ministry, I've taught the concepts of *The Divine Progression of Grace* to people of all ages. What a joy it has been to see middle-aged people (who attended church for much of their lives) come to life as a more comprehensive awareness of grace began to take root. The positive changes are always exciting, but I also grieve over the fact that most—if not all—of their church-going lives have been mired in spiritual mediocrity. What farmer would be content with a field full of plants that bear no fruit—or even worse—bad fruit?

Grace, according to many Christians, is defined as "God's unmerited favor." This is absolutely true and I would never argue otherwise. How awesome it is when the light dawns in our hearts, revealing the profound truth that we don't have to earn God's approval! What burdens lift from our shoulders! The inexplicable sense of freedom that flows from the reality of God's unmerited favor will mark a person for life. And yet, as amazing and life-changing as this favor may be, I would point out that unmerited favor is only *one* dimension of grace. This single error, I believe, has led to a distorted view of grace. From a biblical perspective, the Christian life is never portrayed as simply accepting what God has done for us and leaving it at that.

There have always been—and continue to be—Christian leaders who teach a more complete understanding of grace. For some reason, however, our *collective* understanding of grace remains one-dimensional. The sad result is what seems to be an exceedingly large number of passive, self-centered people who profess the name of Christ, but who lack the devotion and vitality of true Christian living. Although we can do nothing to earn God's favor, the effect that grace has on our lives is never passive. The complete gospel moves men, women, and children beyond mere acceptance and on to spiritually fruitful lives—a topic that we will explore in much greater detail.

HOW DID WE GET HERE?

I can't blame our limited definition of grace on Christian scholars as a whole. When I dig deeper into my biblical resources, I find that the necessary information is available. Tragically, a fuller knowledge of grace unearthed through untold hours of prayer, study, and research has failed to find a home in the hearts and minds of ordinary Christians.

While I won't point a finger at any particular individual, I am compelled to say that the primary fault lies with many of our "builders"— those influential Christian leaders who have helped to define the nature of the gospel in the eyes of the general public. In Christian circles, we have a tendency to trust leaders who build "successful" ministries. If a dynamic evangelist draws massive crowds and has large numbers of people respond to altar calls, we somehow assume that his or her word is gospel. This mentality is fueled by a celebrity mindset. The practices and teachings of a few gifted Christian leaders soon become the standard of truth and practice for the people of God. This can result in a spiritual boom when those leaders get it right, but a painful bust when they miss the mark.

In their efforts to make grace understandable—and accessible—to the average person, key Christian leaders over the past hundred years or so have limited grace to mean unmerited favor and unmerited favor alone. This mindset has become so ingrained that even questioning our contemporary definition of grace can be considered an act of legalistic heresy worthy of social media stoning.

To make matters worse, those who question the common teachings of the day are often branded as "troublemakers" who are then "encouraged" to shut their mouths. The phrase, "Don't ask questions, just believe it," has driven far too many sincere people from Christ. If God's word is true—and I stand convinced that it is—digging deeper is never a bad idea. I can't say that all of the questions I've brought to God have been answered, but many of them have, and my faith has only grown as a result.

I am grateful for all who have given their lives in service to Christ, and I never want to swing a hammer of condemnation at the head of a person whom Heaven honors. In many ways, their examples should be followed. Still, those seeking to help grow Christ's church must examine the *doctrines*, *practices*, and *actions* that influence our effectiveness. Shouldn't we be able to engage in thoughtful dialogue about these issues without falling into the trap of character assassination?

Not one of us has a monopoly on God's truth. Even good people can have bad doctrine and devoted ministers of the gospel can employ unhealthy practices. Anointed success in ministry is no guarantee that a person has a direct hotline to Heaven. God doesn't move in our midst because of our perfect doctrines, lifestyles, or ministry practices; God moves on our behalf because He is faithful to bless us and answer our prayers of faith.

Am I overstating the problem? Perhaps. But with all that God has provided for us through the sacrificial death and resurrection of Jesus Christ, we can do much better than we are doing. With all that is happening in our world, we *must* do better. If we are to truly understand God's ways, we need to move beyond feelings, personalities, and human loyalties to pursue truth objectively. In the process, the Holy Spirit will flood our hearts with the resplendent light of His glory.

Grace has always been a controversial issue, but a significant shift has taken place during the past century. Consider the following quote from Burton Scott Easton in the 1930 edition of the *International Standard Bible Encyclopedia*:

> Most of the discussions of the Biblical doctrine of grace have been faulty in narrowing the meaning of "grace" to some special sense, and then endeavoring to force this special sense on all the Biblical passages . . . Protestant extremists . . . have argued that grace cannot mean anything except favor as an attitude, with results that are . . . disastrous from the exegetical standpoint.[2]

Wow! What was once considered by some to be an *extremist* view in 1930 now represents a *common* perspective for evangelical Christians. Is it possible that Easton and the older scholars had it wrong? Not if you understand the core of his argument. Our definition of grace as unmerited favor simply doesn't fit everywhere the word grace is found in the New Testament. Like the extra 3/8" of height on my steps, the bad fit couldn't come at a worse place.

PREACHING GRACE; PRACTICING LAW

In light of all the scholarly resources available to the Western church, it's difficult to fathom how we have collectively failed to understand a concept so central to the Christian faith. We can at least take heart that the problem is not a new one. God's grace is unnatural and counter-intuitive, running against the grain of our inborn human ways. These natural tendencies have clouded the hearts and minds of many who have heard—and even studied—the gospel ever since its inception.

---

2. Burton Scott Easton, *The International Standard Bible Encyclopedia*, Vol. 2 (Chicago: Howard Severance Co., 1930), 1292.

Not long after its birth, the early church began to wrestle with legalism—a struggle that continues to this day. The Reformation, initiated by Martin Luther, brought with it a desperately needed revelation of grace. Scholars, pastors, and lay people have studied—and heavily relied upon—God's grace since that time. Still—perhaps because of the multifaceted nature of grace—the church at large has been unable to lay hold of this essential doctrine. Painful errors have been all too common as various camps have navigated either toward *legalism*[3] on one end of the spectrum, or *lawlessness*[4] on the other.

Rarely a week goes by when I don't hear of a person whose spiritual and emotional well-being has been damaged through involvement with a legalistic church. You might be inclined to think that I am referring to churches with names like The Fellowship of Never-Ending Rules, but I am not. Some of the saddest stories have come from churches with the word *grace* integral to the name.

An incomplete definition of grace will lead a church to practice law in spite of the fact that they consistently preach a grace message. Why? We humans may be foolish, but we aren't stupid. No one who believes in God wants to go to Hell. Accordingly, people will receive the message of "just ask Jesus into your heart" so that they can obtain their free "eternal fire insurance policies." Ultimately, their behaviors remain unchanged as they move on with self-centered lives, happy to rest on the laurels of what they believe Christ has done for them.

Professing Christians who are not being transformed by God's grace will create all sorts of problems. Church leaders, then, must learn the creative art of *behavior modification*. This involves making endless lists of written and unwritten rules, or at the very least, continually crafting persuasive messages in an attempt to get people to give money, serve in the children's ministry, or stop saying certain undesirable words during church softball games.

Should biblically-based preaching move people to action? Absolutely! But it shouldn't be driven by legalism or manipulation.

---

3. *The American Heritage College Dictionary* (Fourth Ed.) defines *legalism* as: "strict, literal adherence to the law or to a particular code, as of religion or morality.
4. According to 1 John 3:4, *lawlessness* is synonymous with *sinful living*.

True love thrives in an atmosphere of *freedom*, whereas, legalism is all about *control*. Legalism works from the *outside in*. Grace—the antithesis of legalism—works from the *inside out*. Through my years of ministry, I have learned that young Christians who fully grasp the depths of God's multidimensional grace will need wisdom, guidance, and encouragement from Christian leaders, but they won't need to be continually prodded to action.

The Christian gospel is not—and never has been—simply a message of behavior modification. No, it is one of inner transformation in which hard, selfish hearts are exchanged for ones filled with life and love. Grace doesn't make bad people better citizens; it brings the spiritually dead to life. When a human heart is truly transformed, outward actions cannot help but follow. If we are not seeing positive changes in attitude and behavior, something is lacking in our understanding of grace.

Just as that 3/8" really mattered at the base of my wall, so, too, our comprehension of grace is critical in the construction of God's glorious church. If we don't have grace right, we don't have love right. And if we don't have love right, the church will crumble even as we build. Thus, I think it would be wise for us to revisit our building process (1 Corinthians 3:10-11). Specifically, this means a closer look at the meaning of grace throughout the context of the entire New Testament. We'll take a broader look at grace in the next chapter, but before going there please consider the exercise below.

BLAZING A TRAIL TO FRUITFUL LIVING

Take a highlighter and a Bible that doesn't have many personal markings or notes. Then, utilizing an exhaustive concordance (they can be found online), identify each time the Greek word for grace—*charis*—is used in the New Testament. As you read each passage, highlight the word that is translated from the original Greek *charis*.

When this task is complete, take some time to leaf through the entire New Testament while reading each passage that contains a highlighted word. Go through it a second and, possibly, a third time. This activity may take you a few hours, but it will help you blaze a trail to a fuller understanding of grace.

CHAPTER TWO
GRACE IS MORE

But by the grace of God I am what I am, and His grace toward me did not prove vain.

1 Corinthians 15:10a

God has more grace in Him than we have sin in us.

—Source Unknown

I was eleven or twelve years old when I laid eyes on Specimen #217868 in the Smithsonian National Museum of Natural History. Most people would be more familiar with its common name—the Hope Diamond. I don't remember much from that visit to the Smithsonian, but the Hope Diamond's beauty and brilliance made a lasting impression. Associated Press reporter Ron Edmonds gave the following description of his experience with the exquisite and mysterious gem:

> You cradle the 45.5-carat stone—about the size of a walnut and heavier than its translucence makes it appear—turning it from side to side as the light flashes from its facets, knowing it's the hardest natural material yet fearful of dropping it.[5]

I don't imagine that the Hope Diamond would have the same memorable effect if it were flat. A diamond's beauty and value are the products of its multifaceted nature. And so it is with grace.

THE MULTIFACETED NATURE OF GRACE

I think it's safe to say that the apostle Peter knew something about grace. He lived and walked with Jesus—the Son of Man who was full of grace

5. http://usatoday30.usatoday.com/news/science/2003-10-03-hope-diamond_x.htm

and truth (John 1:14)—for over three years. Rather than achieving the greatness that he longed for, Peter sank to painful depths by denying the Lord to whom he had promised uncompromising allegiance. Still, in spite of his self-induced brokenness, God's unconditional love enveloped Peter's heart and restored his soul. Simon Peter knew and experienced God's unmerited favor like few others, and yet he referred to grace as something greater still:

> As each one has received a special gift, employ it in serving one another as good stewards of the manifold grace of God. 1 Peter 4:10

Sometimes, when a passage really strikes me, I like to research the original word meanings and then make my own "BOBS" paraphrase of the passage. Through only thirty years of effort, I have already completed six or seven verses of the BOBS version of the Bible! One of the verses is 1 Peter 4:10:

> As each one has received a grace-gift, use it in serving one another as responsible and effective managers of the multifaceted grace of God, which manifests itself in many different ways. (BOBS)

Being so much broader than we realize, God's grace is *multifaceted*, manifesting itself in multiple ways in and through the life of a Christian. Does grace extend unmerited favor? Yes! Does grace cover, cleanse, and forgive? Absolutely! But God's amazing grace does even more. Grace empowers and grace transforms. Like a dazzling diamond, grace is adorned with multiple, interrelated facets—each with its own unique expression. Sadly, we've minimized the multifaceted grace of God into only one dimension—unmerited favor. This facet of grace is profoundly beautiful and sparkles brilliantly, but it presents an incomplete and therefore, flawed picture.

TEN DIMENSIONS OF GRACE

The word we translate as "grace" is the Greek word *charis*, which has multiple meanings, and accordingly, is translated by Bible scholars in multiple ways. I've titled the list below, *Ten Dimensions of Grace*. My compilation isn't intended to be exhaustive; these are simply the ten facets of grace that stood out to me as I followed the trail of *charis* through the New Testament.

As you review the *Ten Dimensions of Grace*, please note that the passages quoted are from the New American Standard (NASB) version of the Bible—a fairly literal translation—with the English translation of *charis* in boldfaced type. Other versions of the Bible will word some of these passages a little differently, but they should still communicate the same general thoughts.

1. **Grace can be an expression of gratitude, thanksgiving, or praise (Luke 17:9; Colossians 3:16; Hebrews 12:28-29).**

   *Therefore, since we receive a kingdom which cannot be shaken, let us show **gratitude**, by which we may offer to God an acceptable service with reverence and awe; for our God is a consuming fire. Hebrews 12:28-29*

2. **Grace can be favor that may or may not be earned (Luke 2:52; Ephesians 2:8-9).**

   *And Jesus kept increasing in wisdom and stature, and in **favor** with God and men. Luke 2:52*

   *For by **grace** you have been saved through faith; and that not of yourselves, it is the gift of God; not as a result of works, so that no one may boast. Ephesians 2:8-9*

3. **Grace can be a favor done for someone (Acts 24:27, 25:3, 9).**

   *But after two years had passed, Felix was succeeded by Porcius Festus, and wishing to do the Jews **a favor**, Felix left Paul imprisoned. Acts 24:27*

4. **Grace can be a blessing given, or an act of giving to others (1 Corinthians 16:3; 2 Corinthians 1:15, 8:6-7).**

   *So we urged Titus that as he had previously made a beginning, so he would also complete in you this **gracious work** as well. But just as you abound in everything, in faith and utterance and knowledge and in all earnestness and in the love we inspired in you, see that you abound in this **gracious work** also. 2 Corinthians 8:6-7*

5. **Grace involves the manner in which we treat others and speak about them (Ephesians 4:29; Colossians 4:6).**

    *Let your speech always be with **grace**, as though seasoned with salt, so that you will know how you should respond to each person. Colossians 4:6*

6. **Grace enables us to believe (Acts 18:27; Romans 11:5-6).**

    *And when he wanted to go across to Achaia, the brethren encouraged him and wrote to the disciples to welcome him; and when he had arrived, he greatly helped those who had believed through **grace**... Acts 18:27*

7. **Grace equips and empowers us with the ability to serve others more effectively (Romans 12:6a; 1 Corinthians 3:10).**

    *Since we have gifts that differ according to the **grace** given to us, each of us is to exercise them accordingly . . . Romans 12:6a*

8. **Grace strengthens and builds us up (Acts 20:32; 1 Corinthians 15:10; 2 Timothy 2:1; Hebrews 4:16).**

    *But by the **grace** of God I am what I am, and His **grace** toward me did not prove vain; but I labored even more than all of them, yet not I, but the **grace** of God with me. 1 Corinthians 15:10*

9. **Grace teaches us not to sin (Titus 2:11-14).**

    *For the **grace** of God has appeared, bringing salvation to all men, instructing us to deny ungodliness and worldly desires and to live sensibly, righteously and godly in the present age, looking for the blessed hope and the appearing of the glory of our great God and Savior, Christ Jesus, who gave Himself for us to redeem us from every lawless deed, and to purify for Himself a people for His own possession, zealous for good deeds. Titus 2:11-14*

10. **Grace transforms our hearts to reign over sin and bear spiritual fruit (Romans 5:17, 20-21; Colossians 1:3-6; 1 Peter 5:12).**

*For if by the transgression of the one, death reigned through the one, much more those who receive the abundance of **grace** and of the gift of righteousness will reign in life through the One, Jesus Christ. Romans 5:17*

*We give thanks to God, the Father of our Lord Jesus Christ, praying always for you, since we heard of your faith in Christ Jesus and the love which you have for all the saints; because of the hope laid up for you in heaven, of which you previously heard in the word of truth, the gospel which has come to you, just as in all the world also it is constantly bearing fruit and increasing, even as it has been doing in you also since the day you heard of it and understood the **grace** of God in truth . . . Colossians 1:3-6*

Do you see all that grace is? We can only begin to imagine the vast potential of a grace-filled life. God's grace is so multifaceted and so profoundly deep that we cannot contain it to one simple definition. We do, however, find a common theme:

> . . . a single conception is actually present in almost every case where "grace" is found—the conception that all a Christian has or is, is centered exclusively in God and Christ, and depends utterly on God through Christ. The kingdom of heaven is reserved for those who become as little children, for those who look to their Father in loving confidence for every benefit, whether it be for the pardon so freely given, or for the strength that comes from Him who works in them both to will and to do.[6]

I wholeheartedly agree with Burton Scott Easton that a single, concise, academic definition of grace is hardly possible. God is both infinite and mysterious. Also, human nature can be incredibly complex. Both are realities that we must allow for as we seek to understand and define various aspects of the Christian faith. I am not suggesting that we develop a vague, nebulous "believe what you want" perspective of theology, but simply that we realize the limitations of our ability to explain complex scriptural realities. It's nothing short of dangerous to force a concept as essential as grace into a one-dimensional box.

---

6. Burton Scott Easton, *The International Standard Bible Encyclopedia*, Vol. 2, 1292.

GRACE EMPOWERS

Accurately interpreting the Bible requires that we incorporate the context of each passage. We have a tendency to distort what we magnify; therefore, any passage of Scripture must be understood within its context. Far too many errors result from taking a verse of Scripture, pulling it out of its original context, and then unilaterally using it to support a personal viewpoint. This isn't to say that we must quote an entire chapter of the Bible every time we use a verse of Scripture, but that the context should always be taken into account.

If we develop our understanding of grace by incorporating the biblical contexts in which grace is used, we can see that Paul often spoke of grace in the sense of *empowerment* (Romans 12:6 and 1 Corinthians 3:10). Thus, a practical working definition of *grace* might be "the life-flow of God that transforms human hearts and empowers God's people to do all that He calls them to do." Admittedly, my definition doesn't incorporate every dimension of grace, but it does move us closer to a more accurate perspective.

I am by no means suggesting that grace can be earned, or that Christian living should be performance-based. Nor do I seek to minimize the importance of understanding grace as God's unmerited favor. Indeed, many of us could use a fresh revelation of God's favor and its extreme ramifications. My point is simply that it is nothing short of dangerous to minimize the other dimensions of grace—particularly its empowering nature.

Grace enables us both to change and to serve. If we are truly connected to God's grace, positive change is inevitable. Sadly, many of us remain ignorant of what grace can do in and through us. The painful result is that we remain bound, subject to the mentality that our sin is more powerful than God's grace to help us live in victory over the dominion of sin. All too often, we shrink back from serving God, feeling as though we have nothing significant to offer.

Grace is the life-flow of God supernaturally imparted to those who are blessed to receive it. Grace brings to life that which was once dead. We've all seen a branch wither and die as soon as it is cut from a tree. Why does it die? It has been cut off from the flow of life-giving nourishment. Imagine reversing the process—pulling an old, dead branch out of a backyard brush pile and seeing it return to full life. Now picture that branch bearing fruit. Grace doesn't simply forgive a person so that he or she can continue a meaningless, sin-filled existence; grace brings life and, subsequently, fruit where there was once death.

Some professing Christians use the free gift of grace as an excuse for self-willed living. I fear for them! To see grace as a license to sin is to distort biblical truth (Romans 7:14-8:2 and Galatians 5:13-23). Furthermore, it's sobering to realize that we can *insult* the Spirit of grace (Hebrews 10:26-29). Considering the exceedingly steep price that Jesus paid on the cross for us to receive God's grace, we should expect both the heavenly Father and the Holy Spirit to take offense when Christ's sacrificial death is treated with callous contempt.

HYPER-GRACE?

The term *hyper-grace* is commonly employed by those who are concerned that the message of grace is being used as an excuse for self-centered, ungodly behavior. I understand their point but consider the term hyper-grace somewhat of a misnomer. *Hyper*, as a prefix, means "extreme" or "excessive." Any person who has ever tasted the depths of his or her own sin, and then experienced the grace of God can tell you that grace is both extreme and excessive. No, perceptions get distorted due to an understanding of grace that is far too limited. I contend that *one-dimensional grace* better defines our misuse of the concept than does *hyper-grace.*

The true grace of God will never breed sinful behavior or foster a sense of selfish passivity in the people of God:

> *I say this because some ungodly people have wormed their way into your churches, saying that God's marvelous grace allows us to live immoral lives. The condemnation of such people was recorded long ago, for they have denied our only Master and Lord, Jesus Christ. Jude 1:4 (NLT)*

The price that Jesus paid on that horrible cross was intended to accomplish a powerful transformation within each of us. It's not about being a perfect Christian, or even striving to do better. The key lies in learning to *abide* in a vital, grace-filled relationship with Jesus Christ. This abiding—or *connecting*, if you will—is not something that happens automatically for any of us, including those who are genuine believers (John 15:1-11). It is entirely possible for a person to be a Christian and yet fail to abide in Christ for a particular season(s). This is where our confusion lies. The fact that we cannot earn God's favor does not mean that we have nothing to do with the process of abiding in His transformational grace. A careful reading of the Scriptures will show that we can:

- receive grace in vain (2 Corinthians 6:1).

- fall from grace (Galatians 5:4).

- come short of grace (Hebrews 12:15).

I cite these verses not to create fear, but to show that abiding in grace does not happen by default because of a one-time prayer to receive Christ. Consequently, we each play a vital role in determining whether or not we will continuously abide in God's life-giving grace. I absolutely agree that there is nothing we can do to earn grace, but there are things we can do that *position* us to abide in God's transformational grace. Spiritual disciplines such as prayer and Bible reading are not ends within themselves. Those who wish to grow spiritually must, through the disciplines, learn to position themselves to continuously draw upon the life-flow of God.

HOPE FOR THOSE WHO STRUGGLE

There can be more to the plague of sin than willful disobedience. I have met many genuine people who honestly desire to walk with God and live in victory over sin, but find it impossible to do so. The problem goes beyond a simple matter of choice. The collective cry of their frustrated hearts echoes the writings of Paul in Romans 7. I think the J.B. Phillips paraphrase of the New Testament puts it well:

> *In practice, what happens? My own behaviour baffles me. For I find myself not doing what I really want to do but doing what I really loathe…When I come up against the Law I want to do good, but*

in practice I do evil. My conscious mind whole-heartedly endorses the Law, yet I observe an entirely different principle at work in my nature. This is in continual conflict with my conscious attitude, and makes me an unwilling prisoner to the law of sin and death. In my mind I am God's willing servant, but in my own nature I am bound fast, as I say, to the law of sin and death. It is an agonising situation, and who on earth can set me free from the clutches of my sinful nature? I thank God there is a way out through Jesus Christ our Lord. Romans 7:15, 21-25 (Phillips)

At this point, I am compelled to address my own struggles. I spent the entire first decade of my Christian life under the crushing burden of Christian perfectionism. While in my twenties, I became a leader in our church and served in all manner of ways. In my own mind—and in the minds of many around me—my measure of spirituality amounted to how much I was doing for the church. But I was miserable! In spite of my faithful efforts—including a consistent devotional life—Christianity was not working for me. Somewhere along the line, I wisely concluded that the problem was with me and not with God. Brilliant!

Searching for answers, I read books and listened to sermons; I went to Bible studies and talked to older Christians. Nothing seemed to help. Finally, I began to seriously cry out to God, "Please show me what's wrong with me. Help me understand the Christian life. Show me how to walk with You!" Do you know what I discovered? God does indeed provide a way out of our inner struggles, but it is *unnatural*. We cannot break free from sin by obeying rules, trying harder, praying longer, or giving more. The key to freedom involves learning how to continually draw upon God's grace. This is amazing news for those who struggle. The secret of the Christian life lies not in trying harder, but in learning how to stay connected to the life-giving flow of grace.

STAYING CONNECTED

The weight of the New Covenant falls squarely on the shoulders of Jesus Christ (Luke 22:20), but that does not mean that ours is a one-sided relationship. As a person who has experienced the saving grace of God through the cross of Jesus Christ, I am secure in my status as a son of God. I, however, don't always live out a vital relationship with my heavenly Father. I can never earn a relationship with God, but staying close to Him does require something on my part. When I try to walk with God apart from praying and reading the Bible, for example, the fire of my love for Him begins to wane.

Discipline is a necessary part of parenting. Most of the time Debi and I did it well, but sometimes we made mistakes, as imperfect people tend to do. There were times—some of them quite painful—during which my kids and I were not "in fellowship" with one another. Whether because of a mistake on my part, or because their immature minds failed to fully comprehend the reasons for my actions, they weren't always happy with Dad. On more than one occasion, the bedroom door stayed shut for a long time, but the barrier was more than a physical one. They never stopped being my children—we were always *in relationship*, but not always *in fellowship*. Consequently, they failed to receive the fullness of what I had for them.

In His final discourse before going to the cross, Jesus spoke some poignant words to the disciples as He emphasized the need for them to continue to abide in Him. If abiding in a vital relationship with Christ was not automatic for the men who lived with Him for three years, how could we expect that it will happen effortlessly for us?

"I am the true vine, and My Father is the vinedresser. Every branch in Me that does not bear fruit, He takes away; and every branch that bears fruit, He prunes it so that it may bear more fruit. You are already clean because of the word which I have spoken to you. Abide in Me, and I in you. As the branch cannot bear fruit of itself unless it abides in the vine, so neither can you unless you abide in Me. I am the vine, you are the branches; he who abides in Me and I in him, he bears much fruit, for apart from Me you can do nothing. If anyone does not abide in Me, he is thrown away as a branch and dries up; and they gather them, and cast them into the fire and they are burned. If you abide in Me, and My words abide in you, ask whatever you wish, and it will be done for you. My Father is glorified by this, that you bear much fruit, and so prove to be My disciples. Just as the Father has loved Me, I have also loved you; abide in My love." John 15:1-9

Do you see it? Abiding—staying connected to God—is the secret to a fully fruitful life. Conversely, the presence of spiritual fruit in our lives indicates the reality of an ongoing relationship. A person can be "in Christ" in one sense, but not in another. In other words, I can be a Christian, but have times when I am not really walking in fellowship with God. It doesn't mean that I need to "get saved" all over again, but that I need to renew my fellowship with my heavenly Father.

(It may seem like I am splitting hairs, but I dislike the idea of "recommitting" oneself to God. All too often, it seems like we are trying, in our own sufficiency, to do something that we weren't able to do in the first place. On the other hand, to renew one's fellowship with God is to humbly reconnect in such a way that we seek to draw upon His grace. Thus, I prefer confession of sin and a fresh surrender over any attempt to be a more committed Christian.)

GRACE—THE MIDDLE ROAD

Staying connected to God requires intentional effort, but that effort does not involve obeying long lists of rules (laws). I often hear well-intentioned people say that we must have "balance" when it comes to grace. They speak as if law were one extreme and grace another, that the healthy road of life must incorporate a mix of the two. Wrong! Dead wrong! Legalism and grace don't mix. The extremes are not law and grace, but *law* and *lawlessness* (i.e. license to sin). Grace is the middle road. The road of life. The road of power. The way of grace is the path to freedom; it is the *central* way. Those who live by grace will be governed by a very different sort of "rules"—the laws of *faith* and *love*.

The goal of a wise master builder is not simply to modify people's behavior through rules or persuasion; it is to teach them to abide in grace. None of us ever reaches a point of sinless perfection, but when the people of God learn to continually draw upon the ever-abundant flow of His life-giving grace, the church will be vibrant and alive. No power on earth—or in Hell—will be able to uproot what God has established!

LES MISERABLES—A PICTURE OF GRACE

Before moving on to a practical understanding of how to abide in God's life-giving grace, I'd like to close this chapter with an illustration from

Victor Hugo's classic, *Les Miserables*. In the story, Jean Valjean, a naïve woodcutter, is condemned to five years in a horrid prison for stealing a loaf of bread to feed his starving family. Several escape attempts turn five years into nineteen and, Jean Valjean, the loving family man, becomes a hardened criminal. Upon his release from prison, Valjean is given a yellow passport to indicate that he is on parole. French law requires that this passport be shown wherever he goes so the ex-convict quickly becomes a "free" outcast.

Resorting to a life of crime, both by instinct and for the sake of survival, the main character finds himself in a pitiful state until he is directed to the home of Bishop Myriel. The kindly priest takes the criminal in, feeds him a nice meal (using his best silver), and then provides a clean, comfortable bed for the night.

After his first comfortable sleep in 20 years, Valjean awakens with the priest's silver at the forefront of his mind; he simply cannot shake the idea of stealing that valuable silver. After wrestling with his thoughts for a while, the guest becomes a burglar. Quietly slinking out of bed and into the priest's bedroom where the silver is stored, thief Valjean briefly contemplates murdering the priest before finally stealing the silver and fleeing.

After being caught by the police and returned to the home of the bishop, Jean Valjean has the audacity to claim that he was *given* the silver. Surprisingly, the kindly old priest not only agrees that he willingly gave the silver, but he goes on to chastise the criminal for forgetting to take the candlesticks as well. "Why didn't you take the candlesticks? They are worth a lot of money!"

Entirely confused, the police go on their way while a bewildered Jean Valjean stands staring at the priest. In a scene rife with emotion, the hardened criminal breaks down in tears, entirely befuddled by the kind man's actions. Jean Valjean—a man accustomed only to the bitter pill of selfish hate—simply cannot comprehend the undeserved favor that he has been shown by a total stranger—and a priest no less. The priest's kindness doesn't end there, though. He gives Jean Valjean *all* of the silver and sends him on his way, now empowered to embark upon a new existence.

This powerful scene propels us toward a more complete perspective of God's grace. Forgiveness and empowerment are both expressions of grace. God mercifully forgives and cleanses even the worst among us, but He is never content to allow us to slither back into the cesspool of sin from which we've been delivered. Through his empowering grace, our loving Father provides us with all that we need to live godly lives.

BLAZING A TRAIL TO FRUITFUL LIVING

The path to radical change is marked by a comprehensive understanding of the multifaceted nature of grace.

CHAPTER THREE
THE MATURING
INFLUENCE OF GRACE

But the goal of our instruction is love from a pure heart and a good conscience and a sincere faith.

1 Timothy 1:5

Cheap grace is the deadly enemy of our church.... Cheap grace means grace sold on the market like cheapjack's wares. . . . Cheap grace is the preaching of forgiveness without requiring repentance, without church discipline, communion without confession, absolution without personal confession.

—Dietrich Bonhoeffer

I admit it! I am a proud parent. Our children are walking with God and have grown into mature, responsible young adults. They also work in service-oriented professions. I'm not sure there is much else a parent could ask—except, perhaps, for grandchildren. Of course, all parents have those disheartening times when they are dismayed by the attitudes and behavior of their kids, times when all they can do is fall to their knees and cry out to God for grace and mercy. Been there. Done that. It's all part of the parenting territory.

I found the early teenage years to be particularly challenging. In my mind, there are few creatures as scary as middle schoolers—middle school boys in particular. These young people are beginning to develop the physical stature and abilities of adults, but their minds are still childish. They can be likened to the ancient dinosaurs that had huge bodies and pea-sized brains. Due to some vivid memories of my own adolescent years, I am well aware of what a maturing body and an immature mindset can mean. So, when our son was a young teen, as he left the house to hang out with his buddies, I used to point to my head and exclaim, "Son, use your head—because your friends won't use theirs!" Thankfully, we all survived.

THE PLAGUE OF SPIRITUAL IMMATURITY

We can understand that a junior high school boy would act immaturely—he can't help it because his dinosaur brain is still developing—but when fully-grown adults are characterized by immature behavior, there is a problem. It pains me to admit that the church has always been plagued by spiritual immaturity, which I consider synonymous with *fleshly*—or *carnal*—behavior. For young Christians, immaturity can often be tied to little more than a lack of wisdom, but for those more seasoned in the faith, spiritual immaturity indicates a self-centered mindset.

I can't begin to explain the deep sense of disappointment I felt when I first began serving as a leader in the church. I was excited for the opportunity to help God transform human lives, but I instead found a high level of carnality—even among many who had been Christians for thirty, forty, or fifty years. What an unpleasant wake-up call that was!

When their primary focus should have been on touching others and advancing the kingdom of God, far too many were consumed by self-centeredness. Their behavior was petty. They navigated adversity with unnecessary drama. They were tossed about by the "winds of doctrine" and "Christian fads" that frequently came along. And they required attention to the point that I began to feel that a church leader was little more than a glorified babysitter. I soon began to realize that this type of behavior was by no means limited to our local fellowship; spiritual immaturity was rampant throughout our nation. Sadly, to the detriment of us all, it still is. I'd even say that spiritual immaturity in the U.S. is at epidemic proportions.

I hear far too many sad stories about people who have been alienated from church life—and often from Christ—because of immature behavior on the part of church people who profess to be Christian but whose lifestyles speak otherwise. It breaks my heart to see sincere people keep their distance from our loving God because of wayward human behavior. You can say all you want about God being sovereign and in control, but the bottom line is that self-centered, immature behavior among God's people continues to turn genuine seekers away from the one true source of life.

> You who boast in the Law, through your breaking the Law, do you dishonor God? For "THE NAME OF GOD IS BLASPHEMED AMONG THE GENTILES BECAUSE OF YOU," just as it is written. Romans 2:23-24

Paul's emphasis is telling. He claimed that unbelievers blasphemed the name of God because of ungodly behavior on the part of God-professing people. Exactly how we reconcile this reality with the tension between God's sovereignty and mankind's free will, I do not profess to fathom. Still, it remains clear that some people will be turned away from seeking God by the very ones who profess to know and serve Him—the supposed representatives of God who should be helping to reconcile others to Christ.

I realize that I may be offending a few readers, but please hear my heart. Through my years as a campus minister, I met dozens of young people who had walked away from Christianity because of their negative experiences with the church. This is not an issue that we can lightly dismiss. No one is perfect, and we all have the potential for hypocrisy, but if we are truly walking with God, we should be increasingly characterized by spiritually mature attitudes and actions.

It's also quite possible that some readers may think I am calling them immature when I am not. I do not equate having problems, issues, and needs with spiritual immaturity. We all have our struggles. Each of us has been "dealt" a set of circumstances over which we have little or no control. In far too many cases, those circumstances have been pain-ridden and no one comes through these types of things unscathed. Spiritual maturity, though, has nothing to do with having problems. Spiritual maturity relates to how we *respond* to the circumstances over which we have little or no control.

I can't help that I was born into a dysfunctional family environment, or that as a child I lacked athletic ability, or that I grew up in a housing project on "the other side of the tracks." I didn't choose those things. If possible, I would have traded my circumstances—something I constantly wished for—in an instant. But I couldn't. That left me with a choice to either wallow in my perceived misfortune, or bring my issues into the light of God's love. Wallowing breeds immaturity; learning to trust God and deal with our struggles cultivates spiritual adulthood.

Most pastors I know aren't bothered by people who have problems (helping others is a primary reason many pastors have entered the ministry), but they are disheartened by spiritual immaturity. Consider the following quotes from New Testament writers and feel their frustration over the subject:

> And I, brethren, could not speak to you as to spiritual men, but as to men of flesh, as to infants in Christ. I gave you milk to drink, not solid food; for you were not yet able to receive it. Indeed, even now you are not yet able, for you are still fleshly. For since there is jealousy and strife among you, are you not fleshly, and are you not walking like mere men? 1 Corinthians 3:1-3

> My children, with whom I am again in labor until Christ is formed in you— but I could wish to be present with you now and to change my tone, for I am perplexed about you. Galatians 4:19-20

> Concerning him we have much to say, and it is hard to explain, since you have become dull of hearing. For though by this time you ought to be teachers, you have need again for someone to teach you the elementary principles of the oracles of God, and you have come to need milk and not solid food. For everyone who partakes only of milk is not accustomed to the word of righteousness, for he is an infant. But solid food is for the mature, who because of practice have their senses trained to discern good and evil. Hebrews 5:11-14

There is no question that people's problems can weigh down a leader, but I think that spiritual immaturity will do more damage than just about anything else. What is there to do for a person when you've done everything that you know how to do? When you've given all that you can give—and in disproportionate terms? When you've poured out your heart and soul in prayer? To heavily invest in a person and see little or no return in the form of positive change is one of the most discouraging things a Christian leader will experience. I have faced a lot of difficult challenges in my years of ministry, but nothing has taken the heart out of me like spiritual immaturity and the unnecessary conflict which accompanies it. With spiritual immaturity seemingly at all-time heights in the Western church, it is no wonder that a great number of pastors have left the ministry in recent years.[7]

THE GOAL OF OUR INSTRUCTION

The plague of spiritual immaturity stands in stark contrast to the encouraging usefulness of a spiritually mature believer. I am reminded of Dave—a college football coach who played on our church softball team. Dave often amazed me. He never got rattled. When it seemed like a game was beginning to unravel for us, Dave always seemed to make a key defensive play to settle us down. He was like a rock of stability at second base. A spiritually mature believer has this type of impact on others.

A primary goal of the apostle Paul was to help grow those he served into spiritual maturity:

> We proclaim Him, admonishing every man and teaching every man with all wisdom, so that we may present every man complete [mature] in Christ. Colossians 1:28

Spiritual maturity is not about becoming the perfect Christian; it is the result of learning to abide in God's grace and growing in love. If we will stay connected to Him, He will grow us into full spiritual adulthood— the very idea communicated by Colossians 1:28.

In principle, it's all very simple. In practice, however, we find ourselves severely challenged. The key is to abide, but sadly, our one-dimensional definition of grace has left us with the false belief that saying a one-time prayer to receive Christ results in some type of "autopilot" walk with God. It's as though we have a subliminal mindset which proclaims, "I've raised my hand. I've said the prayer. I'm in. The autopilot is on. There's nothing else for me to do. All of the blessings of God should be mine in abundance!" The problem is that the Bible

---

7. http://thegospelcoalition.org/blogs/kevindeyoung/2013/04/18/why-pastors-quit/

teaches something very different. According to no less an authority than the Son of God, we abide by *obeying* His commandments:

> *"Just as the Father has loved Me, I have also loved you; abide in My love. If you keep My commandments, you will abide in My love; just as I have kept My Father's commandments and abide in His love." John 15:9-10*

"If you keep My commandments, you will abide in my love"—a one-dimensional perspective of grace cannot allow for such thinking! After all, Jesus paid everything so that we don't have to do anything—right? Not exactly. We can never earn a close relationship with God, but, as is the case with drawing upon God's grace, we can position ourselves to abide in His love.

"Exactly," we might ask, "*what* commandments was Jesus talking about? The Ten Commandments? All of the rules established by church leaders?" Notice that Jesus spoke of *His* commandments. All too often, we make the mistake of equating Christ's commandments with lists of rules. Jesus' commandments—and really, the entire Bible—boil down to two primary facets of obedience: *to trust* and *to love*.[8] Spiritual maturity is realized as we grow in faith, enabling us to abide in God's transformational grace. In a sense, faith is the raw material that we send into the manufacturing plant, with love being the product that comes off the end of the conveyor belt.

> *But the goal of our instruction is love from a pure heart and a good conscience and a sincere faith. 1 Timothy 1:5*

Problematically, not only do we have difficulty achieving spiritual maturity, we struggle even to define it. A 2009 study by the Barna Research Group found that eighty-one percent of those who identified themselves as Christians described spiritual maturity as "trying hard to follow the rules described in the Bible." According to the Barna Group, "People aspire to be spiritually mature, but they do not know what it means."[9] Talk about heart-breaking! We have an abundance of resources

---

8. Properly identifying Christ's commandments is such an important issue that we will deal with it more extensively in Chapter Nine.
9. https://www.barna.org/barna-update/article/12-faithspirituality/264-many-churchgo-ers-and-faith-leaders-struggle-to-define-spiritual-maturity

and yet most of us remain clueless about the practical workings of the Christian faith. Maturity is not about rules—it's about relationship!

Still, in an odd sort of way, I am encouraged by the results of the Barna Group study. The Western church is not hopelessly lost. We have so much knowledge available to us, so many devoted and gifted leaders, and so many necessary structures already in place. If only we can make a few adjustments to several of our core issues, I believe that the Western church will explode with life. Our understanding of grace is one such issue.

THE DIVINE PROGRESSION OF GRACE

Teachers like to analytically explain concepts with diagrams and charts. Much to our disappointment, however, reality does not always consist of nice little boxes with well-defined lines. More often than not, reality is more like a mess of tangled roots spreading in all sorts of directions. It becomes virtually impossible to know where one thing ends and another begins. Accordingly, we often struggle when truth doesn't fit into our predefined boxes.

Because reality can be complicated, I want to caution you not to get too nitpicky about the various facets of grace. The Hope Diamond has many beautiful facets, but it is still the Hope Diamond. In a similar vein, grace has many different dimensions, but each one is still grace through and through.

In this book, I am focusing on three specific influences of grace—unmerited favor, transformation, and empowerment. This is not to suggest that the other dimensions are unimportant or that the lines between these particular facets of grace can be easily drawn. My goal is simply to help provide additional illumination to a subject that is essential to Christian living.

All that being said, charts and diagrams can be valuable learning tools because they help us get a general idea of how things work. Thus, I am presenting you with an admittedly oversimplified diagram—*The Divine Progression of Grace*—that should help us gain a better perspective of the progressive effect that grace has on our lives.

DIVINE PROGRESSION OF GRACE DEFINITIONS

- **Saving grace** – God's unmerited favor to draw us to Himself (John 6:44; Ephesians 2:8-9).

- **Saving faith** – The faith to believe in the sacrificial death and resurrection of Christ to forgive and cleanse our sins, causing us to be at peace with God (Romans 5:1-2).

- **New creation** – This is the point of salvation. Those who are saved by faith become new creations—the very children of God—as the Holy Spirit comes to dwell in their hearts, infusing their human spirits with life (2 Corinthians 5:17). Only new creatures in Christ can walk by the Spirit.

- **Functional faith** – The Bible teaches that we are saved from "faith to faith" (Romans 1:16-17). Our saving faith grows into a functional faith that learns to trust God in every area of life: identity, provision, guidance, etc.

- **Obedience** – Doing what God calls us to as the expression of our trust in and love for Him (John 14:15).

- **Transformational grace** – The life-flow of God that grows the fruit of the Holy Spirit and gives us the ability to live in victory over the dominion of sin (Romans 5:17, 20-21; 1 Peter 5:12).

- **Fruit of the Spirit** – The abundant life of God manifesting in our lives as godly virtues. This is the process of sanctification by which we live in dominion over the power of sin and are conformed into the eternal image of Jesus Christ (Galatians 5:22-23; 1 Thessalonians 4:7).

- **Empowering grace** – The life-flow of God that strengthens and anoints us with the supernatural ability to advance God's kingdom on the Earth (Acts 1:8; Romans 12:6-8; 1 Corinthians 12:4-11, 15:10).

- **Living Works** – Acts of service, motivated by faith and love, that honor God and help others (Ephesians 2:10).

- **Effective ministry** – Making a favorable eternal impact in human lives (Acts 10:38).

We begin by being drawn to God through His *saving grace*. Regardless of how we view God's sovereignty—as opposed to human free will—most of us will agree that no one comes to Christ unless he or she is drawn by the heavenly Father (John 6:44). Through the process of being drawn, we at some point exercise *saving faith*. This is the necessary point of salvation where the spiritually dead are "born from above" (John 3:3) to become *new creations* (2 Corinthians 5:17) in Christ who are capable of knowing and relating to God. I believe that most evangelicals will track with me to this point, but things can get sticky when we begin to blaze a trail of *functional faith*. The Bible doesn't merely teach that the righteous will simply *have* faith, but that they will *live by* faith:

> "Behold, as for the proud one,
> His soul is not right within him;
> But the righteous will **live** by his faith."
> Habakkuk 2:4 (emphasis added)

How important is this passage? It was quoted twice by the apostle Paul (Romans 1:17 and Galatians 3:11) and once by the writer of Hebrews (Hebrews 10:37-38), who may or may not have been Paul. The importance of living by faith is integral to Christianity as there are many areas of life which put a demand on our trust in God. We need faith to receive forgiveness, faith to believe in God's love for us, faith to secure a sense of identity, faith to trust for provision, and faith to know that God will redeem negative circumstances. The list goes on. We are saved by faith, and it is by faith that the Christian life functions.

A study of Biblical Hebrew will show that the idea of faith communicated in Habakkuk 2:4 also denotes a sense of firmness, steadfastness, and fidelity.[10] True faith leads to *faithfulness*. In the Bible, faith is never seen simply as a mental exercise. Faith always produces something—faithful *obedience*, in particular. Those who believe in God will be faithful to Him; they will be faithful to practice obedience to His word. All too often, Christians in the West think that they possess a depth of faith beyond that which is actually present in their lives. A glaring absence of faithfulness, however, speaks differently.

---

10. Francis Brown, Samuel Rolles Driver, and Charles Augustus Briggs, *Enhanced Brown-Driver-Briggs Hebrew and English Lexicon* (Oak Harbor, WA: Logos Research Systems, 2000), 53.

From this point forward I will make a distinction between *transformational grace* and *empowering grace*. It is a difficult line for me to draw because in some senses the two words can be used interchangeably. Nonetheless, such a distinction helps to clarify the idea that *spiritual maturity* and *spiritual ability* are two different—albeit related—issues. For our purposes, then, *transformational grace* is the sanctifying element in our lives, enabling us to live in victory over sin and bear the *fruit of Holy the Spirit* (Galatians 5:22-23). *Empowering grace* flows from the supernatural anointing of the Holy Spirit enabling us to do things beyond our natural human capacity.

God's gifts to us are *grace gifts*; we can do nothing to earn them. The Greek word is *charisma*. Charisma, according to our contemporary definition, focuses on dynamic *natural* abilities and personality traits. The biblical emphasis, however, is on *supernatural* gifting, enabling us to touch the lives of others in ways beyond the scope of any natural human ability (Romans 12:3-8 and 1 Corinthians 12:4-11).

Living works—as opposed to dead works (Hebrews 6:1)—are specific actions that are motivated by faith and love. Our works do not make us righteous in the eyes of God; they are outward expressions of the inward work of grace. When we combine living works with the fruit of the Holy Spirit, truly *effective ministry* results.

I'll be honest with you. I don't fully understand all of the inner workings of *The Divine Progression of Grace*. (This fact should instill confidence in my readers!) As already explained, these types of diagrams present imperfect representations of reality. A person can receive supernatural abilities from God, for example, without growing into full maturity. This leads one to question exactly where obedience should fall in *The Divine Progression of Grace*. I can't say with absolute confidence—perhaps in more than one place. I do know, however, that we cannot become fully fruitful unless we learn to practice obedience to God as a way of life.

ABIDING

In spite of the difficulties involved with attempting to diagram these concepts, on a practical level, it's quite simple. To abide in Christ means that we stay connected to the flow of His transformational grace, which in time, produces the fruit of love. The emphasis is relational—as indicated by Christ's vine/branches illustration from John 15 that I have already highlighted. When we live in fellowship with God, His grace nourishes our spiritual lives in the same manner that sap nourishes the branches of a grape vine. Without that flow, the branch withers; with that flow, an abundance of fruit will ultimately be borne.

As important as going to Heaven may be, The *Divine Progression of Grace*—as we can see—involves far more. From beginning to end, the core of Christianity centers on the relationship between God and humankind. The thing that makes Heaven to be Heaven is the nearness of God's presence. The idea that Christianity is primarily about moral or religious obligation conflicts with the heart of God's passion for people.

Does this mean that we are free to do whatever we want? Not at all! The secret lies in learning to continually abide in His transformational grace so that we can live in victory over sin and its devastating impact on human lives. Somewhere in this mix we find obedience—both a fruit and a foundation of grace.

The fact that a person is a Christian does not guarantee a lifestyle of continually abiding in grace. While on this earth, we live in fleshly bodies which are tainted by sin. The very idea of obedience is problematic because we all want to do our own thing. A person may be a new creation in essence, but still operate in the flesh from time to time—or even most of the time. It can all be very confusing because, as Christians, we should always abide in Christ. But we don't—not always!

I've been a Christian since 1980, and I still have times (more than I care to admit) when I live according to the flesh rather than by the Holy Spirit of God. We all do. But as we learn to abide in God's transformational grace, we will live more and more in dominion over the flesh, bearing sweeter and more abundant spiritual fruit.

THE CORPORATE DIMENSION OF GROWTH

It is important for those in individualistic cultures to realize that The *Divine Progression of Grace* is a corporate concept. As the body of Christ, we are to create an environment in which we help one another grow. Those who are spiritually mature will go to great lengths to help others rather than looking with contempt on those who don't measure up to their standards. We're here to help each other abide in Christ, to grow in His grace.

> *And He gave some as apostles, and some as prophets, and some as evangelists, and some as pastors and teachers, for the equipping of the saints for the work of service, to the building up of the body of Christ; until we all attain to the unity of the faith, and of the knowledge of the Son of God, to a mature man, to the measure of the stature which belongs to the fullness of Christ. As a result, we are no longer to be children, tossed here and there by waves and carried about by every wind of doctrine, by the trickery of men, by craftiness in deceitful scheming; but speaking the truth in love, we are to grow up in all aspects into Him who is the head, even Christ, from whom the whole body, being fitted and held together by what every joint supplies, according to the proper working of each individual part, causes the growth of the body for the building up of itself in love. Ephesians 4:11-16*

As I read this powerful passage from Paul's letter to the Ephesian church, I can't help but make comparisons with the behavior I've seen in many Christian circles over the years. If our churches were defined by the spirit of this passage, would they be losing so many young people? It's not because churchgoers are too loving and encouraging that people leave organized religion. In all my days, I've never heard someone say, "The problem with Christians is that they love each other too much."

I don't ever want to compromise truth for the sake of unity, but neither do I want to sacrifice love on the altar of truth. Due to the judgmental nature of the human heart, it's easy for us to forget that God's love is redemptive. Truth is not a sword to wave about indiscriminately. The goal of truth is never to put others down, but to help lift them to new heights in Christ.

Are our lives defined by the same priorities held by the God we profess to love? Involvement with a community of believers is something that our New Testament authors assumed would be a common reality for all believers. How can we live out the love God puts within us if we aren't somehow connected to other Christians? No one grows into maturity entirely through self-effort; I believe it is arrogant to think otherwise. Do relationships complicate life? Absolutely! However, relationships also contribute to the maturing process. To give, to receive, to forgive, and to bless are all necessary aspects of the Christian life. Those who truly abide in Christ and stay connected to the flow of His grace will expend their resources in an effort to build others up. If spiritual growth is only for ourselves, it isn't growth at all.

I emphasize the importance of corporate relationships in spite of the fact that I am an introvert. It's the quietness and solitude of the outdoors that I appreciate, not crowds. I've also experienced my share of bumps and bruises through my interactions with other Christians. I know how easy it is to become jaded when a person experiences things that he or she should not experience in the church. Individualism, however, is far more problematic than it is helpful. The Bible clearly teaches that God desires His people to be connected with one another. The only way that the church can grow in a healthy manner is by its members growing into maturity together through the influence of grace.

BLAZING A TRAIL TO FRUITFUL LIVING

The key to cultivating spiritual maturity is not simply to do things for God, but to serve out of an abiding relationship with Him.

CHAPTER FOUR
GOD'S MEASURE OF SUCCESS

Watch over your heart with all diligence, for from it flow the springs of life.

Proverbs 4:23

It is the laden bough that hangs low, and the most fruitful Christian who is the most humble.

—Author Unknown

Start reading the Bible from its beginning and it won't be long before you encounter the topic of *fruit*. Fruitfulness is like a thread that begins in early Genesis and weaves through the tapestry of the Scriptures until ending in Revelation. If fruitfulness really is that important, shouldn't we seek to understand more about it and its relationship to grace? While guarding our hearts from the hammer of condemnation, let us follow the thread of fruitfulness for a bit.

On the third day of creation, God spoke fruit trees into existence. On the sixth day, the concept of fruitfulness was applied to humankind:

*God blessed them; and God said to them, "**Be fruitful** and multiply, and fill the earth, and subdue it; and rule over the fish of the sea and over the birds of the sky and over every living thing that moves on the earth." Genesis 1:26-28 (emphasis added)*

God's very first words to the human race were "Be fruitful . . ." We are inclined to think that this passage only applies to having lots of kids, but there is more to the story. The concept of fruitfulness, we must understand, has both physical *and* spiritual dimensions. God is undoubtedly concerned about the propagation of the human race, but He no less values the character of our lives. Fruitfulness isn't simply an earthly concept; it involves eternal spiritual dynamics.

Creation provides ample evidence that God loves to grow things, but He is especially passionate about nurturing people into spiritual maturity. Our Creator cares about our physical existence—as was evidenced by the earthly ministry of Christ—but the beat of His heart centers on our spiritual fruitfulness. *Spiritual fruitfulness* can be defined as "bearing the sweet, abundant fruit of the Holy Spirit and helping to multiply that good fruit in the lives of those we serve." *Unfruitfulness* would be defined as "bearing the fruit of the flesh and helping to multiply its bad fruit in the lives of others."

ANCIENT ISRAEL'S FAILURE

Ancient Israel was physically fruitful. About seventy people went into Egypt under Joseph's leadership, and more than a million exited with Moses. The nation continued to grow and prosper, but their waywardness collided with God's plan. Ultimately, they were vanquished and banished into exile because the fruit of sin exemplified their lives more than the fruit that God expected. One particular passage from Isaiah spells out God's displeasure all too explicitly:

> *Let me sing now for my well-beloved*
> *A song of my beloved concerning His vineyard.*
> *My well-beloved had a vineyard on a fertile hill.*
> *He dug it all around, removed its stones,*
> *And planted it with the choicest vine.*
> *And He built a tower in the middle of it*
> *And also hewed out a wine vat in it;*
> *Then He expected it to produce good grapes,*
> *But it produced only worthless ones.*
> *"And now, O inhabitants of Jerusalem and men of Judah,*
> *Judge between Me and My vineyard.*
> *What more was there to do for My vineyard that I have not done in it?*
> *Why, when I expected it to produce good grapes did it produce worthless ones?*

So now let Me tell you what I am going to do to My vineyard:
I will remove its hedge and it will be consumed;
I will break down its wall and it will become trampled ground.
I will lay it waste;
It will not be pruned or hoed,
But briars and thorns will come up.
I will also charge the clouds to rain no rain on it."
For the vineyard of the LORD of hosts is the house of Israel
And the men of Judah His delightful plant.
Thus He looked for justice, but behold, bloodshed;
For righteousness, but behold, a cry of distress. Isaiah 5:1-7

Ouch! This is a painful passage to read but it's even worse than it appears at first glance. The Hebrew word translated as "worthless" literally means "stenches"—as in the smell of something rotting.

> . . . this word . . . describes objects that have a foul odor, bad relationships between people creating abhorrence, and the general principle that evil deeds are so rotten that they have a bad smell in God's nostrils.[11]

Western Pennsylvania abounds with wildlife. That's good for hunters but bad for motorists. I think we're second only to West Virginia when it comes to the amount of roadkill seen lying along the highways. Few experiences can equal coming upon a bloated deer carcass on a hot summer day. The flies are so big that they're easily seen from a distance. Then there is the smell—it's enough to turn the strongest stomach. The "worthless grapes" mentioned in Isaiah 5:1-7 can be likened more to a roadkill deer than to a bunch of over-ripe grapes.

The Israelites of Isaiah's era were physically fruitful and yet God was repulsed by their spiritual fruit. Their lives were not characterized by the righteousness and justice that the King of Glory prizes, but by the attributes of the fallen nature. In other words, the Master Gardener was looking for sweet, tasty fruit, but found "roadkill" fruit instead. Injustice, greed, envy, bitterness, judgmental attitudes, the quest for control—all are roadkill fruit. The imagery may not present a pretty

---

11. Louis Goldberg, "195 באש," ed. R. Laird Harris, Gleason L. Archer Jr., and Bruce K. Waltke, *Theological Wordbook of the Old Testament* (Chicago: Moody Press, 1999), 88.

picture, but I'm confident that it presents an accurate one. God would not have sent ancient Israel into exile for a trivial reason.

Fruitfulness, we might say, is *God's* measure of success for human lives. As humans, we tend to focus on outward, measurable things—such as money, cars, houses, status, etc.—as our standards of success. What a huge mistake! God's perspective is totally different. He doesn't see outward success as being bad in itself, but our Creator is deeply offended when we use various measures of success to build a platform for self-validation. In comparing our earthly success—or lack thereof—to others, we are prone to either elevate or marginalize people solely on the basis of how they measure up to humanistic standards.[12]

A disturbing experience during my college years left a profound mark on my heart. I was part of a mission team that visited Port-au-Prince, Haiti, about the time a large cruise ship docked. There, on the bow of the ship, stood a middle-aged American guy wearing a large cowboy hat. It took a minute for us to realize that he was throwing coins into the water below, and that young Haitians were diving for the money. I was especially struck by the arrogant attitude with which that man carried himself. In all honesty, it made me embarrassed for my country. I don't know whether the source of his arrogance was his wealth, race, or nationality, but you can be sure that it had something to do with the manner in which he measured success.

Spiritual fruitfulness cannot exist apart from humility. One of the keys to becoming spiritually fruitful is to admit that our motives stink apart from Christ's divine influence on our hearts. Only as we admit how much pride and selfishness corrupt even our noble deeds, can we allow God to reproduce His character within us. The highest measure of worldly success is abhorrent in the eyes of God if that success is rooted in human greed and pride (Luke 16:14-15).

Fruitfulness has always been central to God's divine plan for humanity, and a careful reading of the New Testament will reveal that God's expectations regarding fruitfulness have not changed under the New Covenant age of grace. In fact, God may actually expect *greater*

---

12. Humanism, as a philosophy, attaches the utmost importance to matters relating to humanity as opposed to anything divine or supernatural.

fruitfulness from us because of all that He has provided through the cross of Christ and the presence of the Holy Spirit. Today's people of God have the ability to bear spiritual fruit in a way that the ancients could not have imagined.

FRUITFULNESS IN THE AGE OF GRACE

When John the Baptist—a hairy, wild sort of man—came on the scene, he challenged the religious leaders to "bear fruits worthy of repentance" (Matthew 3:8, NKJV). Jesus later blasted the Jewish elders and priests saying, "the kingdom of God will be taken from you and given to a nation bearing the fruits of it" (Matthew 21:43, NKJV). Ouch!

To fully grasp the full weight of such words, we need to put these passages into perspective. Both John and Jesus were addressing the elite spiritual leaders of their day—the very men that most people admired and envied. Like the ancient Israelites of Isaiah's era, they had failed to produce the coveted fruit that their Lord and King expected. Can you see that the New Covenant message of grace does not give us a license to be unfruitful? Instead, grace enables us to produce a rich harvest of spiritual fruit. A grace-filled life is a fruitful life—a cherished goal— which the heart of Heaven longs to see become reality. Below are five reasons that I believe fruitfulness matters so much to God:

1. **Fruit is *excess life* and so fruitfulness serves as a sign that true spiritual life is not only present, but also overflowing.** A tree that bears abundant fruit has so much life that it can't be contained. How can we recognize truth as opposed to falsehood? By the love, joy, peace, patience, kindness, goodness, faithfulness, gentleness, and self-control that result. How can we tell the difference between authentic worship and flesh-based religious activity? By the fruit produced in those who participate.

2. **A fruitful life serves as an indicator that a person is truly abiding with God.** The prophet Isaiah referred to Israel as "the *choicest* vine" (Isaiah 5:2) while Jesus called *Himself* "the *true* vine" (John 15:1). A human life that bears a full measure of spiritual fruit is a life connected to God.

3. **The fruitful transformation of a person's life reflects God's glorious work.** The fruit of the Holy Spirit can be mimicked only to a degree. When an obviously sinful and self-absorbed person begins to bear the sweet fruit of the Holy Spirit, the amazing handiwork of God is revealed.

4. **Fruitfulness is one of the primary means by which God draws people to Himself.** Love, joy, peace, etc. spilling over in the life of a church are so sweet to the taste that outsiders find themselves hungering for what that church has to offer.

5. **God loves spiritual fruit!** Just as the sweet, fresh, and abundant fruits of nature bring pleasure to so many people, so God delights to see the sweet fruit of the Holy Spirit abound in the lives of His much-loved children.

It is through spiritual fruit that God's name is glorified (John 15:8) and that His presence is realized (John 13:35). *Truly, one of the greatest gifts that we can give to God is a spiritually fruitful life!*

When a church's fruit fails to match its profession of faith, young people will be sure to leave. Instead of seeing love, joy, and peace exemplified, they are often repulsed by judgmental attitudes, anger, and strife. Sadly, these vices lead to hardened hearts, which then blind the perpetrators to the error of their ways. The result? All of the blame is directed toward those who are leaving. This is one of the painful realities of our day. Of course, we want to blame the demise of our culture on unbelievers, but if those filling our churches are largely unfruitful, how can we expect a world without Christ to be any better? Thankfully, the opposite trend also holds true; people are drawn to the church as they see the life and love of God expressed in a group of believers.

We had some very special groups of young people during the years that Debi and I did college ministry. One particular "generation" really got it—they understood the true meaning of grace. The resulting environment was contagious. One day we had a picnic in our back yard. I fired up the grill and cooked a bunch of hamburgers and hot dogs to help feed about twenty or so young people. Sara, one of our students, had invited her sister Jean to join us for the afternoon. For us, it was a typical get-together. We talked, laughed, and played some yard games. God's love was evident in our midst as it often was. That's not to say that we never had strife, but that our young people were growing into fruitful maturity. Jean grew up attending church, but her heart had been distant from God. That day she was so touched by our typical get-together that she had to pull her car to the side of the road on the way home. "God," Jean cried, "I want what those people have!" I guess I'm foolish enough to believe that this type of experience should be the norm—not the exception—for our Christian organizations.

If the fruit of our lives is fleshly, we really don't grasp the true nature of grace. Paul's letter to the Galatian church provides us with a clear contrast between the roadkill fruit of the flesh and the sweet fruit of the Holy Spirit:

> But I say, walk by the Spirit, and you will not carry out the desire of the flesh. For the flesh sets its desire against the Spirit, and the Spirit against the flesh; for these are in opposition to one another, so that you may not do the things that you please. But if you are led by the Spirit, you are not under the Law. Now the deeds of the flesh are evident, which are: immorality, impurity, sensuality, idolatry, sorcery, enmities, strife, jealousy, outbursts of anger, disputes, dissensions, factions, envying, drunkenness, carousing, and things like these, of which I forewarn you, just as I have forewarned you, that those who practice such things will not inherit the kingdom of God. But the fruit of the Spirit is love, joy, peace, patience, kindness, goodness, faithfulness, gentleness, self-control; against such things there is no law. Now those who belong to Christ Jesus have crucified the flesh with its passions and desires. Galatians 5:16-24

Paul is not referring to a requirement of moral perfection on the part of Christians; he is emphasizing that the fruit of the Spirit should increasingly characterize our lives as we continue to walk with God. If a Christian's life is not increasingly marked by the fruit of the Holy Spirit, then something is out of sync. The source of the problem is usually found through ignorance, self-will, or a combination of the two. If we fail to live out the dynamics of *The Divine Progression of Grace*, we will find ourselves producing the fruit of the flesh no matter how hard we try to do what we think God requires. I don't make such claims to condemn people, but to challenge all of us to dig deeper into grace.

By incorporating the broader context of Paul's writings, we can see that *abiding in grace* is tantamount to *walking by the Spirit* and that *living under law* leads to *living by the flesh*. Bearing the fruit of the Spirit does not make us righteous—acceptable in the eyes of God—but rather indicates whether or not we are truly abiding in Christ. Conversely, the rotten and destructive fruit of the flesh reveals that, regardless of our profession of faith, we are not staying connected to the true vine of God.

Human self-will, of course, presents a huge problem. The desire for "self-sovereignty" passionately burns in every human heart. Indeed, it is the most difficult struggle that any of us will ever face. Christ's willingness to yield to the Father's will in the garden of Gethsemane was as much a victory over sin as was His resurrection. Each of us is called to follow in His steps. Any supposed version of Christianity that doesn't compel a complete surrender of the will to God is more an expression of humanism than of true religion.

WOLVES IN SHEEP'S CLOTHING

Whether due to ignorance or the strength of self-will, bad fruit—especially in the life of a leader—has all of the opposite effects of good fruit. Bad fruit is not to be taken lightly! Unfortunately, too often Christian leaders focus on what they believe God wants to do *through* them without allowing Him the free reign to accomplish what He wants to do *in* them. Jesus addressed this issue in what I consider to be one of the most unnerving passages in the entire Bible:

> *"Beware of the false prophets, who come to you in sheep's clothing, but inwardly are ravenous wolves. You will know them by their fruits. Grapes are not gathered from thorn bushes nor figs from thistles, are they? So every good tree bears good fruit, but the bad tree bears bad fruit. A good tree cannot produce bad fruit, nor can a bad tree produce good fruit. Every tree that does not bear good fruit is cut down and thrown into the fire. So then, you will know them by their fruits.*

Not everyone who says to Me, 'Lord, Lord,' will enter the kingdom of heaven, but he who does the will of My Father who is in heaven will enter. Many will say to Me on that day, 'Lord, Lord, did we not prophesy in Your name, and in Your name cast out demons, and in Your name perform many miracles?' And then I will declare to them, 'I never knew you; DEPART FROM ME, YOU WHO PRACTICE LAWLESSNESS.'" Matthew 7:15-23

This passage does not declare that God is against using people to prophesy, cast out demons, and perform miracles—that would conflict with the context of Scripture—but that such trademarks of spiritual ministry fail to indicate whether a person is truly connected to Christ in an abiding relationship.

A *false prophet*, in my definition, is "someone who proclaims the ways of God, but functions according to the flesh as a way of life." Deception and fleshly living go hand in hand. In other (painful) words, outwardly we can be working for God while *opposing* Him in our hearts due to pride and self-centered motives. How can anyone who professes to love God think that living in opposition to Him with a pride-filled heart is an acceptable way of life?

Often, false prophets are blind to their own folly, convinced that Heaven's stamp of approval marks their ministries. Worse still, false prophets aren't just people who are "out there"—meaning the leaders of cults. Paul *strongly* cautioned the Ephesian church that "ravenous wolves" would *rise from their own ranks* if they allowed it (Acts 20:25-31). Both Jesus and Paul were referring to people who professed to serve God's "sheep" while actually feeding off of them.

The idea of false prophets arising within the church creates all manner of theological difficulties for us. I will not debate whether or not a person can lose his or her salvation, but I will say that we find enough warnings in Scripture to declare fleshly territory to be dangerous ground (Matthew 3:7-10 and 2 Peter 2).

When we think of false prophets, greed, of course, quickly comes to mind because we've seen far too many "spiritual" leaders who have approached ministry as a means to get rich. There is more to the picture however. An insecure leader who seeks to draw a sense of significance through the approval of the people he or she serves is behaving in a wolf-like manner. Practically speaking, I think that ministry is used as an ego trip far more than as a means to get rich.

Before you go and call out all of the "false prophets" that you know, please take a long look in the mirror. The highest agenda in the heart of a false prophet is self, while the core motivation of a fully fruitful leader will always be love. Somewhere in between the two extremes of false prophet and fully fruitful believer, we find a vast array of sincere people who truly desire to serve God but who struggle with impure motives. As long as we live in fleshly bodies, self-centered desires will try to dominate our hearts and minds. Such temptations can be as real for the aged saint as they are for the new believer.

I, for one, do not want to be in the habit of calling people *fleshly beasts* or *ravenous wolves*. In trying to correct those we consider to be devourers, we can easily become destroyers ourselves. Those who bear the fruit of the flesh, regardless of their self-professed motivations, will ultimately oppose and tear down—rather than build up—Christ's church. We dare not viciously attack others, but neither will true love ignore the bad fruits of sin, deception, and spiritual immaturity. Like deadly cancers, if unchecked, they will corrupt and destroy the vitality of our lives. This is where *we* need to be spiritually mature. Our goal is always to edify, not to savagely judge or condemn. Even when a person's negative behavior is long-term, we want to build up, not tear down.

Spiritual fruit grows over time—*process* is a key word—so we must be careful not to make rash judgments based on quick snapshots. Anyone can have a moment—or even a season—of weakness. Also, sincere leaders can struggle to find their identities as they serve under the extreme weight of ministry. In the end, I'm not sure which is worse in the eyes of Heaven—being a false prophet or wrongly accusing someone of being a false prophet. I don't think either option sits well with God. The key lies in doing what Jesus was implying through Matthew 5-7— that is training ourselves (and those we serve) to recognize good and bad fruit. There's no better way to begin recognizing the difference between the two than by being honest with our own motives.

It's generally easy to avoid associating ourselves with public personalities of doubtful character, but things get a lot more complicated with our interpersonal relationships. There are times when we will need to lovingly call out those in our sphere who exhibit signs of stinky fruit. The Bible provides us with instruction on how to do this in a healthy manner (Matthew 18:15-17 and Galatians 6:1).

THE MULTIPLICATION OF SPIRITUAL FRUIT

It is important to understand that fruitfulness involves growth *and* multiplication. Both the good and bad fruit borne in a person's life will be multiplied by hard work, gifts and talents, and technology. A self-absorbed musician's skill, for example, will multiply any bad influence in the lives of others. A devoted worship leader, on the other hand, will multiply his or her good influence in a similar way. Intercessory prayer adds another powerful dynamic that enables Christians to compound the good fruit of their lives.

Every Christian has the potential to bear the same *quality* of spiritual fruit because it flows from an ongoing relationship with Christ. However, because a host of other factors may be involved, not every believer will have the same *degree of multiplication* (Matthew 13:23). Our call is to bear the full potential of fruit that God has created and called us as unique individuals to bear—not to attempt to duplicate the measure of fruitfulness we see in the lives of others who have different gifts, strengths, and resources.

There is yet another element to fruitfulness that we should keep in mind. None of us is the be-all and end-all when it comes to fruitfulness; we're merely vessels being used by God to accomplish His plans and purposes. Due to the finite nature of human ability, we won't see the full cause and effect of our actions. Fruit can be growing invisible to the human eye, or it can mature and multiply long after we have been removed from the picture.

One evening a new Christian named Joe "accidentally" walked into one of our campus ministry meetings while looking for a different meeting. The story of Joe's salvation provides a powerful lesson in the nature of spiritual fruitfulness.

Joe had been a "Deadhead," meaning that he liked to get high and attend Grateful Dead concerts—often at the same time. A lost soul, Joe knew nothing of God and had no Christian friends or relatives. Every day, Joe did see a cafeteria lady—Marie—who loved Jesus. Marie was by no means at the pinnacle of human success. Her mundane job consisted of taking each student's meal card and putting it into a computerized machine to record the transaction. That was it—card in and card out, hundreds of times, day in and day out. In spite of her lack of outward success, the spiritual fruit of love was flourishing in Marie's heart. Marie didn't just process meal cards on a daily basis—she also prayed for the college students who owned them. Marie was particularly burdened for Joe; she could tell how lost he was simply by gazing into his eyes.

One evening, Joe got high and attended a Grateful Dead concert. It was something he had done on a number of occasions, only this particular event was anything but routine. Suddenly, in the middle of the concert, Joe had an epiphany of sorts as a strange new thought popped in his mind. Joe stared at the people around him—many of whom had removed themselves from reality through drug-induced stupors of their own—and asked himself a question that would forever change his life: "Is this all there is to life?"

That watershed moment began a process that opened Joe's heart to the gospel of Jesus Christ. Sometime later, he surrendered his life to God and became a new person in Christ. When the young man returned to the meal cart and gave Marie his card, she immediately recognized the change. "Joe, your eyes are different!" Marie exclaimed, near tears. Joe certainly was a different man.

Today Joe is happily married, the father of three children, and serving as a pastor in a fruitful church. His life is a million miles from a drug-induced stupor as he seeks to multiply in others the good fruit that God is growing in his own life. But Joe's fruit is also Marie's fruit! We don't know if Marie was the only one praying for that young man in his lost state, but we do know that her faithful prayers had a profound impact on his life, and, by the nature of fruitfulness, on the lives of all the people Joe has touched since. That's the way that the *seed principle* of fruitfulness works—the long-term ripple effects are far, far reaching.

While we don't want to ignore the importance of visible fruit, we also need to understand that there is so much that we cannot see. Our call is to be with God and to faithfully live out His will for our lives, to touch those unique spheres of influence that He has entrusted to us. I may not be able, for example, to gain an audience with your neighbor, but if I can influence you, I have the potential to impact the life of your neighbor. That's a trail worth blazing—awakening hearts to the importance of faithful seed-planting.

As scary as the idea of unfruitfulness may be, our potential to bear spiritual fruit is all the more exciting. No grand abilities are required. We simply learn to walk with God, abide in His empowering grace, and step out in obedience as the Holy Spirit leads. Only eternity will reveal the full ramifications of a life lived with God. Won't it be awesome to someday meet all of the people we've impacted through the fruit of our lives? Those who sacrificially give, pray, speak, and serve may one day find themselves being thanked by people who were not even born when such service was lovingly initiated.

THE ROLE OF THE VINE DRESSER

Do you remember our passage from John 15 about abiding in the vine (Jesus)? Who is the *vine dresser*? Our heavenly Father. And what is His goal? It is the same as any farmer or gardener—to nurture the plant to achieve the maximum production of fruit. Once again, we see that fruit-bearing really matters to God! How sad it is that we often (wrongly) accuse God of being an uncaring or absentee Father because we don't understand what He seeks to accomplish in our lives. We tend to focus on physical, temporal things while He always seeks to produce sweet, eternal fruit. Simply understanding this one issue can change the manner in which we handle adverse circumstances.

When I was a teen, my buddy's grandfather, Pap, would take his entire two-week vacation in August to pick blackberries. Each trip into the wild became a grand adventure of sorts. First in importance, was to clothe ourselves with coveralls and long-sleeve shirts, heavy enough to withstand the thorns, but light enough to keep us from sweating too much. We'd also strap on our boots to help protect from snake bites. In the days when safety seemed to have a different meaning, we'd all—

along with Sally the terrier—pile in the back of Pap's pickup truck. I think Sally loved blackberry picking more than all of us. Not only was she able to hang with the guys all day, she could chase small animals to her heart's delight.

Each blackberry picker wore a heavy leather belt to which an empty one-gallon jug (with the top cut off) would be strapped. This allowed us to pick berries with both hands, doubling our efficiency. Pap knew all of the best spots and led us in a constant search for the "mother lode"—that place where the berries were big, tasty, and abundant. Finding such a mother lode made for a short day as we filled our buckets to capacity. Then, on the drive home, we'd sing our own rendition of "Delta Dawn" while enjoying ice cream—topped with fresh blackberries, of course.

Little did I know that those experiences would give me valuable insight into the heart of our heavenly Father. "Be fruitful and multiply!" was His very first commandment/blessing to the human race. God desires that the fruit of the Spirit would develop and mature in us, and then be multiplied in the lives of those we serve. This is what the *Great Commission*—the call to make disciples—is all about (Matthew 28:18-20). Jesus' disciples are to bear the fruit of the Spirit and then multiply their fruit by teaching others what they've learned.

BLAZING A TRAIL TO FRUITFUL LIVING

Redefining success to mean "spiritual fruitfulness" will help us to get on track with God's design for our lives.

CHAPTER FIVE
BLAZING A TRIAL TO GROWTH

And we know that for those who love God all things work together for good, for those who are called according to his purpose. For those whom he foreknew he also predestined to be conformed to the image of his Son . . .

Romans 8:28-29a

The only people that God sends away empty are those who are full of themselves.

—Dwight L. Moody

The need for godly character is not limited to Christian leadership; a godly leader will be in big trouble if his or her people are not growing to spiritual maturity. A primary goal of a leader, then, should be to work with God to *form* the lives of people—to instruct, challenge, nurture, and pray for them to achieve the maximum production of spiritual fruit in their lives. This effort amounts to what some call "spiritual formation"—a term quite common in some Christian circles, but almost non-existent in others. Regardless of what terminology we use, in light of the Great Commission, spiritual formation should be at the top of our priority list.

Spiritual formation, in my own words, is "the intentional process by which a Christian grows into the likeness of Christ (i.e. fruitful maturity) through an abiding relationship with God and through interaction with other Christians." If you find my self-made definition to be inadequate, consider the following statement by the late Dallas Willard who had many profound things to say about spiritual formation:

> Spiritual formation for the Christian basically refers to the Spirit-driven process of forming the inner world of the human self in such a way that it becomes like the inner being of Christ himself.[13]

Ideally, the process of spiritual formation is intentional, involving a partnership between the Holy Spirit and the people of God. Personally, I find 1 Corinthians 3:6 to be one of the most profound verses in the entire Bible:

> *I planted, Apollos watered, but God was causing the growth.*

Paul got it! He understood that fruitfulness must be a collective effort between God and humankind. Indeed, one of the keys to truly fruitful service lies in understanding the difference between *God's* role and *our* role. We dare not attempt to do what only God can do, while it is sheer foolishness to wait for God to do what He has called us to do.

God calls us to abide in His grace and to do the things—teach, challenge, nurture, and pray—that will enable others to also abide. Growth won't happen without us playing a role, but, ultimately, true spiritual fruit springs only from the life that God imparts through the Holy Spirit of grace.

Christian discipleship must be active—otherwise nothing ever progresses. At the same time, it must be relational but not controlling. A person who is pressured and manipulated toward certain expected behaviors will never grow to full maturity. We can, however, support, teach, and coach one another to grow through difficult times. How we need wisdom to "plant" and "water" in ways that honor God and grow people!

FRUITFULNESS IN THE MIDST OF ADVERSITY

No matter how much a person desires to bear spiritual fruit, real and lasting transformation is never easy. Why? Various forces constantly work against growth. Some of the opposition is external. The devil and his lackeys will vigorously oppose the process of spiritual formation because the very thought of a spiritually mature Christian strikes terror in their dark hearts. Some humans don't appreciate spiritual growth

---

13. Dallas Willard, *Renovation of the Heart: Putting on the Character of Christ* (Colorado Springs: Navpress, 2002), 22.

very much either; humanistic goals almost always conflict with the advancement of God's kingdom. Unfortunately, no less opposition comes from within our own selves. Not only is the old fallen nature averse to change, it sees true spiritual growth as nothing less than a death threat. Thankfully, God is greater than them all!

That there are opponents to spiritual growth shouldn't surprise us. When Adam ate from the tree of the knowledge of good and evil, God proclaimed a curse over humanity's fruit-bearing efforts:

> ". . . Cursed is the ground because of you;
> In toil you will eat of it
> All the days of your life.
> Both thorns and thistles it shall grow for you;
> And you will eat the plants of the field;
> By the sweat of your face
> You will eat bread,
> Till you return to the ground,
> Because from it you were taken;
> For you are dust,
> And to dust you shall return." Genesis 3:17b-19

Just as the command/blessing to be fruitful and multiply was both physical and spiritual, so is the curse two-dimensional. While we honestly desire love, joy, and peace to characterize our hearts, selfishness, anger, and anxiety vie for dominance. I sometimes think that I am making progress in my spiritual growth until I need to call a company that has terrible customer service. Such experiences have a tendency to reveal the true depths of a person's heart. How do you know when you've arrived spiritually? When your heart remains peaceful and loving after an hour-long interaction with the customer *non-service* of a phone or utility company!

Fruit trees need to be fertilized and we are no different. Unfortunately for us, *manure* makes some of the best fertilizer. In other words, we cannot be truly successful in the eyes of eternity without going through a lot of crap in this life. ("Crap" is the least offensive word I could find to accurately convey my intended meaning.) So much for our idea of the blessed Christian life!

Manure is actually valued in a farming environment. In a suburban neighborhood with a bunch of backyard gardeners, it might even be treasured. I remember times when I'd bring home a truckload of horse manure for my garden, and my neighbors would suddenly emerge from the shadows. I would often hear, "Hey neighbor, are you planning to use *all* of that?" Each one truly appreciated his or her share of poop.

Spiritual manure, on the other hand, is never sought after. We generally do not appreciate adversity in spite of scriptural admonitions to value it (James 1:2-3). I suppose it's a matter of human nature. Regardless of how we feel about difficulties, it's essential that we recognize the profound work that our heavenly Father seeks to accomplish through challenging times. What a powerful expression of our Father's glory— He mysteriously turns even the worst-smelling stuff thrown at us into sweet, abundant fruit!

SPIRITUAL CHAMPIONS

I don't believe that God tries to bring misery and adversity into our lives—there is more than enough to go around in our fallen world. It's more like He refuses to entirely spare us from the mess we (the human race) have created. Instead of insulating us in a carefree existence, our loving Father grants us the grace to be *overcomers*, to grow into the stature of spiritual champions. A champion cannot exist apart from adversity; there can be no such thing as an overcomer if there is nothing to overcome (see the Christ's letters to the churches in Revelation 2-3).

I think that we often misinterpret what it means to be a victorious overcomer in Christ. For some reason, we believe that a true spiritual champion is never beset by personal problems or struggles. Some people will believe that because they struggle, something about them is uniquely flawed. In fact, Christians who have deep-seated, ongoing issues might begin to feel that they have been disqualified from bearing any type of significant fruit for God. Others will feel a sense of betrayal— that the Christian leaders they so trusted have painted a false picture of reality. In the end, all who view God as a heavenly fairy who needs only to wave His magic wand so that they can "live happily ever after" will be sorely disappointed.

We are all cut from the same cloth of human nature, but we're also unique individuals. Each of us is born into this world with a different genetic makeup, family structure (or lack thereof), and set of physical circumstances. A young black man who grows up fatherless in a violent inner city environment will probably have more external adversity— and therefore internal struggles—than an upper middle class white child born to a loving, two-parent family in the suburbs. Of course, outward images can often betray inward realities. A young, upper middle class girl abused by her father is going to have her own set of seemingly insurmountable struggles to overcome.

What does it mean to be a victorious overcomer in Christ? No matter what we go through in this life, no matter how distant the promises of God may feel, our loving Father will grant us the grace to live in victory over bitterness, hatred, despair, and any other dark mindsets that attempt to consume our lives. The key to overcoming adversity and bearing spiritual fruit lies in learning to believe God in the midst of difficulty, thereby drawing upon His abundant grace.

In Romans 8, we find what I believe is one of the most powerful promises in the Bible:

> *And we know that God causes all things to work together for good to those who love God, to those who are called according to His purpose. For those whom He foreknew, He also predestined to become conformed to the image of His Son, so that He would be the firstborn among many brethren; and these whom He predestined, He also called; and these whom He called, He also justified; and these whom He justified, He also glorified. Romans 8:28-30*

In all of my days, I have never found anything offered by this world that even comes close to this promise from our faithful God. However, we must note the promise is not that *all things will be good in our lives,* but that *God will work all things for our good*; that He will use every imaginable circumstance to conform us into the eternal image of Christ (i.e. make us spiritually fruitful). We may not entirely understand our circumstances, or even why a fruitful life is so important, but we can rest in the promise that our loving Father is always at work on behalf of those who love Him.

All of this is very good news for the average person. Bearing the fruit of the Spirit is rooted in our abiding relationship with Him, not in our natural abilities. Those born into adverse circumstances are not disqualified from fruitful service to God. Our failures, inabilities, and weaknesses need not disqualify us from fruitful lives. On the contrary, all of these things can help lay a *necessary* foundation of humility that challenges us to draw upon God's grace and keeps us from boasting when He uses us in powerful ways.

Those who know only earthly success without failure or difficulty will soon be beset by the deadly curse of *self*-confidence—as opposed to *Christ*-confidence. Their success will become their downfall. Not so when fruitfulness is our measure of success; spiritual fruit flourishes only when fertilized by humility.

LEARNING THE SUFFICIENCY OF CHRIST

Would you say that the apostle Paul lived a fruitful life? The question, in many ways, is absurd. If we could somehow measure the spiritual fruit of all the people who have ever lived, Paul would certainly be one of the top five inductees into *The Eternal Fruit Bearers Hall of Fame*. And yet, Paul often had significant struggles as he stepped out to serve God. He was a man of profound faith, but even the great apostle Paul wrestled with intense fears.

> *And when I came to you, brethren, I did not come with superiority of speech or of wisdom, proclaiming to you the testimony of God. For I determined to know nothing among you except Jesus Christ, and Him crucified. I was with you in weakness and in fear and in much trembling, and my message and my preaching were not in persuasive words of wisdom, but in demonstration of the Spirit and of power, so that your faith would not rest on the wisdom of men, but on the power of God. 1 Corinthians 2:1-5*

> *For we do not want you to be unaware, brethren, of our affliction which came to us in Asia, that we were burdened excessively, beyond our strength, so that we despaired even of life; indeed, we had the sentence of death within ourselves so that we would not trust in ourselves, but in God who raises the dead . . . 2 Corinthians 1:8-9*

Do we understand the message that Paul was trying to communicate to the Corinthian church? When we succeed, our natural tendency is to gain a sense of *self*-confidence that is rooted in pride, which in turn hinders us from becoming spiritually fruitful. In His wisdom, our loving Father will allow us to experience times of intense weakness—and even failure—in order to firmly establish us in the sufficiency of Christ. He always provides the grace that we need to overcome, but the process is often messy.

Embedded in Paul's story is an often overlooked message. Many understand—at least in theory—that God can do significant works of ministry through those with terribly flawed pasts. But what they often fail to realize is that when we step out in obedience to God, we will soon find ourselves in situations *intended* to bring the deep-rooted issues of our lives to the surface. This isn't because God is cruel, but because He seeks to transform the very core of who we are.

The more fruitful we become in Christ, the more usable we become for God's purposes. As painful as the struggle to grow into fruitful maturity may be, seeing God touch others through our difficulties breathes life into every painful memory. Almost anyone who has been down a similar path will testify that few things compare to being used to help others at the culmination of an intense personal struggle.

For as long as I can remember, I have believed in the existence of God. Still, at various times, I've struggled to trust Him for things such as forgiveness, a sense of identity, material provision, and favorable outcomes for specific circumstances. Long after I gave my life to Christ, living by faith continued to be a major challenge. Isn't it odd then that God would call me away from a full-time career as a chemist into the uncertain world of college ministry with no guaranteed salary? And isn't it odd that after becoming firmly established in campus ministry, Debi and I would then be called to start over by launching SfMe Ministries from scratch—with an even less certain income?

I wish I could say that I have made all of these transitions gracefully, with my feet barely touching the ground as I glided through the trials of life. Such is not the case. For this introverted, non risk-taker, such major steps of faith have created all sorts of angst. In many ways, the core of my being has been turned inside out. Still, in spite of my struggles, I have grown in ways that I never imagined, doing things that I never dreamed. Better yet, God is giving me a growing platform to touch others as I continue to learn and grow in the midst of my difficulties. My struggles may conflict with the image of ministry often portrayed by Christian leaders, but that just happens to be my reality. I'm not sure that I'll ever really "arrive" as a Christian leader, but I do believe that I can impact others—not in spite of my weaknesses, but because of them.

PAUL'S THORN IN THE FLESH

History has revealed that the greater the work God seeks to do *through* us, the deeper the work that He must do *in* us. We can see this essential principle illustrated, once again, through the life of the apostle Paul:

> *Because of the surpassing greatness of the revelations, for this reason, to keep me from exalting myself, there was given me a thorn in the flesh, a messenger of Satan to torment me—to keep me from exalting myself! Concerning this I implored the Lord three times that it might leave me. And He has said to me, "My grace is sufficient for you, for power is perfected in weakness." Most gladly, therefore, I will rather boast about my weaknesses, so that the power of Christ may dwell in me. Therefore I am well content with weaknesses, with insults, with distresses, with persecutions, with difficulties, for Christ's sake; for when I am weak, then I am strong.* 2 Corinthians 12:7-10

Paul's "thorn in the flesh" mentioned in this passage has become a controversial topic. We sometimes read too much into the text. The Greek word translated as "messenger" is *angelos*, which can refer to a person, but usually speaks of an angelic spirit.[14] In this case, it would be a fallen angel—that is a demon. The goal of the demon was to harass Paul in order to stop him from proclaiming the life-changing message of the gospel. All the while, God had a different goal—to keep Paul abiding in His grace. In spite of Paul's frustrations and protests, God did not answer his repeated request to remove the demon from his life.

---

14. Robert L. Thomas, *New American Standard Hebrew-Aramaic and Greek Dictionaries: Updated Edition* (Anaheim: Foundation Publications, Inc., 1998).

We must note that this was a unique situation and Paul's ongoing struggle was not due to any lack of faith; the apostle was quite familiar with treading over demonic powers. No, something bigger was at play. Paul would influence so many lives that, through His mercy, God needed to protect His faithful apostle from becoming "full of himself." Thus the messenger from Satan, although intent on destroying Paul, ultimately served God's sovereign purposes by helping Paul grow in grace. How I love it when Heaven turns Hell's plans upside down!

GRACE THROUGH WEAKNESS?

From the context of 2 Corinthians 12:7-10, we can highlight a broad principle: we draw more fully upon the power of God's transformational grace as we walk in a greater measure of humility. While weakness and adversity appear to hinder the work that God calls us to, they can actually *increase* our long-term fruitfulness by training us in the way of humility.

I love the Bible, but there are some things about it that rub me the wrong way. This is one such concept. What red-blooded male *boasts* about his weaknesses? Not only does this mentality run against the grain of human pride, males learn from a young age that showing weakness makes them targets for bullies. Such is the cruel world in which we live.

"The in-laws" (my wife's affectionate term for our daughter-in-law's family) own a small farm a few miles out of town. Recently one of their three male ducks hurt his little duck leg. Upon seeing his injury, the other two mallards began attacking the one who (mistakenly) considered the others to be friends. Only through the father-in-law's human intervention was the duck's life spared.

Sadly, the tendency to attack the weak is also common among people. I suppose that those who don't know the love of Christ have an excuse, but this type of behavior is very disturbing when exhibited by the people of God. It's a sad fact that even Christians can be "pouncers" who lurk in the shadows, waiting for a perceived opponent to show some sign of weakness or struggle. As soon as the moment presents itself, they strike with toxic venom! God doesn't operate this way, but sin sure does (Genesis 4:7).

In light of the vulnerability that weakness brings, Paul's mindset is all the more puzzling. To boast of his weaknesses instead of hiding them was risky behavior indeed. Why did Paul do it? God had given him revelation not only of heaven, but of how to abide in grace.

I'll be honest with you—I'm not quite there yet and I don't think I'm alone. Whether due to my stupid male pride, or to the fear of being judged, I cannot freely boast about my weaknesses. Only little by little do I inch closer as I more fully lay hold of the dynamics of grace.

The Creator of the Universe knows how to transform people. Somehow, He is able to take our flawed areas—the ones that we think disqualify us from being fruitful—and use them to make us *more* fruitful. I think, at least in part, the mystery can be understood by realizing that our struggles and weaknesses compel us to rely more fully on the sufficiency of God's grace instead of on self-sufficiency. Whether we refer to personal shortcomings, difficult times, or demonic opposition, God's empowering grace will enable us to do whatever He calls us to do. The process breaks down, however, when we lift ourselves up in pride, laboring hard to hide every perceived crack in our armor.

FLAWED BEAUTY

During my college years, I had a good friend who majored in studio art. As the primary assignment for a sculpting class, Karen took an old granite tombstone and created a beautiful design. With a master plan in mind, she began chipping away at the hard stone.

Imagine Karen's dismay when a simple tap with a hammer and chisel broke a large piece of granite away from the sculpture. In an instant, her entire plan was ruined. With no choice but to move forward, Karen redesigned her sculpture according to what the granite would allow. The end result was a beautiful piece of work chosen for display in the university art show. Who knew?

If my friend Karen was able to salvage a flawed piece of granite to create a masterpiece, how much more is the all-knowing Sculptor of the Universe able to create amazing works of glory from our flawed human lives? Even our fault lines can serve to reveal God's greatness; they need not disqualify us from becoming fruitful.

The great college basketball coach, John Wooden, once told his players, "Don't let what you cannot do interfere with what you can do." What excellent advice for someone who wants to serve God! The fact that a person falls short in *many* ways does not mean that the individual lacks in *every* way. All too often, we allow our shortcomings in one area to stop us from effectively serving God in another. Is it possible that God allows such deficiencies so that we won't become puffed up with pride?

I am sufficient as a public speaker, but I am not dynamic. Time after time, I've found myself frustrated because my marginal ability as an orator has hindered me from gaining a broader platform to share the life-changing truths that God has revealed to me. Tempted to give up, I finally "reinvented" my ministry self as a writer. Publishing my work has been a slow, tedious process, and I still have a lot to learn, but I dare not render myself unfruitful because I fail to meet some people's expectations for public speaking ability.

I am inspired by the heroes of our faith listed in Hebrews 11. They were flawed people who endured long formative seasons of difficulty before coming into the fullness of their callings. Some served God in quiet obscurity. Others weathered seasons of extreme adversity and testing. In spite of the difficulties, in spite of the darkness, and in spite of the lack of visible fruit, they persevered. Coming to the end of themselves, they learned to draw upon the all-sufficient grace of God. Then, in the fullness of time, each produced a rich harvest of fruit—the influence of which continues to our day.

BLAZING A TRAIL TO FRUITFUL LIVING

On our journey toward fruitfulness, we must learn to process the weaknesses, shortcomings, and adverse circumstances of our lives through the eye of faith.

CHAPTER SIX
LEARNING TO REST IN CHRIST'S SUFFICIENCY

"Come to Me, all who are weary and heavy-laden, and I will give you rest. Take My yoke upon you and learn from Me, for I am gentle and humble in heart, and YOU WILL FIND REST FOR YOUR SOULS."

Matthew 11:28-29

No soul can be really at rest until it has given up all dependence on everything else and has been forced to depend on the Lord alone.

—Hannah Whitall Smith

I would be remiss if I failed to mention the importance of spiritual rest when it comes to bearing spiritual fruit. A mango tree does not labor hard to produce mangos. The process is all very natural as the roots, trunk, branches, and leaves work together to produce excess life for our benefit. In a similar sense, bearing the sweet fruit of the Holy Spirit is the "natural" result of a supernatural process that comes from abiding in Christ.

Hebrews 4:9 speaks of a "Sabbath rest" for the people of God. The substance of this topic could fill a book all by itself. The idea of a non-working day of physical rest under the Mosaic Law illuminates a greater spiritual truth in the New Covenant: Jesus Christ has become our Sabbath rest. While the previous "six days" were characterized by our need to work for righteousness, the "seventh day"—the day of salvation (2 Corinthians 6:2)—is to be one in which labor ceases. That doesn't mean we should stop working for God, but that we should stop working for our righteousness as we surrender control and cease all efforts to make ourselves acceptable in Heaven's eyes.

Truly effective labor flows out of spiritual rest; however, such rest is not to be confused with a passive lifestyle. While spiritual fruit is borne from spiritual rest, the multiplication of fruit requires effort. Life begins by *being with* God which, as love mandates, is followed by *doing things for* God as we are *empowered by* God.

Once again, we return to the centrality of Christ's sufficiency. Our lives bear spiritual fruit as we learn to draw upon the transformational grace of God. This happens only as the reality of God's unmerited favor dawns in our hearts. In that favor we rest. In other words, we don't strive to bear spiritual fruit in an effort to gain God's favor; we rest in the confidence that our favor has *already* been gained through faith in Christ's life, death, and resurrection. Everything—our relationship with God, the transformation of our lives, and our service to God—flows out of trusting in the sufficiency of Christ's work on the cross.

Christianity is not a self-improvement project. Nor is it about striving to be a perfect person. We seek to align ourselves with God's design, to stay connected to the vine, and to draw upon all that He has for us by trusting in all that He has done for us. The problem—and it's a big one—is that the idea of spiritual rest runs contrary to our natural bent. We don't want to receive God's favor as a gift. We want to *earn* it. Therefore, we either refuse to accept that our natural tendency is to produce roadkill fruit, or we vigorously work to cut away any bad fruit that may appear. The human heart must constantly see itself in a favorable light—an exhausting proposition in itself.

THE NEED FOR A "BLOODY RELIGION"

Christ's sacrificial death was a bloody mess, but it's the centrality of the cross that marks the difference between true Christianity and manmade religion. There are those who seek to remove the crucifixion from Christian thought and practice. Doing so promises the opportunity for humans to relate to God on *their own* terms—not His. The transformational power of grace is then discarded as we open the door for self-sufficiency to flourish.

To remove the *blood* of Jesus is to remove the *life* of Jesus, disconnecting us from His grace. This can be a difficult concept to grasp—especially in a world where hamburgers come fully cooked within two minutes of ordering. Do we understand that animals die and are butchered—a bloody, messy process—so that we can eat meat? In a similar vein, Christ's sacrificial death was ugly but also necessary if sinful humans are to experience true life.

Many a well-intentioned Bible reader has begun at Genesis 1:1 only to be bogged down by the tedious book of Leviticus. Reading about ancient laws, rituals, and sacrifices can sometimes feel like eating sand. And yet, the sacrificial system of the Old Testament provides much needed insights for us as Christians.

From the very first sin, animals died that we might live (Genesis 3:21). Or do we somehow think that God clothed Adam and Eve with animal skins without killing the animals from which those skins came? Not long after, Cain brought God an offering of *his own* choosing, while Abel sacrificed animals from his flock (Genesis 4:1-5). The Bible doesn't specify exactly why God regarded Abel's offering and rejected Cain's, but His response makes more sense when we consider ancient thought.

Sin is integrally linked to death (Genesis 2:15-17 and 1 Corinthians 15:56). For sin to be covered, life must be imparted through the shedding of blood. Forgiveness of sin does not come without a price. Animal sacrifices, therefore, *atoned* for the sins of humans. Leviticus 17:11 provides a powerful glimpse of this concept:

"For the life of the flesh is in the blood, and I have given it to you on the altar to make atonement for your souls; for it is the blood by reason of the life that makes atonement."

This principle—the life of the flesh being present in the blood—was understood by virtually every ancient culture. According to H. Clay Trumbull, "It was not merely that the taking away of blood was the taking away of life; but that the taking in of blood was the taking in of life, and of all that life represented."[15]

---

15. H. Clay Trumbull, *The Blood Covenant: A Primitive Rite and Its Bearings on Scripture* (Kirkwood, MO: Impact Christian Books, 1975), 126

Consequently, we don't work for life; we receive life. Sadly, this understanding was perverted to the point that barbaric practices prevailed in ancient times. It was not uncommon for a warrior to devour the heart and/or liver of a worthy enemy in an effort to gain his strength and vitality.[16] A similar mindset was involved with drinking blood. The ancients understood the principle that the life of flesh is in the blood, but they sought to establish their own means of atonement apart from God's manner of provision.

Through the Levitical sacrifices, the life of an animal's blood temporarily covered human sins. Unfortunately (for the animal), the animal had to die for the life of its blood to be utilized. As unpleasant and unfair as it may sound, this is the ugly reality of sin. In a sense, the reeking stench of rotting flesh had to be covered by the fragrant aroma of meat roasting over a fire. Without the aroma of the sacrifice, the stench of death would remain indefinitely. The sacrificial system of the Old Testament temporarily pleased God because it atoned for human sins. Still, animal sacrifices never fully reflected God's passion for life.

Under the Levitical system, a sacrificial animal had to be perfect to be accepted by God. The innocent and perfect died that the guilty and flawed might live. In the same way, Jesus lived a perfectly sinless life so that His one-time sacrificial death might atone for the sins of all humans. The all-sufficient Christ became the sacrificial Lamb of God whose life nullified the death of human sin. In other words, the curse of sin was broken so that the ground of our hearts might bear sweet and abundant fruit.

As much as God wants the fruit of the Holy Spirit to proliferate in our lives, we must clearly understand that spiritual fruit *never* establishes our righteousness—or acceptability—in the eyes of God. It is here that an accurate understanding of the unmerited favor dimension of grace is essential. *Regardless of how spiritually mature we may become, our acceptance by God is always based on the sufficiency of Christ through His sacrificial death on the cross.* Without the cross, it is impossible for us to maintain any type of relational connection with God. Without the cross, we are lost in our sins, destined to be mired in death.

---

16. Ibid., 128.

ACCESS TO THE THRONE OF GRACE

To learn—to know and experience—the sufficiency of Christ is to abide in grace. Through the sufficiency of Christ—and only through the sufficiency of Christ—we have instant and immediate access to God's throne of grace during times of need.

> *Therefore, since we have a great high priest who has passed through the heavens, Jesus the Son of God, let us hold fast our confession. For we do not have a high priest who cannot sympathize with our weaknesses, but One who has been tempted in all things as we are, yet without sin. Therefore let us draw near with confidence to the throne of grace, so that we may receive mercy and find grace to help in time of need. Hebrews 4:14-16*

When are our greatest times of need? When we are overcome by sin! The worst thing a person can do when struggling with sin is attempt to run away from God. Do we realize the abject foolishness of trying to run from the only One who can truly meet our desperate needs? It would be like a person who is dying of thirst fleeing from a fresh mountain spring until he or she is no longer thirsty. Our only real hope lies in turning back to the wellspring of life.

Being that the Creator of the Universe sees and knows everything, we deceive only ourselves when we attempt to hide our sins. When we bring our struggles to our heavenly Father, it's not like we're providing Him with new information. I can't imagine God saying, "Oh, I didn't realize you were doing *that!*" His gaze penetrates the very depths of the soul. Perhaps that's why we feel so uncomfortable when we know we're in the wrong; the holy light of God shining on the ugliness of human sin can create a most unpleasant experience.

For some twisted reason, we feel that we must clean ourselves up before coming into His presence. Do we not understand that such a mindset reveals a deadly fallacy? In light of Hebrews 4:14-16, consider my one-question "self-test." (You can relax; it's not all that complicated, and I won't grade your answer.) The question is: *Do you come to God's throne of grace with the same degree of confidence when you are struggling as when you feel that you are doing well spiritually?*

Let's suppose that you have a great week, doing everything that you think God expects of you. You read large portions of the Bible, boldly share your faith, and significantly help others in desperate need. When it comes time to pray, do you approach the unseen throne of God with confidence? Of course you do. Now let's imagine that the following week is the polar opposite. You stay up too late watching TV and miss your morning Bible reading, you shrink back in fear when given the opportunity to present the gospel, and you lie to protect your image. Do you approach the throne of God with the same measure of confidence as when you felt you were doing well? You should!

Whether we feel that we are being holy, fruitful, or productive for God or not, our access to His throne of grace always rests upon the sufficiency of Christ. In other words, the fully fruitful believer leans just as heavily on the blood of Jesus as does the person who is struggling to break free from sin. Indeed, it is this type of unwavering trust in Christ's sufficiency that enables us to abide in His grace, overcome sin, and bear the fruit of the Spirit. Do you want to become a victorious overcomer in life? Learn to rest in the sufficiency of Christ *regardless* of how well you think you are doing.

What marvelous news this is for the soul who has tasted the depths and horrors of sin! What profound encouragement for the man or woman who feels like a fruitless failure in the eyes of eternity! Only through the life, death, and resurrection of Jesus can we find real rest from the never-ending demand for perfection.

GRACE TO HELP IN TIME OF NEED

Accessing God's throne of grace need not be difficult. We simply approach God in prayer and acknowledge our need for Him. I find it unfortunate that some Christians contend that a believer who is struggling with sin should never confess that sin to God or ask for forgiveness. After all, if Christ died for all sins for all time, is it not an act of unbelief to confess our sins and to ask Him to forgive us? Shouldn't we simply believe in what He has done for us? Simply put, the answer is *no*.

Even if such a belief were true in principle, it is dangerous when put into practice. Why? Human pride. Confessing our sins to God—and to others—and asking for forgiveness provides an opportunity for us to humble our hearts so that we may draw upon His transformational grace. Attempting to believe in Christ's forgiveness without "doing business" at the cross can allow human pride to flourish under a pretense of faith. Pride, as we will soon see, is the archenemy of grace. If we attempt to use faith and grace as excuses to walk in pride, we effectively invalidate the power of the New Covenant to transform human lives. In addition, failing to bring our sins to the cross prevents us from bringing much-needed closure to our moral failures.

If you become aware of sin in your life, don't wallow under a cloud of guilt and condemnation. Instead, go directly to God in prayer, fully confess your sin(s), and ask Him to forgive your wayward behavior. If it is a long-term struggle, I suggest you record the day and time in a journal so that you can close the door on your guilt. Only then is it time to stand in faith on God's promises for forgiveness while resting in the sufficiency of Christ (Proverbs 28:13 and 1 John 1:5-10). It will not profit you to attempt some type of penance, or to continually beg for forgiveness. The matter is settled in Heaven and so should it be in your heart.

If for some reason, you still cannot move beyond your struggles with sin and condemnation, it is time to confess your behavior to a trusted friend, leader, or counselor who is mature in Christ. Why might this be necessary? God opposes the proud and gives grace to the humble (James 4:6 and 5:16). Sometimes we need to take the extra step of crucifying our pride by exposing our shortcomings to another person.

I remember a time when I could not break free from a personal sin regardless of what I tried. I prayed. I fasted. I confessed my failures to God. I stood on His promises. Things that normally worked seemed of no value, and my frustration level skyrocketed. This was a significant issue that I could not ignore, so I asked a trusted friend if we could talk. After confessing my sin to him and receiving prayer, I finally found the freedom for which I had been searching.

As is often the case with medicine, we may be tempted to reason that if a little confession is good, then a lot of confession would be better. For example, a person might think that posting personal struggles on social media will get God's attention by showing how serious the individual is about the issue. In most cases, such a move would be nothing short of foolish. There's no need to allow uncaring and untrustworthy people into the sensitive areas of your life. (One exception would be public sins. If you've done something that everyone already knows about, or that has negatively affected a large group of people, then a public confession might be warranted.)

God is gracious and compassionate; He will never despise a broken and contrite heart (Psalms 51:17). When we choose to humble ourselves, we are positioned to draw upon our Savior's transformational grace. The process may be difficult and painful, but He will work on our behalf in marvelous ways. If we refuse to humble ourselves and bring our sins into the light, we will know Him only from a distance. Be fully warned: human pride is too cunning for us to avoid the practice of confession. Those who seek to be fully fruitful dare not ignore this reality!

GOD IS PATIENT

As much as God expects you to bear fruit, He is amazingly patient with the growing process. The sacrificial Lamb of God is also your faithful *high priest* who bridges the gap between a holy God and sinful humanity. Jesus walked this earth in human flesh for over thirty years, was tempted in every natural manner, and willingly took upon Himself all of our sins, fears, and diseases. Trust me, Jesus the Christ understands the depths of your struggles. For the person who wants to walk with God—and even for many who don't—His patience seems to know no bounds.

I learned a little about God's patience several years ago through a decision to grow blueberries in my backyard. I planted several bushes, expending a lot of effort to build an enclosure out of chicken wire. I didn't want "evil" birds to eat the fruits of my labors. One of my berry bushes gave me fits as it struggled to grow. In fact, it seemed to do almost nothing for over two years, having only a short little stub that appeared to be dead. I began to wonder whether there was any value in continuing to nurture that particular plant. I was about to rip it out and plant a new bush when I remembered the following parable from the book of Luke:

And He [Jesus] began telling this parable: "A man had a fig tree which had been planted in his vineyard; and he came looking for fruit on it and did not find any. And he said to the vineyard-keeper, 'Behold, for three years I have come looking for fruit on this fig tree without finding any. Cut it down! Why does it even use up the ground?' And he answered and said to him, 'Let it alone, sir, for this year too, until I dig around it and put in fertilizer; and if it bears fruit next year, fine; but if not, cut it down.'" Luke 13:6-9

After finding and reading this passage, I decided to give that little sprig another year. I am so glad that I did! The next year the bush began to grow, eventually becoming one of my best producers. That experience spoke to me so much that I named the bush *Kristy* after a friend who had been struggling for a long time to walk with God and was finally learning to abide in His life.

God doesn't stop forming someone until that person draws his or her final breath. Until that time, the Master Gardener will use everything—and I mean *everything*—to make His children fruitful. If you look at your life and see nothing but bad fruit, you are not without hope. You now have an enviable truckload of humility that has etched your dire need for God's grace upon your heart.

Please also note that timing is a critical element when it comes to achieving the full potential of fruitfulness. An apple tree won't fully mature for several years—as many as ten for some varieties. In spite of the obvious lack of fruit, those first years of growth are by no means wasted; the tree simply bides its time as it grows to full maturity.

You might spend a long time serving God with little or no "external" fruit to show for your efforts. Such formative seasons of slow growth and elusive fruit are never to be despised because they are meant to teach you to labor from a place of spiritual rest. When the appropriate time comes, God will bring the multiplication in ways you never imagined. Because you are becoming fruitful over a long period of time, and because humility is being instilled through the rigors of adversity, visible success will not corrupt the core of your being. If you are struggling in your service to God, please take heart; your delayed success might just be a gracious gift from your loving Father.

BLAZING A TRAIL TO FRUITFUL LIVING

We can increase the lasting fruitfulness of our labors by learning to rest in the sufficiency of God's grace in good times and in bad.

CHAPTER SEVEN
THE CORE ISSUES OF OUR EXISTENCE

"They have healed the brokenness of My people superficially, saying, 'Peace, peace,' but there is no peace."

Jeremiah 6:14

There are a thousand hacking at the branches of evil to one who is striking at the root.

—Henry David Thoreau

I learned how to drive in a 1975 maroon Chevy Vega with an aluminum block engine and 3-speed manual transmission. The car had sat idle for a while, causing the clutch cable to rust. That crazy clutch pedal took nearly all of my leg strength to operate!

For those unfamiliar with manual transmissions, the clutch enables the engine and the wheels to engage or disengage. When the clutch pedal is fully depressed, a person can speed the engine to a million revolutions per minute (rpms), but go absolutely nowhere. As the clutch pedal is slowly released, the transmission hits what is usually called the "friction point." Only then does the transmission begin to engage so that the engine can drive the wheels.

Learning to hit the friction point just right is somewhat of an art. I literally jerked my passengers around as I was learning to drive—partly due to my inexperience and partly due to the stiffness of that rusty clutch cable. And getting stopped on a hill was never fun—especially when the car behind me pulled right up to my bumper. Thankfully, we all survived, apparently whiplash-free.

ENGAGING SPIRITUAL FRICTION POINTS

Did you know that people have *spiritual friction points*? They are the places where we live—the points of contact between our inner motivations and God's transformational truth. Spiritual growth doesn't result simply from accumulating knowledge; it comes only as truth touches the inner places of our hearts that move us to action. When God's word touches a spiritual friction point, those who are willing begin to move from where they are toward a more fruitful existence.

For example, devoted Christians are often plagued by feelings of condemnation centering on their inability to be perfect. The world of self-condemnation is where many of us live, and it is full of bad feelings that assail our hearts like the insects and diseases that attack fruit trees. The answer? Applying God's truth to our point of need.

> *Therefore there is now no condemnation for those who are in Christ Jesus. For the law of the Spirit of life in Christ Jesus has set you free from the law of sin and of death. Romans 8:1-2*

What freedom and peace flood the hearts of those who grasp the reality of God's forgiveness and grace! Freed from the heavy weight of condemnation, they are then able to move forward in their Christian growth and service. This is but one area of life in which touching a spiritual friction point with truth will result in genuine change.

A person can spend his or her entire lifetime learning about Christian living, but if spiritual friction points are never properly engaged, that person will make little or no real progress toward fruitfulness. He or she will confuse the accumulation of knowledge with growth, and, spiritually speaking, remain perpetually immature. Looking back over my own life, I can now see that real change started when God's word began to touch the root issues at the core of my being.

While I needed the strength of my entire leg to move the clutch on my old Chevy Vega, God needs only a word of truth to touch the appropriate places in our hearts. That is only the beginning of the process, though. Once our spiritual friction points are identified, it can still take a long time for us to learn how to "operate" smoothly. Even when we know what to do, life can still be rather jerky at times. Still, being aware of these key points will help us to focus our attention on issues that are relevant to growth.

DEALING WITH OUR CORE ISSUES

As God began to address the core issues in my life, I came to realize a similar need in the body of Christ at large. Generally, it seems that spiritual friction points are either ignored, or they are addressed in a clumsy manner. The result is a large number of people who genuinely want to walk with God and live in victory over sin, but who find themselves bogged down in the muck and mire of fleshly behavior. Several sad scenarios can result when we fail to properly address our root motivations:

1. **We withdraw into our own little worlds, thinking that we are uniquely and hopelessly flawed.** Through an isolated existence, we often lead double lives—presenting images of what we think people expect, but acting like the real us when watchful eyes are focused elsewhere.

   The truth is that we are all born with the same bent toward sinful behavior. Various contributing factors, however, can magnify undesirable tendencies. Someone who has experienced the trauma of physical abuse, for example, will often face an accentuated struggle with the need to be in control. In other words, none of us really has it all together, but some have a more difficult time than others *keeping it together*. Even for a fully devoted Christian, just functioning on a day-to-day basis might feel like an overwhelming task. Thankfully, while we may carry scars of past hurts, we are not destined to wallow in pain and misery. Our loving Father is willing and able to bring healing, wholeness, and freedom. Where sin abounds, grace abounds all the more (Romans 5:20).

   Of course, it doesn't have to be our own sins that compound our struggles. To one degree or another, we've all paid an unfair price because of the self-absorbed behavior of others. How blessed we are that God's sovereign grace knows no bounds; He can redeem even the worst injustice. Joseph, for example, suffered unfairly, but God provided the grace to face the unjust betrayal by his brothers.

Only in the end did the Master's plan become fully evident—
and what a marvelous plan it was! Joseph's faithful perseverance
reaped a massive harvest (Genesis 37-50).

2. **We give up trying, choosing to walk away from God and the
    Christian faith.** It's better to be a happy sinner than a miserable
    one—or so we think! Walking away from God is a bad plan that
    will lead to a road filled with regrets. I've interacted with some
    people who have turned their backs on God; it is nothing short
    of tragic. I understand how disillusionment can lead to such a
    place and think that many who doubt have valid questions and
    accurate perceptions. Unfortunately, by leaning on their own
    intelligence—yet another manifestation of human pride—they
    arrive at faulty conclusions. In the end, they offer no real hope or
    meaning for life. There is only a sad, mournful monologue that
    asks a million questions while providing no substantive answers.

3. **We bounce from "Christian" fad to fad, searching for the next
    new thing that will propel us and the church to victory.** I've
    watched this disturbing process for many years. Failing to realize
    that God has already provided all that we need through the cross
    of Christ, we latch onto the next great revelation of truth, the
    next great celebrity Christian leader, or the next great spiritual
    movement—all with the hopes of seeing long-awaited change.
    Sadly, in the wake of each new fad we find a trail of disillusioned
    and damaged souls. Fads are not true paths to fruitfulness. We
    want to blaze a road for generations to follow, not rabbit-trails
    that disappear into the woods, leading followers astray.

Should we be open to fresh trends that help grow the body of
Christ? Absolutely! But don't look for the next new thing to fix
the church and make it all better; the "new" thing that we need
has already come to us in the form of the *New Covenant*. Those
who seek personal and corporate transformation must delve
deeper into the workings of the New Covenant gospel of grace.
The complete gospel, as we shall see, touches us where we live.

4. **We run from person to person, looking for comfort and encouragement in the midst of our seemingly overwhelming difficulties.** Our focus becomes feeling better about ourselves and our situations. We listen to upbeat music, try to think happy thoughts, and look for people to pat us on the back. And while this approach can be helpful to an extent, it might be compared to ignoring nutritious food in lieu of sweets. I ate more than my share of dark chocolate bars during the long, tedious process of writing this book. They really did help me stay better focused, but I didn't dare allow them to form the bulk of my diet!

A sugar high is short-lived; its momentary boost will be followed by a letdown, which then requires another "fix." The resulting cycle? An ever-worsening addiction to sweets. Christians who ignore the meat of God's word while focusing only on what makes them feel better will soon be entrapped by an "encouragement addiction." Rather than relying on God as the primary source of their strength, survival will seem impossible apart from encouraging words and happy meetings.

All this being said, I have no problem with ministries that exist solely for the sake of encouraging people; God knows we need them in this discouraging age. We all need to be encouraged and uplifted. The church must be a place where we draw comfort, encouragement, and strength from one another. But if spiritual *dessert* forms the bulk of our spiritual diet, we will soon find ourselves in a spiritual *desert*. As important as encouragement and relational support are, they cannot facilitate healing, wholeness, and freedom unless we allow God's truth to penetrate the core issues of our hearts.

Regardless of what other people do, or don't do, you must fully embrace truth—even when it hurts. If you want friends, join a social club. If you need a spiritual lift, turn on a Christian TV program. But if you want to know God, if you desire to live fruitfully, and if you seek to make a lasting mark in this world, then you dare not avoid dealing with the core issues of your heart.

ORIGINAL SIN

As much as we hate to admit it, every human heart possesses natural tendencies that are *opposed* to God. That's right—opposed to God. Humanists laud the *human spirit* that shines as the pinnacle of the evolutionary process. Conservative Christians call it the *sin nature*—the unfortunate result of Adam's and Eve's original sin. That is because the Scriptures treat human nature (aka *the flesh*) not as a cherished friend to be celebrated, but as a deadly foe to be overcome.

> *For those who are according to the flesh set their minds on the things of the flesh, but those who are according to the Spirit, the things of the Spirit. For the mind set on the flesh is death, but the mind set on the Spirit is life and peace, because the mind set on the flesh is hostile toward God; for it does not subject itself to the law of God, for it is not even able to do so, and those who are in the flesh cannot please God. Romans 8:5-8*

Wow! This passage presents an intense thought: our natural human way of thinking and operating is *hostile*—not friendly—toward God. The fiercest, most deceptive enemy a person will ever face is not the devil, but rather his or her own fallen *self*. Herein lies the great struggle of the ages. Those who wish to know God will face an *inner* opposition that must be overcome. Otherwise, we will proclaim Christ while our lives are characterized by self-determination. All the while, we use religious trappings as "fig leaves" to cloak our self-seeking agendas.

As you can already sense, addressing the issue of original sin is not a "feel good" experience. It won't be accompanied by vanilla bean ice cream covered with pretty red and green sprinkles. Focusing on the dynamics of human nature will bring us face to face with the unpleasant reality of what is often called "the human condition." In more ways than one, the human condition stinks, and yet it is by no means hopeless. The bad news is that something within our own natures stands violently opposed to the Giver of Grace. The good news is that if we can learn how to "disengage" the flesh and "engage" the Spirit, favorable changes will surely follow. God's grace enables us to move beyond the roadkill stench of the human condition, enveloping our day-to-day lives in Heaven's fragrant aroma.

BACK TO THE BEGINNING

Many of the issues we face today are rooted in ancient history—as are the solutions to many of our perplexing problems. Biblically, Romans, Galatians, and all other books of the New Testament are founded upon the text of the Old Testament. Early Genesis is especially important because that is where we find not only the origins of humanity, but of human nature as well.

Due to my scientific background, I understand well that an intense debate rages over the scientific accuracy of the creation account. Too often, though, we miss the central focus of early Genesis—the dynamics involved with the relationship between God and humanity. If the human race fails to embrace the key messages of Genesis, it is to our own detriment. The entire Bible rises to the pinnacle of insight and understanding as it reveals the painful dynamics of human nature.

Approaching Genesis from this perspective, I have found it to be a profound document. How could the ancients have understood so much about human behavior? From the few short pages of the creation story, I have learned more about the core dynamics of human nature than from the psychology, sociology, and anthropology classes I took in college. If we truly want to pursue higher learning, it begins with the Bible. Two short passages from Chapter Two of Genesis will help us get started:

> *Then the LORD God formed man of dust from the ground, and breathed into his nostrils the breath of life; and man became a living being. The LORD God planted a garden toward the east, in Eden; and there He placed the man whom He had formed. Out of the ground the LORD God caused to grow every tree that is pleasing to the sight and good for food; the tree of life also in the midst of the garden, and the tree of the knowledge of good and evil. Genesis 2:7-9*

> *Then the LORD God took the man and put him into the garden of Eden to cultivate it and keep it. The LORD God commanded the man, saying, "From any tree of the garden you may eat freely; but from the tree of the knowledge of good and evil you shall not eat, for in the day that you eat from it you will surely die." Genesis 2:15-17*

IMPORTANT OBSERVATIONS FROM GENESIS TWO

These six verses of Scripture provide the groundwork for understanding the relationship between the Creator of the Universe and the human race. Consider the five brief observations below:

1. **Chapters One and Two of Genesis give us a glimpse of God's *desire* for the human race.** That the name *Eden* is synonymous with the concept of paradise is entirely accurate. In fact, *Eden* means "pleasure" or "delight" in the original Hebrew language.[17] God intended a luxurious, delightful, and fruitful existence for His human children. No pain. No suffering. No death.

   The first two chapters of Genesis are especially significant because we have grown accustomed to viewing our Creator through the lens of a sin-stained existence. Recently, a woman in our area died while giving birth to twins. A day or two later, a sixteen-year-old girl was killed in a car accident. Tragic! How do we process heartbreaking events like these and still maintain our sanity? If we see God as the source of death and destruction, or if we somehow feel that He is uncaring or powerless, we are in trouble. If, however, we understand that our heavenly Father desires only good for us—as observed in the early Genesis account—then our hearts awaken with hope!

2. **Humankind was given almost total *freedom* with only *one* (protective) boundary—the command not to eat from the tree of the knowledge of good and evil.** This command might be compared to putting a fence around a dangerous sinkhole in an effort to protect the neighborhood children. Notice the simplicity! No long list of rules or regulations. No need to walk across hot coals to enter God's presence. There was only one protective boundary. Both life and religion can become terribly complicated to the point of exhaustion. God's original design, however, was profoundly simple and free of burdens.

---

17. Wilhelm Gesenius and Samuel Prideaux Tregelles, *Gesenius' Hebrew and Chaldee Lexicon to the Old Testament Scriptures* (Bellingham, WA: Logos Bible Software, 2003), 609.

3. **The *tree of the knowledge of good and evil* represents the knowledge of *everything*.** Good and evil would have been seen as two extremes—with the knowledge of everything in between.[18] I took calculus in college and still remember a thing or two. That which is finite cannot possibly contain infinity. Something has to give. In spite of the amazing capabilities of the human brain, finite humanity could not possibly, without boundary or limitation, absorb and handle infinite knowledge. Attempt to fill a balloon with an infinite amount of air and it will explode!

4. **Eating from the tree of the knowledge of good and evil meant that a torrent of *death* would be unleashed upon our formerly pristine world.** God is not like the parent who warns his or her child ten times and then ignores their disobedience. God is true to His word because His character is without inconsistency. He says what He means, and He means what He says. The terrible tragedy of a mother dying while giving birth to twins is not the result of neglect on God's part, or of some flaw in His character. Death and tragedy remain integral to our existence because humanity chose to ignore God's stern warning. This is not to say that the woman was guilty of some unique, overbearing sin. We all live in a fallen world. Until the kingdom of God comes in its fullness, every person born into existence will be overtaken by death. To be spared an untimely death is to delay the inevitable and a life is never truly saved unless it is saved for all eternity. The days in which we walk this earth are both a gift and an opportunity for us to reconnect with our Creator according to His desired purposes for our lives.

5. **God placed the *tree of life*, from which humankind could have eaten at any time, in the *middle* of the garden.** The gift of life was every bit as accessible as was the plague of death. In addition, Adam and Eve had an almost unlimited menu of choices before them. Only *one* tree was off limits. Just one.

---

18. John C. Rankin, *First the Gospel, Then Politics . . .* , Vol. 1 (Hartford CT: TEI Publishing House, 1999), 101.

The garden of delights was to be Heaven on earth. In Eden we see freedom, loving relationships, and abundant fruitfulness. God intended to establish the perfect society in which nothing was lacking. Relationships were defined by love and trust; fear of vulnerability did not exist. In so many ways, the delightfulness of Eden is still God's end goal. In spite of our temporary "detour" down the highway of sin, Heaven will one day provide the complete fulfillment of both His desire and ours.

There is even more to the story, however, than eternal bliss in Heaven. Herein lies one of the profound secrets of grace: by fully embracing the life, death, and resurrection of Jesus Christ, we can taste Eden here and now. We may not be able to experience all of its fullness until Heaven, but grace brings us back to the garden of delights.

THE NATURE OF LOVE

We can't begin to fathom the amount of pain that has been inflicted on humanity—and on God—because our human parents ate from the tree of the knowledge of good and evil. A person might wonder why a loving Creator would have placed this mysterious tree in the middle of the garden if He knew where it would lead. Strangely, at least in part, the answer is *love*. From the very beginning, we can see one of the primary ways in which we were created in God's image; since God is love (1 John 4:8), every human has been given the freedom and capacity to love.

The very nature of love demands freedom; if it is forced, then, by definition, it is not love. Only those relationships built upon the foundations of love and freedom will be healthy. Freedom is what makes love profoundly beautiful, but it can also make it terribly painful. The freedom to love also means the freedom to *not* love, opening the door for evil to exist, and to flourish. God made the existence of a perfect, peace-filled society to be dependent upon how the human race chooses to relate to its Creator.

We have just answered the age-old question, "If God is both good and powerful, then why does evil exist?" Evil exists *because* God is good and powerful! God did not create evil, but He did allow the potential for evil to exist by creating humankind in His very own image—with the freedom and capacity to love. And while all that God does is somehow motivated by love, human freedom has a less than stellar track record.

Many of those who malign our Creator due to the prevalence of evil would be outraged if He chose to take back their freedom. Imagine God gathering all of the world's people together for a meeting and saying something like, "Okay, folks. It's been brought to My attention that there is an awful lot of death and destruction in this world. I didn't realize that things were so bad, but I think I can manage an effective fix. All I need to accomplish this noble task is to take away your free will." The response would be nothing short of outrage!

We can't have it both ways. Either we have the freedom to love—and to not love—or we live in a world that is programmed and controlled by its Creator. As much as we may say we want this Earth to be a more hospitable place, I can't see many people giving up their freedom— at least not willingly. Thankfully, the good that flows from love is far greater than the pain, suffering, and death that flow from evil.

God placed the tree of the knowledge of good and evil right in the middle of paradise, possibly next to the tree of life. The opportunity to love was provided, but the choice to not love became the order of the day. That's how the original sin came to be. The first sin then established patterns that would be repeated through the ages by each new generation. By taking a closer look at how the original sin transpired, we can uncover the secret of what drives evil and, by default, the human condition.

Now the serpent was more crafty than any beast of the field which the LORD God had made. And he said to the woman, "Indeed, has God said, 'You shall not eat from any tree of the garden'?" The woman said to the serpent, "From the fruit of the trees of the garden we may eat; but from the fruit of the tree which is in the middle of the garden, God has said, 'You shall not eat from it or touch it, or you will die.'" The serpent said to the woman, "You surely will not die! For God knows that in the day you eat from it your eyes will be opened, and you will be like God, knowing good and evil." When the woman saw that the tree was good for food, and that it was a delight to the eyes, and that the tree was desirable to make one wise, she took from its fruit and ate; and she gave also to her husband with her, and he ate. Then the eyes of both of them were opened, and they knew that they were naked; and they sewed fig leaves together and made themselves loin coverings. Genesis 3:1-7

UNEARTHING THE ROOTS OF SIN

If we want to understand the dynamics of the human condition, Genesis 3:1-7 is the perfect place to start. It is here that the roots of human nature were planted, and so a little digging can unearth a wealth of information. Satan—that deceptive author of destruction—is the serpent referred to in verse one (see Revelation 20:2). The hiss of the serpent's voice beguiled Adam and Eve as they turned their backs on God in favor of what they thought was a more promising future. The lies and half-truths that Satan presented in the garden form the roots that determine the fruit of human behavior:

1. **God cannot be trusted – the root of *unbelief*.** Even those who profess a strong belief in God find it difficult to trust Him in various areas of life. This does not make logical sense. If we truly believed that God is all knowing, all loving, and all powerful, we would never have a moment of unbelief. And yet, we do—we all do.

2. **I can be like God – the root of *pride*.** Adam and Eve had been created in the *image* of God, but they did not possess the same infinite *nature* as God. The serpent's temptation promised the opportunity to be like God *apart from* God. In other words, humans could become gods in their own right, making the real God obsolete. The temptation toward deity was at the core of the serpent's effort, and so I will explore this issue in greater detail.

3. **God is not enough to meet my needs; I need something more – the root of *idolatry*.** We are not content to worship, trust, and obey the unseen Creator of the Universe; we need material gods. Idols in "primitive" cultures tend to be representations of what people believe the gods to be. The idols of "more civilized" cultures are often human personalities, material possessions, and corporate entities.

4. **Because this fruit looks good, it will be good for me – the root of *lust*.** Self-determination plays a key role in this particular root; we decide what's best for ourselves. Something enticing becomes the focus of our desire and everything else fades into oblivion. Whether we speak of food, a sexual encounter, or material possessions, we want what we want because we think it will somehow do us good. Only afterward, do we taste the bitter fruit of our actions.

5. **I will be wise if I eat from the fruit of the tree – the root of *deception*.** We think that we see it all and know it all. This is especially true of—but not limited to—those who are intellectually gifted. Our sense of intellectual elitism blinds us to the truth (i.e. reality) of God's word. How much information does the universe contain? What percentage of that information does humanity possess? Intelligent thought is essential; intellectual pride a fool's errand.

6. **I will not die – the root of *death*.** Because Adam and Eve disregarded God's warning, death is now integral to our human existence. We know that all who are born will one day go to the grave, but death also manifests as sickness, emotional dysfunction, violent tendencies, etc. Humanity cannot escape death's bitter taste regardless of our exhaustive efforts, creative imaginations, and wishful longings.

There may be other lies and half-truths beyond the six listed, but these provide more than enough insight into our human brokenness. Unearthing each particular root would provide a fascinating study in itself, but we'll focus primarily on one temptation: "you will be like God," (or "you will be as gods").

The irony of humanity's desire to be like God warrants further attention because, being created by God in His own image, the human race was *already* like Him. Thus, we can see something deeper and more sinister at work. I refer to a quest for independence from God. In other words, the goal is to be like God apart from God, to remove Him entirely from the picture so that He is no longer necessary to our existence. We'll also touch briefly on the issue of idolatry as it relates to our study on grace.

Because Adam and Eve trusted Satan over God, humanity joined a treasonous plot against the kingdom of God. As a result, the kingdom of darkness gained a foothold in the earth. Worse still, the human race forfeited its relationship with its loving Creator to become the abused offspring of the devil. The innate image of God in which they had been created was indelibly tainted by sinful roots—roots that continue to foster death and dysfunction. As much as humanity wants to believe that it can fix itself, no lasting solution is possible apart from divine intervention.

Apart from the dynamic work of God's grace, even our most noble endeavors will be tragically corrupted by the influences of sin. Comprehending the roots of the fallen nature is a necessary first step, but real and lasting change will be found only when the truth of God's word is lovingly brought to bear in the dark and broken places of our hearts. As much as it may hurt, those who wish to reap the harvest of a fruitful life must be willing to allow God to touch the friction points of their hearts.

BLAZING A TRAIL TO FRUITFUL LIVING

We will move forward in our spiritual growth only as we allow God to lovingly touch the core issues of our existence with His truth and grace.

CHAPTER EIGHT
THE ARCHENEMY OF GRACE

But God demonstrates His own love toward us, in that while we were yet sinners, Christ died for us.

Romans 5:8

This is God's universe, and He does things His way. You might have a better way, but you don't have a universe!

—J. Vernon McGee

George Washington is widely recognized as the *Father of the United States of America*. If ever a human approached greatness, it was Washington. As a soldier, he fought valiantly and, as a commander, Washington cared deeply about his men. More than anyone else, it was George Washington's steady hand of leadership that guided a ragtag Colonial Army to victory in the face of insurmountable odds. Our infant nation was still in a chaotic state at the end of the Revolutionary War and so, as the first president of the United States, Washington skillfully helped the fledgling government overcome a large war debt among a host of other obstacles.

You may be surprised to learn that George Washington did something even more significant to cement the true greatness of his character in human history; he opposed a group of people who wanted to make him the *king* of the United States.

Fruitful people wield power wisely, but they do not thirst for it. Sadly, various manifestations of pride—the archenemy of grace—have brought down many a capable soul. If you wish to leave a legacy that genuinely reflects God's glory, you must learn to resist the siren call of pride that would woo you to the rocks of destruction. Pride may titillate the desires of the human ego, but it opposes God's grace and, if allowed to have its way, will leave you unfruitful in the eyes of eternity. Do you want to experience the full progressive work of grace? Seek a deeper understanding of human pride and adjust your life accordingly.

FAILED COUP D'ÉTAT

The temptation to be like God apart from God was at the heart of the serpent's deceptive effort in Eden. Where did Satan get the idea of using such an effective temptation? Really, it was nothing new. The enticement simply mimicked the desire that led to the dark one's own personal fall from glory. In order to better understand this, we must manage a glimpse into a time and place beyond the bounds of our human existence. The story is shrouded in mystery, but it is also highly illuminating.

The prophets Isaiah (14:3-21) and Ezekiel (28:12-17) both made reference to the downfall of the greatest angel of all time. These passages serve dual purposes through what some call *near and far prophecy*. The idea is that both passages have *near* and *far* applications. Originally, they were addressed to real people (the kings of Babylon and Tyre) who lived in the backdrop of human history, but they also pointed toward something—or someone—on a grander scale. A closer look at a portion of Isaiah's prophecy reveals its painful relevance to every human who has ever lived.

> *"How you have fallen from heaven,*
> *O star of the morning, son of the dawn!*
> *You have been cut down to the earth,*
> *You who have weakened the nations!*
> *But you said in your heart,*
> *'I will ascend to heaven;*
> *I will raise my throne above the stars of God,*
> *And I will sit on the mount of assembly*
> *In the recesses of the north.*
> *I will ascend above the heights of the clouds;*
> *I will make myself like the Most High.'"*
> *Isaiah 14:12-14*

The Latin translation of the phrase "star of the morning" is *Lucifer*—one of the names given to the evil one who often disguises himself as an angel of light (2 Corinthians 11:14). By combining these passages with Revelation 12:1-17 and a bit of church tradition, we can paint a picture of what was once the most splendid of all angels—one who likely served as the primary worship leader in all of Heaven.

We can't know the specific details, but at some point, Lucifer looked upon God's magnificence—quite possibly as the host of Heaven, under his direction, worshiped their Creator—and set his sights on the throne of God. We don't know if he was driven by a sense of desire or entitlement—or both—but Lucifer fully intended to become the object of all glory and to have dominion over all things. The devil's actions went beyond mere infatuation with an enviable position. His blind pursuit of glory and power meant only one thing—a violent coup attempt. Stupid move.

Convincing a third of the angels to join his plot, Lucifer committed high treason by attempting to overthrow the King of Heaven. This was no insignificant matter. Treason is the worst possible crime against a government, and the kingdom of Heaven, as the summation of all that is good, is the greatest of all governments. Love, trust, and peace—the things we all long for—are representative of God's kingdom. Therefore, Lucifer's "cosmic coup" attempt was nothing less than an outright assault on all that is good. Thankfully, his vain effort failed miserably. There never has been and never will be a balance of power in the Universe.

THE ROOTS OF SIN

Satan's quest can be summed up by only three defining words: *"I will ascend!"* This simple phrase provides us with profound insight into the primary intentions of evil and, consequently, the roots of human sin. As Adam and Eve swallowed the fruit of the forbidden tree, the motivations of the serpent's heart were supernaturally imprinted on the fabric of human nature. From this point forward, human nature, at its very core, would be at war with its Creator. Every man, woman, and child would crave ascension to the throne of glory and roadkill fruit would forever plague humankind.

To this very day, the cosmic coup continues in the form of human pride; people of all ages, races, and nationalities want to ascend to the place of highest supremacy. This is not to say that every person wakes up with a well-defined plan to overthrow his or her Creator, but that Lucifer's cry of "I will ascend!" is echoed at the inner core of every human heart. When this desire is given the freedom to run its course, human conflict and hostility toward God both result.

This brings us to another imperfect diagram—*The Humanistic Progression of Sin*. As with *The Divine Progression of Grace*, I have analytically separated the root desires of the human heart for teaching purposes. And, once again, even though such a diagram has genuine value, reality is far more complicated.

THE HUMANISTIC PROGRESSION OF SIN

I ⟶ GOD IS THE CENTER OF ALL THINGS ⟶ HUMANS ARE SELF-CENTERED

WILL ⟶ GOD IS SOVEREIGN OVER ALL THINGS ⟶ HUMANS LUST FOR POWER AND CONTROL

ASCEND ⟶ GOD IS THE GLORY OF ALL THINGS ⟶ HUMANS CRAVE GLORY

↗ KINGDOM RIGHTEOUSNESS (SELF-RIGHTEOUSNESS)

↘ SOCIAL RIGHTEOUSNESS (IDENTITY)

"I" → **self-centeredness** – God is the center of all things, but He isn't self-centered. This is amazing in itself. God's other-centered nature was displayed through the selfless life of Jesus Christ. Never has this earth known a man of such courage, compassion, and love. It's difficult for us to fathom how the One around whom all things revolve can be characterized by such a humble other-centered mindset.

We, on the other hand, expect the world to revolve around us. True life, in our minds, is about *our* interests. When I'm backed up in traffic, for example, the most important agenda on that road is mine. When I'm waiting in line at a grocery store, I must battle against thoughts such as, "That cashier is so slow! This is going to take forever!"

I'm just being honest and acknowledge that your heart is likely to be more selfless and noble-minded than mine. Still, we find plenty of anecdotal evidence to show that humans are basically self-centered. Consider a group of two-year-olds arriving at a birthday party. Declared with the authority of kings and queens, shouts of "Mine! Mine!" will soon fill the air. We don't have to teach our kids to look after their own interests—that all comes quite naturally. Our bigger challenge is to instill within them other-centeredness—no small task for any parent.

Of course, as image-bearers of God, we are all capable of love. Through the ages, people of all sorts and beliefs have made amazing sacrifices for the benefit of others. The problem is that self always finds its way into the picture. Those who commit sacrificial acts will begin to celebrate their great selflessness. Their pride produces an attitude that peers down on the less altruistic from its high and noble perch.

"Will" → **self-sovereignty** – God *reigns* over all, but He doesn't *control* everything that happens. In other words, God doesn't make all things happen, but nothing happens that He doesn't permit. Each person is responsible for his or her own choices, and all actions will one day be called into account.

Somehow, through a vast multitude of human decisions, God manages to steer our free choices to accomplish His sovereign purposes. How does He do that? I don't have a clue. I guess that's what makes Him *God*. Humans don't come close to possessing the powerful abilities seen in their Creator. To fulfill our desires for self-sovereignty, we must *overrule* the desires of others. The result is a need—if not a compulsion—to control our own lives and circumstances, the people around us, and, ultimately, the sovereign King of Glory. Grace-filled love and the need to control make terrible bed partners.

The human quest for control is a study in itself. Some people lust for power with no concern about offending Heaven. Others realize the destructive nature of their controlling desires, but the tendency is so ingrained that they have a terrible time letting go. This is especially true of those who have experienced the pain of traumatic events. Various forms of depression, anxiety, and compulsive behavior often result.

The desire to be in control is innate to both sexes, although it often manifests differently. Men generally seek to control by anger, violence, and intimidation. Whether by fear or by force, they *will* get others to do what they want. Because women don't possess the same physical strength as men, they resort to more subtle tactics such as nagging and manipulation. "Bless your heart, son, you are free to do whatever you want. It will probably kill your mother, but don't worry about me. I'll get over it when Jesus ushers me into glory." Men are obvious—like dogs—in their efforts to control. Most women are subtle—like cats.

"Ascend" → **self-glorification** – God is the glory of everything, yet He is mysteriously humble. Human self-glorification finds its expression in a quest for *perfection*. God is perfect and those who want to be like Him apart from Him seek self-validation by attempting to live up to a host of unattainable standards. The quest for self-glorification, self-significance, self-righteousness—or whatever you want to call it—manifests itself through two primary expressions. The first is in relationship to God; the second is in relationship to other humans.

1. **Kingdom Righteousness** – Every government has its own set of law codes by which its citizens must abide. Laws are the rules that govern our behavior. If I decide to become a citizen of Scotland, for example, I must learn and abide by the laws of Scotland. To be righteous in the eyes of the state, then, means that my life is in a condition acceptable to the governing authorities. The same is true for the kingdom of Heaven.

Those who care about spending eternity in Heaven will often try to live up to law-based standards by which they can consider themselves to be acceptable to God. From the New Testament context, this undesirable tendency can be defined as "living under law." This mindset is often expressed in typical statements such as, "I believe I will go to Heaven because I am basically a good person." What we fail to realize is that the standard of Heaven must be—and is—nothing short of absolute perfection.

Do you see it? God is perfect so if I seek to attain heavenly heights by my own merits, I must be morally perfect. From the day of my birth until I take my last breath, I can never lie, steal, or do anything that falls short of moral perfection. Being "basically good" doesn't cut it for a place as marvelous as Heaven because our prideful tendencies would one day surface to the point of revolt—something that God could never allow. The last thing He wants is to allow the plague of sin that has ravished the Earth to corrupt the pristine beauty of Heaven.

As we begin to understand the full gravity of pride, our overwhelming need for God's saving grace becomes evident. Jesus, the Son of Man, lived a perfect life and died as a perfect sacrifice so that we might be clothed in *His* righteousness. Morality is not our means to be accepted by God, but rather our *response* to being accepted by grace as we enter into a New Covenant relationship with Christ.

2. **Social Righteousness** – A second dimension of righteousness involves our relationships with other people. By measuring up to certain societal standards, we seek to put ourselves in a condition acceptable to our culture (or subculture). We're still living under law as we try to meet a slew of unwritten standards in regard to appearance, performance, wealth, status, etc. While breaking a law of the state may result in a fine, breaking the laws of culture will likely lead to being ridiculed and ostracized. As we can see, the quest for social righteousness involves seeking a sense of personal validation—i.e. a sense of *identity*.

The pursuit of a favorable identity has a huge impact on our ability to bear sweet spiritual fruit. Think about it. The primary lie in the garden of Eden was, "You will be like God." Is this not about identity? All of the sin, suffering, pain, and death in our world are the results of an identity issue. The gospel, then, must somehow touch the core of a person's identity.[19]

While God is obviously concerned about our kingdom righteousness, our measure of social righteousness isn't even on His radar—except to the degree that it impacts our spiritual well-being. Things like appearance and social status contribute nothing to our acceptability in the eyes of Heaven. Social righteousness is a deadly trap; our tendency to seek after a worldly sense of significance profoundly affects our ability to live in victory over sin.

PRIDE OPPOSES GRACE

Collectively, the three roots of self-deification—self-centeredness, self-sovereignty, and self-glorification—form the heart of human pride. Other aspects of pride, such as self-determination and self-sufficiency also enter into the mix, but the core motivation is always the same. *To be like God apart from God*—that is our desire. Pride seeks to be independent from God—the giver of grace. Humanistic thought will look favorably on many aspects of personal pride, but Heaven reckons it the archenemy of grace and, consequently, the archenemy of love.

We can't begin to number all of the people who have suffered and died because of the various expressions of human pride. How many wars have been fought? How many individual lives and families destroyed? How many churches corrupted? How much pain and suffering wrought? Human pride always stifles the flow of God's life-giving grace. Sadly, the inherent motivations of pride continue to be passed from generation to generation and constitute a primary source of human dysfunction.

We all understand that children will be self-centered, but when fully grown adults behave in self-absorbed ways, we recognize it as a

---

19. My DVD small group study titled, *The Search for Me: A Journey Toward a Rock Solid Identity,* provides a more in-depth exploration of this vital issue.

sign of immaturity. There's even an academic term that has become all too common in our culture—*narcissism*. If God is to create the perfect society in Heaven, something must be done about our archenemy. Human pride can never be pacified or redirected; it must be slain. Regardless of how spiritual or noble it may appear, any "version" of the gospel that does not effectively kill human pride will ultimately poison and destroy all that is good, including our churches.

Don't be deceived! We are all born into the human condition. Forging a path of independence from the One who is full of grace and life will only facilitate the grip of death and its pitiful expressions. The Scriptures clearly and broadly proclaim this truth, and yet, somehow we miss—or conveniently ignore—it. Failing to account for the severe consequences of pride constitutes an error of epic proportions.

> *For though the LORD is exalted,*
> *Yet He regards the lowly,*
> *But the haughty He knows from afar. Psalms 138:6*

> *But He gives a greater grace. Therefore it says, "GOD IS OPPOSED TO THE PROUD, BUT GIVES GRACE TO THE HUMBLE."*
> *James 4:6*

Not only is this principle clearly broadcasted throughout the Scriptures, we also see it exemplified in every aspect of God's dealings with humanity. The coming of our Savior was announced by John the Baptist—a man who lived in the desert and owned few (if any) possessions. John had no official position in the Jewish religious system, but was empowered by God to make a huge impact on the general public. And what about the woman chosen by God to give birth to the Christ? She was a teenage girl of no wealth, significance, or status.

The King of Glory came to earth apart from the religious establishment, born in a stable filled with manure and overrun by flies. Angels announced His birth to a group of lowly shepherds who likely smelled as bad as the animals they herded. For thirty years, the Son of God dwelt in obscurity in the one-horse town of Nazareth, working as a tradesman. He had no position, no reputation, and no connections. None of this transpired by chance. Just as the serpent had meticulously planned every detail of his garden temptation, so too, the Christ had deliberately ordered every detail of His entry into the human race.

Can it be any clearer? Human pride opposes our Creator and severely hinders us from staying in the flow of His transformational grace. Much has changed through the course of human history, but one thing has not; God still regards the lowly and He still knows the arrogant from afar. If self-centeredness is our goal, we will be far from abiding in grace. If it is control that we seek, we will be far from abiding in grace. If a quest for glory flavors all that we do, we will be far from abiding in grace. When human pride is free to reign, roadkill fruit will always result. This is the spiritual friction point that none of us can ignore without serious and painful consequences.

Admittedly, there are times when I lose my bearings and begin to focus on the seemingly unfair realities of life. As it is with card games, some people are "dealt" amazing hands, being born with money, privilege, good looks, and multiple talents. Others seem to have been given so little. With no family to speak of, and few natural abilities, they barely squeak through life until the grip of death pulls them under.

It all appears unfair and hopeless until I begin to focus on the value of humility. Because those who are admirable in the flesh are easily prone to pride, they are the ones *least* likely to realize their desperate need for God's grace. On the contrary, people who have been dealt "lesser hands" are more likely to look to the heavens for help. In the end, I find myself wondering exactly who was dealt the bad hand.

The good news of grace is that the cross of Christ puts every human on equal footing. Jesus Christ came to earth clothed in humility and He lived in total victory over pride. He now calls us, as vessels of love, to follow in His steps. The quest for a fruitful life is indeed noble, but, as you can already tell, it will turn us inside out!

BLAZING A TRAIL TO FRUITFUL LIVING

Those who wish to stay in the flow of God's transformational grace must slay the roots of pride—self-centeredness, self-sovereignty, and self-glorification—in their hearts, because pride is the archenemy of grace.

CHAPTER NINE
CLASH OF THE KINGDOMS

"The thief comes only to steal and kill and destroy; I came that they may have life, and have it abundantly."

John 10:10

If you have not chosen the Kingdom of God first, it will in the end make no difference what you have chosen instead.

—William Law

It might surprise you that I—a conservative evangelical Christian— don't think that eternal salvation is the primary message of the New Testament. Don't get me wrong. I see the salvation message as integral to Christianity. I think, however, that we have put too little emphasis on the bigger picture of what God seeks to accomplish. This loss of focus has cost us dearly. What do I mean? Most of us have heard of a little prayer that is recited on Sundays by millions of people worldwide. It goes like this:

"Our Father which art in heaven, Hallowed be thy name.
Thy kingdom come, Thy will be done in earth, as it is in heaven.
Give us this day our daily bread.
And forgive us our debts, as we forgive our debtors.
And lead us not into temptation, but deliver us from evil: For thine is the kingdom, and the power, and the glory, for ever. Amen."
Matthew 6:9b-13 (KJV)

The gospel is the good news of God's kingdom coming to earth in and through Jesus Christ. By participating in that kingdom, we are saved from the dominion of sin—and its eternal consequences—and are restored to a new, dynamic relationship with God. At the point of salvation, a person's citizenship is transferred from the dark domain to the kingdom of light (Colossians 1:13). As important as eternal salvation may be, it is not a stand-alone concept, and so we've made a huge mistake by trying to isolate it from the message of the kingdom. The two are intended to be one.

THE KINGDOM OF GOD

A careful reading of the New Testament will show that the kingdom of God stood as a central theme.

- John the Baptist preached the kingdom (Matthew 3:1-2).

- Jesus taught His disciples about the kingdom (Acts 1:1-3).

- Jesus told His followers to pray for the advancement of God's kingdom on earth (Luke 11:2).

- Christ's followers, including Paul, preached the kingdom (Acts 8:12 and 19:8).

I could easily provide more evidence of this reality, but I think that the short list above adequately supports the fact that the kingdom of God was the central focus of nascent Christianity. If you remain unconvinced, try an exercise similar to the one I suggested at the end of Chapter One. Highlight every place you find the word *kingdom* in the New Testament of a relatively clean Bible and then review each passage.

The message of the kingdom is often ignored because of the "problems" that such a message creates. In part, the concept of God's eternal kingdom coming to earth is difficult for people to grasp. We're accustomed to human domains with written laws and physical boundaries, but God's kingdom is spiritual in nature. How can a person be a citizen of an invisible kingdom? What does that look like in daily life? How does the kingdom influence our earthly governments? All are questions that have confounded theologians over the years.

There is yet another critical reason the message of the kingdom is conveniently ignored. The concept of a kingdom cannot be adequately addressed without recognizing the supreme authority of a king. The term itself, *king-dom*, speaks of a king's domain. In addition, the authority of

God's kingdom far surpasses that of any human realm. To proclaim the message of the kingdom is to welcome the supreme authority of Christ over human lives. No higher authority exists. But since humans want to be their own gods, they balk at bending their knees in submission, regardless of how benevolent His authority may be. *Our willingness to embrace Christ's lordship marks a key friction point that impacts our forward movement in the progressive work of grace.*

Regardless of how earthly rulers and leaders may feel, the kingdom of God is progressing across the globe as the church grows rapidly in Africa, Asia, and South America, etc.. The complete fullness of the kingdom is for a day yet to come, but its advance is *now.*

As individuals, our participation in the kingdom continues to be voluntary. Rather than seeking to control all that we value, we willingly invite the King of kings and Lord of lords (Revelation 19:16) to reign over every aspect of our existence. In a sense, we still get to choose between the tree of life and the tree of the knowledge of good and evil. And the consequences of this choice continue to be far-reaching.

THE HUMAN CONDITION'S PAINFUL REALITY

If the message of God's kingdom is good news, the message of the dark domain is hopeless. Pride has given the evil kingdom a deadly foothold in this world. In fact, the human race faces quite the quandary. Our continued quest for independence from our Creator has left us with the horrible problem of the human condition which encompasses the core issues of existence inherent to all people.

Regardless of gender, race, ethnicity, social standing, etc., humans struggle with questions like: Who am I? What is the meaning of life? How can I be free? What will happen to me when I die? Why is this world filled with so much pain, suffering, and evil? We seek noble and glorious answers to these questions, but the deeper we dig, the more futile our existence seems. We look for hope, but apart from Christ, our solutions remain shallow.

The heart-breaking reality of the human condition goes beyond the fallout from diseases and natural disasters; an exceedingly large amount of human suffering is the result of *humans acting against humans.* For example, historians have estimated that over 60 million people died as the result of World War II.[20] Beyond that conservative number are those wounded, maimed, raped, and otherwise emotionally scarred. As massive as World War II was, its casualties are nowhere near the total number of humans that have been killed and injured by other humans as the direct result of ethnic and national violence.

War is but one dimension of human conflict. Governments routinely oppress and kill those viewed as threats to their grip on power. Infanticide, abortion, and sexual abuse—moral crimes against the powerless—never seem to go away no matter how civilized we become. Neither should we overlook the problem of greed. How much human suffering has resulted from exploitation by greedy individuals and corporations? The numbers are staggering—beyond our ability to measure. All are due to grace-starved people mistreating other people. Perhaps the greater wonder is that the human race hasn't yet destroyed itself! As a whole, the human condition can be summed up in one word—*death*. It's just as God said it would be—in dying we are dying.[21]

Australian biologist Jeremy Griffith—a Secular Humanist[22]—does an excellent job explaining the human condition:

> While it's undeniable that humans are capable of great love, we also have an unspeakable history of brutality, rape, torture, murder and war. Despite all our marvellous accomplishments, we humans have been the most ferocious and destructive force that has ever lived on Earth—and the eternal question has been 'why?' Even in our everyday behaviour, why have we humans been so competitive, selfish and aggressive when clearly the ideals of life are to be the complete opposite, namely cooperative, selfless and loving? In fact, why are we so ruthlessly competitive, selfish and brutal that human life has become all but unbearable and we have nearly destroyed our own planet?![23]

20. http://www.nationalww2museum.org/learn/education/for-students/ww2-history/ww2-by-the-numbers/world-wide-deaths.html
21. Genesis 2:17 can be literally translated to say, "dying you shall die." – see Spence-Jones, H. D. M. (Ed.), *Genesis* (London; New York: Funk & Wagnalls Company, 1909), 46.
22. "Humanist" is capitalized to distinguish Secular Humanism from other forms.
23. http://www.worldtransformation.com/human-condition/

Both Humanists and Christians acknowledge the gravity of the problem. In his article, Griffith goes on to say that people are selfish, aggressive, and competitive because they are looking for opportunities to prove that they are good. I am impressed by his insight. From here, however, the philosophical views of Humanism and Christianity diverge.

Griffith concludes that the answer to our problem is to realize that *human nature is good* and that the conflict within our hearts is the natural outcome of a wonderful evolutionary process. Thus, the solution to the problem of human conflict is to stop trying to prove that we are good and to celebrate the goodness that already defines us. If we can only learn to put off the negative label of "evil" and fully love ourselves, our angst will be healed and we'll all become happy, loving, and supportive.

I would summarize contemporary humanistic thought toward religion as follows:

The idea of a savior (from sin) is unnecessary because humans are good within themselves. Further still, religious belief—Christianity in particular—has made a horrible contribution to the human condition. Indeed, a belief in God may even be the *cause* of the human condition. Not only does it burden people with guilt, but it labels them as being evil. If only we can remove religion (i.e. God) from the picture, world peace will finally be within our grasp.

While I applaud people like Jeremy Griffith for caring about the state of humanity, I fear that they continue to eat from the tree of the knowledge of good and evil. Why do we see hostility toward Christianity in some secular circles? Why do atheists sue local governments to remove statues of Jesus and plaques listing the Ten Commandments? Secular activists aren't just out to establish their own supremacy—they believe that they are doing society a favor by seeking to remove all influence of religion.

Once again, the hiss of the serpent beguiles our intellectual pride with the message that we can be good apart from God. Again, we see the endless assault of the cosmic coup against the kingdom of Heaven. God is blamed for the horrible situation that the human race has created. We destroy one another and fault Him for our actions. Talk about injustice!

As noble as Humanist ideals may sound to some people, atheism is powerless to eradicate the problem of human pride—the root source of the human condition. Unwavering confidence in our own superiority continues to propagate the power of death throughout the sphere of humanity. *The Humanistic Progression of Sin* is alive and well and, as a direct result, the human race is not. The sad state of the human condition will continue to be ours until we fully embrace the rule of God's eternal kingdom. Humankind will continue to be selfish. Humankind will continue to lust for power and control. And humankind will continue to seek its own glory.

WE ARE THE PROBLEM!

Why do we see so much conflict in our world? So much injustice? So much oppression? Because seven billion humans are saying, "I will ascend to highest Heaven and erect my own kingdom." This world doesn't have enough room for seven billion gods! People oppress and kill other people because we are living out the repeated patterns of self-centeredness, self-sovereignty, and self-glorification that took root on the day Adam and Eve ate the forbidden fruit.

Coming to grips with the ugliness of the human condition can be most unpleasant. At first, we want to keep a positive spin on things, to put on a smiley face and believe that the world is a happy place. Eventually, depending on our individual circumstances, the painful reality of the human condition is realized—usually by early adulthood. Three responses appear to be typical of most people:

1. **We sink into depression because it all seems very hopeless.** Reality stinks and there is nothing we can do about it.

2. **We try to escape reality by creating alternate realities through various means such as entertainment and substance abuse.** Our lives are consumed by sports, fantasy, and media of all sorts.

3. **We seek to improve the state of the human condition through science, politics, and various movements.** Devoted people have made great strides in helping to ease human suffering, and almost any such effort has value. At the same time, unless we can put

a stop to human oppression, our overall effort can be compared to fixing a leaky water pipe with electrical tape. If the fix does happen to work, it won't for very long.

The human condition is our reality—the pain-filled fruit of humanity's desire to be like God apart from God. The kingdom of Heaven is God's reality. God's answer to our problem is to bring the kingdom of Heaven to earth through the sovereign rule of Jesus Christ. This is the central message of the New Testament. Our only hope—and it is a glorious hope at that—lies with the King of kings and Lord of lords who has triumphed over the power of death and darkness for all time.

ALIGNING WITH GOD'S REALITY

The kingdom of God is Heaven's reality freely offered to the human race. Humanism is man's reality imposed upon the Universe. If we are to abide in Christ and His life-giving grace, God's reality and that of humanity must become one. I can assure you, however, that God will never conform to our selfish and self-destructive desires.

If we want to know and experience the glorious blessings of God's eternal kingdom, we must align ourselves with *His* reality. This is why spiritual friction points matter—they touch the key areas of life that enable us to move forward in our faith by aligning with God's design. When we do, two especially significant things happen:

1. **Heaven comes to earth.** The kingdom of God is the fruit of Heaven's reality coming to earth. Herein a fuller context of salvation is realized. While our modern version of the gospel focuses on us going to Heaven, Christ emphasized *Heaven coming to us.*

   We read in the New Testament that people were saved, healed, and delivered when the kingdom of God advanced. Lives broken by sin were put back together by God. Broken relationships were often restored. Hope and love flourished. We won't experience the full benefits of the kingdom until after Christ returns, but I can assure you that we have only begun to taste of what is possible on this side of Heaven.

2. **The enemies of God explode with anger.** Human and demonic
    spirits always seek to leverage control through manipulation,
    fear, intimidation, and violence; they are outraged when they lose
    territory. I believe that much of the political and social upheaval
    we see in the world today involves a backlash against the forward
    progress of God's kingdom on earth. The princes of men and of
    demons, agonized by its advance, have unleashed a furious assault
    that will ultimately fail.

Understanding these things helps us to see The Lord's Prayer in a
new light. Prayer enables us to advance God's reality on earth without
violating the free will that He gave to humankind in the garden of Eden.
The Lord's Prayer, specifically, addresses several core issues of life by
helping us align with *The Divine Progression of Grace*, thereby reversing
The Humanistic Progression of Sin. Jesus taught His disciples to pray in a
format that facilitates the restoration of His divine order. We make God
the center of all things, we surrender to Him as the sovereign ruler of all
things, and we worship Him as the glory of all things.

Our loving God has made powerful provision for the self-inflicted
state of the human condition. All of this, of course, requires functional
faith. Maintaining an unhealthy focus on the sad state of our world will
do no good. We must place our full confidence in our sovereign God
and the furthering of His kingdom. Faith moves the progressive work of
grace forward; progress breaks down when we cease to believe.

The world has darkened considerably since September 11, 2001.
Terrorist bombings are now an almost daily reality. Once stable
governments are in upheaval and once solid economies are riddled
with debt. Natural disasters seem to have grown in intensity, claiming
hundreds of thousands of lives. Anxiety and discouragement are the
cumulative effects of these and other troubles. A primary goal, then, for
any fruitful believer is to overcome the worry of our age by focusing on
God's goodness and the advancement of His kingdom (Matthew 13:22-
23 and Daniel 2:44). We're not here to merely "hold on" until Jesus
comes back to rescue us; we're here to grow in God's grace so that we
might impact the lives of others. Are problems increasing in our world?
I think so, but so are opportunities to eternally impact human lives!

The advancement of God's kingdom also requires *truth*. To embrace God's kingdom is to voluntarily surrender to His reality (truth). Truth reveals the beauty of God's reality and the painful foolishness of ours. We can't align our lives with God's reality if we don't realize the need. Much to our discomfort, truth can cause us considerable pain as we peer into the evil motivations of our own "cosmic coup" hearts. Truth, therefore, must always be enveloped in love and grace.

Surrender is not possible apart from faith, but neither is it genuine apart from obedience. God often calls for obedience at the spiritual friction points of our hearts because it facilitates forward progress toward spiritual maturity. When we obey the commands of God as found in His word and through the leading of the Holy Spirit, a powerful activation takes place.

As we align with God's design, we are better able to help others align as well. This is integral to the discipleship process. For people to conform to God's reality, for His kingdom to truly advance on earth, God's people must extend grace to those mired in sin. Repentance requires self-honesty, and self-honesty depends upon being loved unconditionally. Fear of being judged makes us shy away from truth, furthering the problem of self-deception.

IT'S ALL ABOUT GLORY

At the center of our struggle to fully embrace the kingdom of light—to allow ourselves to be fully exposed—lies our need for significance (glory). We can gain a fuller understanding by returning to the "birth" of the human condition as found in early Genesis:

> When the woman saw that the tree was good for food, and that it was a delight to the eyes, and that the tree was desirable to make one wise, she took from its fruit and ate; and she gave also to her husband with her, and he ate. Then the eyes of both of them were opened, and they knew that they were naked; and they sewed fig leaves together and made themselves loin coverings.
>
> They heard the sound of the LORD God walking in the garden in the cool of the day, and the man and his wife hid themselves from the presence of the LORD God among the trees of the garden. Then

the LORD God called to the man, and said to him, "Where are you?" He said, "I heard the sound of You in the garden, and I was afraid because I was naked; so I hid myself." And He said, "Who told you that you were naked? Have you eaten from the tree of which I commanded you not to eat?" The man said, "The woman whom You gave to be with me, she gave me from the tree, and I ate."
Genesis 3:6-12

Before Adam and Eve ate from the tree of the knowledge of good and evil, they were "naked and unashamed" with no fear of vulnerability (Genesis 2:25). What changed? Why were they suddenly naked, ashamed, and full of fear? Before eating of the forbidden fruit, Adam and Eve had been clothed in God's glory. But in choosing to isolate themselves from their Creator, they lost their covering of glory. They had been physically naked the entire time, but, spiritually speaking, our ancient father and mother went from being fully clothed to being fully exposed. Worse still, the hideous picture they saw of their spiritual selves terrified their souls.

Taking things a step further, Adam and Eve both became aware of an unattainable standard. Our Creator is perfect in every way. Those who seek to be like God apart from God must, by their own efforts, reach for a standard of absolute perfection. Any such standard was irrelevant when they were clothed in the King's glory, but now their naked flesh felt painfully exposed. Still, it gets worse. Humanity had just "inherited" the serpent's evil nature. Not only were they exposed and made aware of a standard of perfection, they could not have been further from meeting that standard.

Adam and Eve shrank back in fear, trying in vain to cover their spiritual nakedness with fig leaves. Before, they had walked with their Creator in peace, but now they couldn't bear to be in His presence. Dishonesty is often driven by a glory deficiency, so when confronted by their perfect God about their sin, the last thing Adam and Eve wanted was to admit their inglorious state. A little quick thinking and the first blame was cast. Herein lies the great inner conflict of the human heart; beset by a glory deficiency, we can never attain to God's measure of glory, and yet we can never stop trying.

The problem of a glory deficiency goes beyond Adam and Eve. The power of sin that affects us all dwells within the futile compulsion to attain to God's place of highest glory. The apostle Paul addressed this issue in a way that is often overlooked:

For all have sinned and fall short of the glory of God. Romans 3:23

Why did Paul add "and fall short of the glory of God" to "all have sinned"? Acquiring the glory of God is the *goal* of the sinful nature. The cosmic coup is embodied in a quest to ascend to Heaven's throne and rule over God. I am not suggesting other dynamics of sin are unimportant, but that a glory deficiency empowers sin.

The dynamics of God's kingdom will not allow human flesh to boast in itself. Boast, however, is what our fallen natures must do in their pursuit of glory. How does a coach rally his team to "leave it all on the field" even to the point of sacrificing their physical bodies? He paints a vision of glory—that elusive championship title. Without question, sports at all levels have many valuable benefits, but let's face it—no team ever runs off the field shouting, "We're number nine! We're number nine!"

When I first began to think seriously about writing books, I took a continuing education class at our local university. The professor caught me off guard as he discussed the motivations for becoming an author. "Why do we want to write books?" he asked. "Because we want to see our names in print!" In other words, it's all about pursing a sense of significance (i.e. glory). I have my own struggles with pride, but that really was not my motivation for desiring to write. I saw writing as a platform to touch lives and just assumed that's what everyone wanted. How wrong I was.

THE QUEST FOR CONTROL

Why did Cain murder his brother (Genesis 4:1-8)? Envy overran his heart. Cain's actions were the outward fruit of an inward root. The firstborn son of the human race killed his brother due to a glory deficiency. Already, the human condition had taken its deadly toll. The words that God spoke to Cain just before he murdered his brother continue to echo through the corridors of time:

"If you do well, will not your countenance be lifted up? And if you do not do well, sin is crouching at the door; and its desire is for you, but you must master it." Genesis 4:7

Cain's glory deficiency compelled him to murder his brother in a vain attempt to control the situation, to make it more according to his liking. Is not the human tendency toward control self-evident? Do we not realize how it clashes with the design of God's kingdom? If we are to experience the life, love, and wholeness that result from grace's progressive work, we must learn to lead and govern with the wisdom and humility of Heaven.

The human bent toward control can be especially deceptive. Aside from an outright lust for power, it is entirely possible for us to want the *right* thing but to apply our efforts in *wrong* ways. For example, Christians who want their nation to be spiritually fruitful must learn to navigate the world of politics without resorting to the controlling methods that define the political landscape.

Lord Acton once said, "Power corrupts, and absolute power corrupts absolutely." What an accurate summation of the human quest for control! I believe this to be one of the great challenges for human governments. Those who rise to positions of power will be severely tempted as a lust for more power seeks to grip their hearts with ironlike strength. A government that does not have checks and balances clearly established is destined to be ruled by a despot—if not in its current generation, then in the next. George Washington understood this well and multiple generations have reaped the benefits of his decision to refuse the kingship of the United States.

In many ways, the history of human governments can be defined by a ceaseless battle for control between those who oppress and those being oppressed. The seeds of revolution are sown as the oppressed feel increasingly violated and voiceless. Those seeds then sprout into violence as the oppressed gain the courage, power, and opportunity to throw off the yoke of their callous masters. Sadly, without the transformation of human hearts, history is bound to repeat itself. In other words, the *oppressed* will one day become the *oppressors*. Only the humility of men like George Washington can break this deadly cycle of oppression.

Some people consider the United States Constitution to be a noble document. The truth is that the framers of the Constitution had a rather *low* view of human nature. Having experienced the tyranny of European monarchies, they sought to establish a different form of government by distributing a balance of power between three branches. On a governmental level, systems must be set in place to protect the citizenry from oppression. Human nature is so inclined to lust for power, however, that this is no easy task even with such systems in place.

THE UNIQUE GOAL OF CHRISTIAN LEADERSHIP

The goal of Christian leadership is to advance God's kingdom in every aspect of life. Surrendering control to God is necessary, but godly leadership should never be equated with passivity. Any time God has plans for a situation, a "spirit(s) of control" will try to dominate. Healthy leaders, then, will govern to facilitate the advancement of His kingdom and His kingdom alone. This approach is anything but natural and requires faith, courage, and vigilance.

All of our intellectual activity and all of our hard labor—even all of our religious endeavors—mean little in the long run if we do not learn mastery over the dominion of sin. This is why *The Divine Progression of Grace* matters so much. Grace does not provide an excuse to sin. Instead, God has provided us with the ability to live in dominion over sin through the means of His transformational grace. By learning to draw upon the sufficiency of grace, we can find the freedom and dominion that we all long to experience.

Better yet, we can realign our lives through the cross of Jesus Christ so that God's "axe" is laid to the tangled mess of sinful roots that make for a miserable existence. By the means of His abundant grace, God gives us the ability to find freedom from, and victory over, the dominion of sin. The kingdom of light will always reign over the kingdom of death and darkness.

BLAZING A TRAIL TO FRUITFUL LIVING

By proclaiming the gospel of God's eternal kingdom rather than a detached message of salvation, we can help people align with God's reality, propelling them toward a more fruitful existence.

CHAPTER TEN
GOD'S ANSWER TO OUR PROBLEM

"My covenant I will not violate, nor will I alter the utterance of My lips."

Psalms 89:34

If you believe what you like in the gospels, and reject what you don't like, it is not the gospel you believe, but yourself.

—Augustine

Spend enough time around the Western church and you'll find a large number of genuine people who are searching for the next "new" thing that will transform the face of Western Christianity. This tendency has created a fad mentality in Christian circles that rises and falls with each newly elevated Christian "superstar." What too few people seem to realize is that we already have all that we need in the gospel of Jesus Christ. The problem is that we have assumed a level of understanding about the good news of Jesus Christ that we may not actually possess.

The word *gospel* literally means "good news." Typically, we think about eternal damnation—which is very bad news—as the result of sinful living and proclaim the gospel as God's answer to our problem. That is as it should be, but in the process we have mistakenly come to think of the gospel as merely an *introductory* message into the Christian faith. But the gospel is so much more! The good news of Jesus Christ is intended to be a *way of life*—the means by which we continually experience the fullness of God's abundant life (Luke 4:18-19). Our problems don't end when we receive Christ and neither does the role of the gospel. Let us revisit the gospel by returning to its roots.

REDISCOVERING A COVENANT WORLDVIEW

We will begin with the concept of *covenant*.[24] A *covenant* can be defined as "a sacred and binding relationship in which friends, enemies, possessions, and even identities become shared." Historically, *blood* covenants were especially meaningful. Through ancient eyes, a covenant was considered to be unbreakable (Galatians 3:15). Each party in the relationship was considered to be worthy of *complete trust*. In the eyes of Heaven, trust is so sacred that those who break a covenant bring terrible curses upon themselves.

In the West, we tend to think in terms of *contracts*, which differ significantly from covenants. A contract is designed primarily with a person's *own rights* in mind, whereas, a covenant emphasizes the *other's well-being*. Love and trust should go hand in hand.

We see evidence of what I call a *covenant worldview* throughout history. The blood brotherhood of Native Americans, for example, was a particular expression of a blood covenant. The treaties between Native Americans and the U.S. government were thought by the natives to be unbreakable covenants, and so they reacted with violent disbelief when those treaties were violated. Government authorities weren't just breaking contracts; they were betraying a sacred trust.

A covenant worldview once permeated virtually every part of the ancient world, but it has been largely lost in our day. Perhaps our two closest examples would be the marriage covenant and the supreme level of loyalty we see in some branches of the military. Sadly, marriage is no longer valued as a lifelong, love-filled commitment and the brotherhood of military service is often betrayed at a number of different levels—especially at the higher levels of authority. All too often, those in power will do whatever they can to protect their image and position.

A covenant is rooted in trust and if there is anything that this world lacks, it is trust. As a result, we see breakdowns at almost every level of

---

24. Two books have helped me to better understand the covenant concept and its prevalence in the ancient world. *The Blood Covenant* by H. Clay Trumbull is a scholarly work—not an easy read—that I have found to be most helpful. *The Power of the Blood Covenant* by Malcom Smith provides a more readable explanation, although, I tend to disagree with some of Smith's conclusions regarding the nation of Israel.

society. A politician gets elected on the basis of noble promises, only to reveal his true colors after taking office. A corporate executive cares far more about her personal compensation package than about the laborers who break their backs to make the company successful. A head coach promises to stay with the program for the long haul, but announces his departure the following week. A pastor proclaims the glory of sin-free living, but sleeps with vulnerable women who approach him for counsel. A wife sneaks off for a tryst with a "caring" coworker. Such painful breaches of trust are far too common.

JOSHUA AND THE GIBEONITES

Perhaps no story illustrates the unbreakable nature of a covenant better than that of Israel's relationship with the Gibeonites (Joshua 9-10). Joshua was leading the nation of Israel into the Promised Land, conquering every opposing kingdom with relative ease. This terrified the Gibeonites, so they sent representatives to make a treaty (i.e. covenant) with Israel while pretending that they had traveled from a far-off land. Actually, their homes were only about twenty miles down the road.

Without consulting God for guidance, Joshua and his leaders took the bait, exchanging oaths with the Gibeonites to forge a treaty between the two nations. Only after the covenant was established, did Joshua learn that the Gibeonites lived in their neighborhood. Needless to say, the Israelite leaders were outraged by the trickery, but they were now bound together with the Gibeonites by a sacred union. The deceivers would become the servants of Israel, but not a hair on their heads was to be harmed.

When five neighboring kings caught news of the covenant, they attacked the Gibeonites, whom they now considered to be their enemies. Do you know what Joshua did? He risked the fate of Israel by marching his army through the night and attacking the armies of those kings the next day. What did God think about all of this? He was honored by the fact that Israel stood faithful to the covenant—even though it had been established under false pretenses. During the battle, God sent hailstones from the heavens to help defeat the enemy armies. Then, even more amazing, at Joshua's request, God had the sun stand still for a period of time so that the Israeli army could complete its triumph!

Somewhere from 200-400 years later (depending on the historical source consulted), King David found himself befuddled by a famine that was oppressing the nation of Israel (2 Samuel 21:1-14). When David inquired of God, he discovered the famine was the result of divine judgment against Israel because the previous king, Saul, had violated the covenant with the Gibeonites by putting some of them to death. Only after several of Saul's descendants were killed in retribution for his injustice, did the famine finally lift. We may think the consequences to be overly severe, but the story provides powerful insight to how highly the God of Heaven values covenant faithfulness.

While the absolute faithfulness required of a covenant may seem extreme to some, the erosion of trust resulting from the lack of a covenant worldview continues to have painful and far-reaching implications. And if the covenants between humans were considered to be ironclad, how much more should we consider a covenant established by God to be absolute?

A GLIMPSE OF GOD'S FAITHFULNESS

One of the biggest problems with a cultural erosion of trust is that our feelings of uncertainty are erroneously projected onto the God we profess to know and serve. We tend to lack, therefore, a functional faith in God that enables us to gracefully navigate the more extreme difficulties of life. We may trust Him for salvation, but beyond that we often struggle to believe that our heavenly Father will take good care of us, or that sacrificial obedience is worth the steep price that it exacts. In general, we don't trust Him because we don't know Him.

The faithful nature of a covenant relationship provides us with a much-needed glimpse into God's character. Through covenant we come to see that He is our *immovable rock*—one that will never shift or falter. If, for some reason, you feel that God has failed you—or that He has abandoned you because you have failed Him—you don't understand the nature of a covenant relationship with God. Apart from a covenant worldview, we find it virtually impossible to understand God's ways. The ability to make Christianity culturally relevant has its limits; at some point we must educate people about God's way of thinking.

A covenant worldview can, in a sense, be compared to the Rosetta Stone when it comes to trying to comprehend the nature of God, and thus, the teachings of the Scriptures. For a long time, scholars tried in vain to decipher Egyptian hieroglyphics—a form of writing too difficult to crack. Everything changed, however, with the discovery of the Rosetta Stone by a French soldier in 1799. Because the same passage was recorded in three different languages, the mystery of hieroglyphics finally unfolded.

In a similar way, longstanding points of confusion suddenly become clear as we begin to develop a covenant mindset. More and more, we see a loving and faithful heavenly Father as opposed to one who is capricious and unjust. Accordingly, an accurate and healthy perspective of our heavenly Father makes all the difference when it comes to learning to abide in His transformational grace.

Because many in our modern age know so little about the concept of covenant, it will do us good to briefly review the series of covenants that have defined the relationship between God and humanity since the beginning of creation. I will highlight seven primary covenants, but please be aware that I am not providing a comprehensive list.

THE COVENANTS OF THE BIBLE

Although the word covenant isn't used in the first three chapters of Genesis, covenant language is employed and the idea of covenant is inherent to the story. The *Edenic Covenant* was a sacred and binding relationship between God and the human race in which He created us in His image and made provision for all of our needs. Great blessings are in store for those who honor a covenant, while terrible curses await those who would stoop so low as to break one. Adam and Eve violated that covenant as they unwittingly joined in Lucifer's rebellion and committed high treason against the kingdom of Heaven.

The punishment of Hell, as unloving as it may seem, is the result of violating the Edenic Covenant. The curses of Genesis 3:14-19—pain in childbirth, male oppression of women, the curse of thorns and thistles plaguing our attempts to bring forth both physical and spiritual fruit, and finally death—were also the direct results of violating the first covenant between God and the human race. All of these curses can seem unfair and unloving when we lack the foundation of a covenant worldview. I can't begin to express how much it saddens me that people mistrust God because of our collective failure to understand His faithfulness.

While the creation story unfolded against the backdrop of the Edenic Covenant, a second covenant is also integral to the story—the *marriage covenant*—that mystical union between a man and a woman:

> *The man gave names to all the cattle, and to the birds of the sky, and to every beast of the field, but for Adam there was not found a helper suitable for him. So the LORD God caused a deep sleep to fall upon the man, and he slept; then He took one of his ribs and closed up the flesh at that place. The LORD God fashioned into a woman the rib which He had taken from the man, and brought her to the man. The man said,*
>
> *"This is now bone of my bones,*
> *And flesh of my flesh;*
> *She shall be called Woman,*
> *Because she was taken out of Man."*
>
> *For this reason a man shall leave his father and his mother, and be joined to his wife; and they shall become **one flesh**. And the man and his wife were both naked and were not ashamed.*
> *Genesis 2:20-25 (emphasis added)*

The marriage covenant (addressed in greater detail in Chapter Thirteen) was established as the foundation for the family, which is intended to be a covenant concept in itself. Through the nurture, safety, and security of a loving family, children can be reared to advance God's purposes—including the propagation of the human race—on earth. In principle, the nuclear family represents the ideal environment to grow children to physical and spiritual maturity. In practice, however, sin has had a destructive impact on the family from both within and without.

In spite of humanity's devastating disobedience in the garden, God immediately began to draw the human race back to Himself through a series of redemptive covenants. This brings us to the *Adamic Covenant*, which pointed toward Jesus as the ultimate victor over the serpent.

The LORD God said to the serpent,
"Because you have done this,
Cursed are you more than all cattle,
And more than every beast of the field;
On your belly you will go,
And dust you will eat
All the days of your life;
And I will put enmity
Between you and the woman,
And between your seed and her seed;
He shall bruise you on the head,
And you shall bruise him on the heel." Genesis 3:14-15

The serpent's curse was to become our blessing. From the very moment that Adam and Eve sinned, God instituted a plan to redeem the human race from the curses that it had brought upon itself by violating the Edenic Covenant. This redemption would come at a price, though, and no one would pay a higher premium than God Himself.

Jesus Christ—the seed of the woman—would one day trample the devil, thereby disarming every power of the dark lord over God's people. Jesus changed everything! Satan—the once majestic worship leader of Heaven—has been reduced to a pitiful state (though we dare not pity him) who functions much like the *Wizard of Oz* from that old movie classic. He gives the appearance of greatness and intimidating power, and yet his majesty is nothing more than the veiled product of smoke and mirrors. Jesus Christ fulfilled the Adamic Covenant for the sake of those who would become citizens of His kingdom. The serpent's destiny, then, is not to rule over the followers of Christ, but to eat their dust.

Next came the *Noahic Covenant* in which God displayed the rainbow as a reminder of His promise to never again flood the entire earth (Genesis 9:8-17). Not only can we enjoy the beauty of this faithful reminder after a storm, the rainbow forever captures the attention of the heavenly host. In fact, a rainbow rests over the very throne of God (Ezekiel 1:26-28 and Revelation 4:1-3). I don't believe it is there to remind God of His promise, though. God's faithfulness is ingrained in

His character. The rainbow over God's throne reminds us—and all of Heaven's angels—of our Creator's absolute faithfulness.

The Noahic Covenant was then followed by the *Abrahamic Covenant* in which God promised to bless Abraham and his descendants (Genesis 12-17). *Promise* is a keyword in the Abrahamic Covenant, emphasizing both God's faithfulness and the importance of our trust in His character. Through the Abrahamic Covenant, faith (trust) emerged as the foundation of humanity's relationship with God.

> *Then he believed in the LORD; and He reckoned it to him as righteousness. Genesis 15:6*

Things took another fascinating turn with the establishment of the *Mosaic Covenant* (*Old Covenant*). If the people of Israel would only obey the Mosaic Law, they would be "a kingdom of priests and a holy nation" (Exodus 19:6). It is important to note that the Mosaic Law was "ordained through angels by the agency of a mediator, until the seed would come to whom the promise had been made" (Galatians 3:19). The Law, in other words, was not God's first choice for the human race. Rather, it served to point the way toward a covenant that would become the culmination of all covenants.

THE ORIGINS OF LAW

The Mosaic Law was not unique in its day; archaeologists have uncovered several other law-codes that some scholars claim predate the time of Moses. The Code of Ur-Nammu, the Laws of Eshnumma, the Code of Lipit-Ishtar, and the Code of Hammurabi all involved various punishments—some of which were quite harsh—for failing to meet their community standards. The laws of a nation are used to govern the behavior of its citizens. Laws are needed to keep selfish people from destroying each other. This is why early civilizations began to formulate their own law codes. The choice was a simple one: create laws or self-destruct.

The problem—and it's a big one—is that law, in its many forms, is embodied by the tree of the knowledge of good and evil. These are deep and difficult things to fathom, but I find it impossible to fully comprehend grace without establishing a basic understanding of law.

Think about it. How many laws were there before Adam and Eve ate from the tree of the knowledge of good and evil? One—just one. After they ate, however, a drastic change occurred. Suddenly, the father and mother of humanity became acutely aware of evil in contrast to good. This awareness is expressed in the form of the human *conscience*, which literally means "with knowledge."

A MORAL COMPASS WITHOUT A TRUE NORTH

Some people believe that the conscience was given by God to humanity from the very beginning of time. Others feel that it somehow developed through a natural evolutionary process. Beginning with nothing, an immeasurable material universe mysteriously appeared. Life then formed spontaneously and, what was once a single-celled organic creature became amazingly complex. Somewhere along the evolutionary line, humans naturally developed a high level of conscious, intellectual thought, which includes an innate sense of moral justice and obligation. In my mind, both perspectives fall terribly short.

Before eating the forbidden fruit, Adam and Eve possessed an innocence that might be compared to that of a young child who does not yet grasp the concepts of good and bad. All they knew was relationship—with God and with each other. There was no pressure to perform, no compulsion to present a positive image, and no sense of superiority—or inferiority for that matter. There was certainly no guilt. Adam and Eve knew nothing of right and wrong. They had only the choice to trust or not trust, to love or not love. Everything changed after they ate from the tree! Suddenly, an acute awareness of social and moral standards beyond number overwhelmed their souls.

A conscience serves as an internal moral compass of sorts, but it lacks a "true north." The human conscience is subject to manipulation by humanity itself; therefore, we dare not confuse it with the voice of God. A sanctified conscience can be of some value, but even a mature Christian must be wary of his or her own conscience. There will be times when a person's actions and motives may be entirely offensive to God, but there is not a twinge of guilt. At other times, an individual may be plagued by a nagging sense of guilt and condemnation even though God takes no offense at his or her actions.

The natural laws that govern human behavior are compulsory. In other words, if I jump off my roof, thanks to the law of gravity, I will plummet to the ground. Moral law is quite different. We are hounded by lofty standards of expectation, but nothing forces us to respond accordingly. Neither do we find within the conscience the power to meet the standards it imposes.

The moral laws, societal laws, and the Law of Moses are all linked. Some scholars argue that Moses borrowed from other law codes to produce his own. I propose that they are mistaken. God looked on as human civilization developed, and in a sense said, "Do you want law? All right, I will give you law." Through the Mosaic Law, God began to relate to the human race according to our predetermined paradigm of rules and regulations that would be obeyed through independent human effort.

God established a law-based covenant, not because it reflected His mindset, but to protect us from ourselves while bringing us face to face with the futility of living according to our own human wisdom. The Mosaic Law was not to be the law code to end all law codes, but rather, a "schoolmaster" intended to point us in the direction of the coming Messiah and the establishment of the New Covenant (Galatians 3:24).

Let me be clear—there is nothing wrong with the Mosaic Law (Roman 7:12), or even with the concept of law in and of itself. Human pride is where the issues lie. The only "fault" found with the Old Covenant (Hebrews 8:7-8) was its inability to transform the human heart. Consider the following quote from the *Expositor's Greek Testament*:

> The old covenant was faulty because it did not provide for enabling the people to live up to the terms or conditions of it. It was faulty inasmuch as it did not sufficiently provide against *their* faultiness.[25]

Law is not the problem. Human nature is the problem. Even secular laws are necessary. Society cannot declare a free-for-all and expect nobody to get hurt. Both conscience and government legislation have their necessary benefits. The only way that a society can exist is through

---

25. Marcus Dods, "Hebrews," in *Expositor's Greek Testament* (Grand Rapids: Eerdmans, 1951), 4:323.

both internal and external laws. Anarchy never fixed anything. We face several significant drawbacks, however, with a law-based existence:

1. **Law can get very complicated and burdensome.** In the garden of Eden, there was almost total freedom with only one protective rule. Under the Mosaic Law, there were *613* commandments. Jewish leaders added many more, creating an increasingly constrained existence for the chosen people of God. Now that full-time employees in air-conditioned offices are typing laws with word processors, the number of government regulations has increased exponentially. Typing and printing a page is considerably faster than engraving it on stone. Imagine how long it would take to carve the United States' tax code on a rock!

2. **Laws restrict freedom.** This is necessary if people are selfish and/ or foolish, but laws can also be used to control people in ways never intended by God. The Bible validates the need for various types of authority, but never does it give humans the right to exercise complete *dominion* over other humans.

3. **The sinful nature of pride is awakened, aroused, and empowered by law.** This powerful reality is too often neglected in Christian circles. Not only is law powerless to change hearts, the manner in which the sinful nature responds to law is where the pride finds its deadly expression. Tell me not to cross a line, and I will want to cross it. Give me a list of rules, and I will boast if I follow them and despair if I fail.

4. **Law breeds judgment.** Law-based living requires perfection. A person only needs to break one significant law of the land to be declared a "lawbreaker" who is worthy of condemnation and punishment. Whereas a limited measure of judgment took place before the giving of the Mosaic Law; a virtual landslide of judgment followed afterward. Previously, God had judged only those societies that became excessively wicked and violent. After the giving of the Mosaic Law, however, almost every disobedient act met with severe punishment.

Further still, living by law breeds judgmental attitudes in human hearts as we constantly measure people by their ability to meet various written and unwritten standards of appearance and performance. As we judge others, we are inclined to either applaud or condemn ourselves. Law, as a standard for approval, will always facilitate judgment against those who fail to meet its exacting nature.

GOD'S TRUE CHARACTER

Even though there was nothing inherently wrong with the Old Testament Law, it does not provide an accurate representation of God's heart. This confuses people. Many of us assume that God the Father—typically represented as "the God of the Old Testament"—is somehow less loving than Jesus. Through a horrible mischaracterization, we envision God the Father as being harsh and vindictive in contrast to a sweet, syrupy Jesus. Consequently, we see Jesus as a non-judgmental buddy and God the Father as a strict authority figure just waiting to bring down the hammer as soon as we step out of line.

Jesus made it clear that He and His Father are *one* in nature (John 14:1-11). This means that there is no harsh "God of the Old Testament" who stands in contrast to the loving "God of the New Testament." The difference between the Old and New is not the nature of God, but the nature of the *covenants* between God and man. Do you see it? Under the Old Covenant, God related to humanity through a law-based paradigm chosen by the human race when Adam and Eve ate from the tree of the knowledge of good and evil. Under the New Covenant, the very same God relates to His redeemed children in a way that reflects His true nature.

Are we deeply disturbed when we read of the harsh judgments meted out by God in the Old Testament? We should be! We accurately perceive that something is desperately wrong in the picture. We, however, arrive at inaccurate conclusions when we assume some sort of unsavory character on God's part. If the Mosaic Law were the end of the story, we might have reason to doubt His goodness, but the Law wasn't intended to define the nature of God's relationship to humanity.

Instead, its purpose was to point us toward something greater—the New Covenant in Christ.

That the human race lives by the driving force of law remains one of the bitter consequences of eating from the tree of the knowledge of good and evil. Had Adam and Eve focused their attention on the tree of life, a very different scenario could have resulted. Living by law involves the pursuit of *merited favor*, trying to please God at a distance through our own self-sufficient efforts. Epic fail!

Even worse, our existence is replete with judgment as we continue to fall short of law's exacting standards. Sadly, we often see God as the source of a futile and painful law-based existence. Because of sin's destructive consequences—including the fear it instills—and because God is repulsed by the nauseating nature of human sin, we collectively find ourselves relating to God only from a distance. The unfortunate result is separation from the only true source of life. Our human quest for independence from God continues to give us what we seek in the form of the human condition.

It is the tree of life—not the tree of the knowledge of good and evil—that reveals God's heart. In a very real sense, this tree of life is embodied in the person of Jesus Christ. Jesus—the One *full* of grace and truth—has provided the means to disarm and defeat the archenemy of pride. The New Covenant of grace through Jesus Christ is God's final and complete answer to the problem of the human condition. It is the covenant to fulfill all covenants.

BLAZING A TRAIL TO FRUITFUL LIVING

If you want to better understand God's faithful love, read through the Bible with a keen eye open for the concept of covenant.

CHAPTER ELEVEN
THE UNIQUE NATURE OF THE NEW COVENANT

And in the same way He took the cup after they had eaten, saying, "This cup which is poured out for you is the new covenant in My blood."

Luke 22:20

Reality, in fact, is usually something you could not have guessed. That is one of the reasons I believe Christianity. It is a religion you could not have guessed.

—C.S. Lewis

We often think that the standards of the Mosaic Law are difficult to meet, but the situation is actually *worse* than it seems. Have you ever read the Sermon on the Mount and thought its standards impossible to meet? You are not alone. Jesus made it clear that DIY righteousness will not make Heaven's grade. No matter how hard we try, we can *never* render ourselves favorable to Heaven. To be like God apart from God requires *absolute perfection* on our part. Dare we use the term "perfect perfection" to emphasize the impossibility of achieving such a standard?

Like a thermometer, the Law has the ability to reveal a person's "spiritual temperature," but unlike a thermostat, it can do nothing to turn up the heat. If I begin, for example, to honestly read through the Ten Commandments, I may soon realize that I have failed miserably in my efforts to obey them. I may have taken God's name in vain, lied, and coveted my neighbor's ox (well, sort of). The Ten Commandments, though, offer nothing that empowers me to obey them. I am left entirely to my own flesh-based efforts.

Run, John, run, the law commands
But gives us neither feet nor hands,
Far better news the gospel brings:
It bids us fly and gives us wings.

This short verse, often attributed to John Bunyan, speaks volumes about the vast difference between our natural human paradigm and God's New Covenant gospel of grace. Does God expect people to live differently when they become Christians? Absolutely! But through the means of divine grace, the Holy Spirit both *empowers* Christ's followers to obey His will and *transforms* their hearts so that they want to do His will. All of this is made possible because Jesus, the Son of Man, initiated a "religion" unlike any other.

The series of covenants between God and humanity find their fulfillment in the New Covenant. In using the term "new," we don't just mean new as in time—like a new car—but new as in being *uniquely different from anything that existed in the past.*[26] The New Covenant is unlike any other covenant that has ever been made by man or God.

I find it unfortunate that we have come to use the term "New Testament" to name the part of the Bible that contains the New Covenant. We are left with the imagery of a Last Will and Testament—instructions that a person leaves for others after he or she has died and moved on from this world. The word *covenant* carries a very different connotation—the concept of an ongoing *relationship*.

The New Covenant of grace enables us to relate to God in a manner that we never imagined, and with an intimacy we never thought possible. Through the New Covenant, imperfect humans can live out a daily abiding relationship with the perfect and holy Creator of the Universe. The flawed and the flawless coexist in a way that the sinful mind is stretched to comprehend.

JESUS—OUR COVENANT REPRESENTATIVE

Not everyone participated in the ceremony when two ancient groups of people entered into a blood covenant. Often a *covenant representative*

---

26. Barclay M. Newman Jr., *A Concise Greek-English Dictionary of the New Testament* (Stuttgart, Germany: Deutsche Bibelgesellschaft; United Bible Societies, 1993), 90.

would stand in for the entire group.[27] The two individuals would cut themselves and somehow mingle their blood together. Often, they would rub some type of substance into their wounds (later cultures used gunpowder) to leave a lasting mark of remembrance. Only the covenant representatives paid the price, but the benefits and requirements of the covenant applied to all.

Jesus, the Son of Man, fulfilled every requirement needed to not only meet the exacting standards of the Mosaic Law, but of highest Heaven as well. Thus, as our covenant representative, the pressing weight of the New Covenant falls upon His shoulders—not ours. In this shines another sparkling facet of Christ's sacrificial death on the cross. Jesus died as the perfect Lamb of God so that the highest standards of Heaven could be met on our behalf. Through His perfection, the Son of Man has established an eternal relationship with the pure, holy, and just God of the Universe. We are privileged to enter into that New Covenant through faith in Jesus Christ—our covenant representative.

All who enter into the New Covenant through Jesus Christ take on new identities and stand before the heavenly Father wearing *Jesus'* robe of righteousness. It depends not upon self-effort, but upon our willingness to admit our fallen state and to fully embrace God's provision through the cross. Through faith, the power of pride is disarmed, and we are transformed by grace to bear sweet and abundant fruit for God. Transformation is not something that we can even begin to achieve through our own law-based efforts. Those who wish to walk with God and reverse the power of the curse can do so only through a revelation of the gospel of Jesus Christ. The New Covenant stands as God's ingenious answer to the horrific problem of the human condition.

Through faith, the life of Christ's blood vanquishes the death of our sin, not only covering the stains of our past, but washing them as white as snow. Through faith, our sinful underbellies are exchanged for His robe of righteousness so that we have confident access to God's throne of grace. Through faith, our once-corrupt hearts are transformed into holy temples in which the Holy Spirit dwells. Through faith, we bury our

---

27. Malcolm Smith, *The Power of the Blood Covenant: Uncover the Secret Strength in God's Eternal Oath* (Tulsa, Oklahoma: Harrison House, 2002), 73-77.

covenant-breaking pasts and are reborn as the covenant children of the King. And through faith, our internal motivation changes from a law of self-righteousness to the law of love. None of this happens because we've earned anything; it's all due to the unmerited favor of God. The ingenious solution of the gospel stands as the only effective antidote for human pride, and, consequently, the human condition. Through the blood of Jesus, the worst of Adam and Eve's descendants can stand before the throne of Heaven with the same confidence as those deemed by humanity to be the best.

Oh, the amazing beauty of grace! By grace, we find peace with our Creator and stand guilt-free before His throne. By grace, the Holy Spirit gives us the strength and courage to fulfill the will of God. And by grace, God puts within our hearts the desire to obey His wise directives. When God's people understand and abide in grace, the Christian life flourishes. But when they mistake the paradigm of human law for God's design, religion becomes foul, festering with harsh and judgmental attitudes.

As appealing as the New Covenant of grace may seem, not all people want to accept its reality. A primary part of the problem lies with the innate human desire to use law as a means of self-validation (glorification). By its very nature, the flesh wants, through law-based efforts, to validate itself. Herein lies another friction point of the soul that we all must face. Do we acknowledge the self-absorbed nature of sin that dominates our hearts, do we walk away from all religion and into a self-willed secular existence, or do we use religious effort as a law-based platform to establish our own sense of self-righteousness?

CHRISTIANITY IS UNIQUE

We are overwhelmed by a long list of philosophies regarding what Christianity is and what it isn't. During my college years, for example, I acknowledged the historical reality of Christ's death and resurrection, but saw no need to worship Him as the King of the Universe any more than I'd need to worship a friend who had given his life for mine. Would I owe a debt of gratitude? Obviously. But anything beyond that seemed extreme through the eyes of human reasoning that flowed from my self-will. We have many valid questions about the nature of God and Christianity, but the conclusions that we draw are often rooted in humanistic reasoning instead of true wisdom.

All too often, when it comes to the exclusive nature of Christianity, we want the amazing benefits of the New Covenant without the covenant itself. The New Testament clearly states that a personal relationship with God is possible only through faith in Jesus Christ (John 14:6 and Acts 4:10-12). Anyone who does not embrace the Christian faith is left on the *outside* as a self-condemned, treasonous covenant-breaker. Biblical Christianity is, without question, *exclusive* in this sense. Those who attempt to arrive at a different conclusion must either convolute the Scriptures or reject their authority.

In our efforts to soften the blow of what appears to be overly harsh and unreasonable doctrine, we sometimes try to explain away certain teachings of the Bible. In this case, we may erroneously conclude that God cannot be both loving and wrathful at the same time. (Try telling this to a father whose infant child has been molested and murdered by a repeat offender!) The only reasonable recourse is to deny the existence of Hell or to reserve it for those "human animals" who are *really bad*.

The obvious next step is to equate Christianity with all other belief systems. "All roads," we say, "lead to God. A loving Jesus would never have it any other way." It doesn't matter if a belief system contradicts biblical teaching; we need only find a small plot of common ground to contend that it is essentially equal to Christianity. This is, after all, the only "reasonable" approach if we are to walk the same non-judgmental path that Jesus walked. Or so we think.

SALVATION MUST BE EXCLUSIVE

Biblical Christianity does indeed share some common ground with most other religions but it remains unique in one critical facet: Christianity stands alone as *the religion of grace*. Every other religious belief system involves living up to some type of standard(s) by which we can either become acceptable to God, or achieve a higher order of existence. Each system of belief, then, is law-based at its core. And the problem with law-based religion is that it fails to defeat pride. Still, that's not the worst of it. Law-based living actually *fuels* the power of sin.

The sting of death is sin, and the power of sin is the law; but thanks be to God, who gives us the victory through our Lord Jesus Christ. 1 Corinthians 15:56-57 (see also Romans 7:5)

Religious doctrine may be used to modify human behavior to a certain extent, but, apart from grace, the problem of the human condition will perpetuate. We dare not ignore this reality! Jesus is the *only* tree of life. Every other system of belief proceeds from the tree of the knowledge of good and evil. They may look appealing, and they may promise life and wisdom. They may even emphasize that which is good to the exclusion of evil, but law-based religions cannot impart life to those who are spiritually dead.

People who seek to enter the family of God cannot "self-adopt." Only through a personal relationship with our covenant representative— Jesus—can we become viable members of God's family. Jesus alone is our tree of life. He alone is full of grace and truth. He alone can cleanse our sins and render us acceptable in the eyes of Heaven. And, standing as an eternal truth, Jesus alone has the ability to give us dominion over the devastating power of sin. Any attempt to appease Heaven apart from faith in Christ will fuel pride and end in corruption.

Independence from God ultimately leads to a self-centered chaos devoid of His grace-filled presence. This, I believe, is the ultimate essence of Hell—an existence separated from God, filled with regrets, and characterized by the fruit of the forbidden tree for all eternity. Hell is the full expression of the human condition having run its course apart from the redemptive influence of Heaven. I don't like the idea of Hell any more than the next person, but it is a reality nonetheless. The call of a Christian, then, is not to condemn others, but to expend our energies and efforts to *prevent* others from being condemned.

Proclaiming the exclusivity of salvation through Christ alone often offends those who hold other beliefs. To contend that one belief system is right and all others are wrong appears very harsh—if not arrogant. The spirit of the gospel, though, is neither harsh nor arrogant. Consider that the three qualifications for salvation are to be a sinner, to admit you are a spiritual failure, and to exercise faith in Christ's saving work on the cross. No, it is law—not grace—that breeds harshness and arrogance.

The Christian faith is much bigger than any of us. God's truth stands eternal regardless of what we say, feel, think, or believe. It doesn't matter how offended we are or how angry we become. We discover life and freedom only by aligning ourselves with God's reality, not by trying to constrain Him to ours. If the writers of the New Testament did not believe this, ten of Christ's disciples and the apostle Paul would not have died as martyrs. If they truly thought that salvation existed apart from Christ, they would have preserved their own lives and simply pointed others in the appropriate direction.

It is not without personal difficulty that I have worked through these concepts, and so I leave you with three additional thoughts to help bring additional perspective to this heavy issue:

1. **Christianity is a reasonable faith.** I do not espouse a blind confidence in the person of Jesus Christ. The historical evidence for the life, death, and resurrection of Christ is available for those who are willing to accept it at face value. Also, I have presented logical arguments that explain the roots of human nature and how the New Covenant gospel of grace provides the only viable answer to our extreme need. There are, no doubt, theories that compete with the gospel of grace, but we remain hard-pressed to find any system of belief—or non-belief—that explains our human existence the way that Christianity does. In the end, no law-based belief system offers a viable solution for the pride-induced problem of the human condition.

2. **Christianity is *inclusive* as well as exclusive.** What is the Christian requirement for salvation? *Faith* in Jesus Christ! Pedigree, wealth, appearance, and social status are non-issues. It doesn't matter what gender, race, or nationality you are. It doesn't even matter if you've had a dastardly moral track record. You may feel that you are the lowest of the low, but your moral failure doesn't disqualify you from becoming a Christian—it serves only to reveal your desperate need for Christ (which really isn't any greater than it is for the rest of the human race). Access to God's throne of grace is *joyfully* granted to *all* who are willing to embrace the person of Jesus Christ!

3. **People are left on the outside not due to any failure on God's part, but because of human indifference and opposition.** I can't imagine anything beyond the extreme effort that God has already made. Jesus humiliated Himself by stepping down from the throne of Heaven, confining Himself to human form, and experiencing a tortuous death as a treasonous covenant breaker. Heaven did not pay such a steep price to keep us from accessing God's presence. If people don't embrace the inclusive nature of Christianity, it is not because God is keeping them on the outside. Laws which punish possession of the Bible and conversion to Christianity come from humanity—not from God.

    In addition, consistent with the dominion that He gave to the human race, God uses *people* to reach people. If people aren't being reached, then the people to be reached are either closed to the truth, hindered from receiving the truth, or being slighted by those who already have the truth. In fact, it's entirely possible that God desires to use *you* to eternally touch the lives of others. If you are unwilling to be used, can God be blamed?

Attempting to make the gospel of grace entirely non-offensive undermines its power to transform broken lives. While we never want to unnecessarily antagonize others, we dare not deny the timeless truth of the New Covenant that towers far above any human idea, institution, or culture. There can be no apology for the life-giving message of the gospel of grace.

CHRISTIANITY IS NOT LEGALISTIC

The gospel does not just offend those outside of church. Sadly, the compulsion toward law-based living is so ingrained in human nature that legalism has made its way into Christian practice—and even doctrine. In many Christian circles, being a "good Christian" is all about measuring up to a long litany of written and unwritten standards of behavior. Don't we understand that Christ died to free us from such a stifling mindset? If our view of the Christian faith is not founded upon a revelation of grace, the good news of Jesus Christ will conflict with our religious sensibilities.

Law-based living and lawlessness can be equally destructive. Law empowers sin; lawlessness welcomes it. Law makes life complicated; lawlessness breeds a sense of futility. To reject grace is to choose judgment. Grace—the middle way—is where the transformational power of God does its marvelous work.

Finally, because there are so many needs in our world, and because our one-dimensional definition of grace has left us with a passive mindset, leaders will often burden people with a sense of obligation in an effort to spur them to much-needed action. I can recall plenty of times when I did something not because I really cared, but because I felt guilty for not acting. Living such a law-based existence robbed me of the life and vitality that flow from walking with God. Worse still, I thought that my heavenly Father was the source of the pressing sense of obligation that burdened my soul. How wrong I was!

Again, the victorious Christian life is not achieved by mixing law and grace, but by learning to continually abide in God's transformational grace. This is the unique message of the New Covenant. The way of grace is where fruitful living is to be found. And not only is that way full of hope, it is profoundly simple. We'll catch a glimpse of that simplicity in our next chapter.

BLAZING A TRAIL TO FRUITFUL LIVING

Let us put aside both legalism and lawlessness as we move toward a mindset characterized by the New Covenant gospel of grace.

CHAPTER TWELVE
FROM LAW TO LIBERTY

Jesus answered them, "Truly, truly, I say to you, everyone who commits sin is the slave of sin. The slave does not remain in the house forever; the son does remain forever. So if the Son makes you free, you will be free indeed."

John 8:34-36

Interwoven is the love of liberty with every ligament of the heart.
—George Washington

How we love our freedom! Of course, the definition of freedom can vary from person to person. Some view freedom as a license to do whatever feels good. Those who are more noble-minded realize that personal freedom should not adversely impact the lives of others.

Regardless of which definition of freedom appeals most, we would all do well to realize that, from the very beginning, freedom was *God's* idea. Isn't it ironic, then, that *freedom* and *Christianity* are two words many people feel contradict one another? Only the person who has been delivered from bondage to sin can understand that, at its very core, the gospel is a message of freedom.

THE GOSPEL AS OUR FOUNDATION FOR LIVING

The gospel of Jesus Christ is our foundation for living and the means by which we can experience real and lasting freedom. Embracing the gospel is not a one-time event, but a *daily* endeavor as we learn to draw upon the strength of God's grace. Consider the following passage from Paul's letter to the Roman church:

For I am not ashamed of the gospel, for it is the power of God for salvation to everyone who believes, to the Jew first and also to the Greek. For in it the righteousness of God is revealed from faith to faith; as it is written, "BUT THE RIGHTEOUS man SHALL LIVE BY FAITH." Romans 1:16-17

The gospel is the *power* of God for salvation—something that includes going to Heaven and much more. Through faith in Christ, we are able to break free from the grip of sin and effectively touch this world for Christ. The gospel centers on the life, death, and resurrection of Jesus Christ (1 Corinthians 15:1-11), but centuries before Jesus walked this earth, the gospel was being announced. Let's look at two Old Testament prophetic passages that point toward the New Covenant gospel of grace:

"For I will take you from the nations, gather you from all the lands and bring you into your own land. Then I will sprinkle clean water on you, and you will be clean; I will cleanse you from all your filthiness and from all your idols. Moreover, I will give you a new heart and put a new spirit within you; and I will remove the heart of stone from your flesh and give you a heart of flesh. I will put My Spirit within you and cause you to walk in My statutes, and you will be careful to observe My ordinances." Ezekiel 36:24-27

"Behold, days are coming," declares the LORD, "when I will make a new covenant with the house of Israel and with the house of Judah, not like the covenant which I made with their fathers in the day I took them by the hand to bring them out of the land of Egypt, My covenant which they broke, although I was a husband to them," declares the LORD. "But this is the covenant which I will make with the house of Israel after those days," declares the LORD, "I will put My law within them and on their heart I will write it; and I will be their God, and they shall be My people. They will not teach again, each man his neighbor and each man his brother, saying, 'Know the LORD,' for they will all know Me, from the least of them to the greatest of them," declares the LORD, "for I will forgive their iniquity, and their sin I will remember no more." Jeremiah 31:31-34

What great, exciting promises for all humanity! Take note how God uses "I will" in these prophetic passages:

"I will take and gather you . . . I will bring you . . . I will sprinkle you . . . I will cleanse you . . . I will give you a new heart . . . I will put a new spirit within you . . . I will remove your heart of stone . . . I will give you a heart of flesh . . . I will put My Spirit within you . . . I will cause you to walk in My statutes . . . I will make a new covenant . . . I will put My law within them . . . I will write My law on their heart . . . I will be their God . . . I will forgive their iniquity . . . I will remember their sin no more."

Now, contrast the intent of God's "I wills" with those of Lucifer from Isaiah 14:13-14:

"I will ascend to heaven . . . I will raise my throne above the stars of God . . . I will sit on the mount of assembly . . . I will ascend above the heights of the clouds . . . I will make myself like the Most High."

Whose kingdom do you want to govern your life? Satan's agenda is entirely self-absorbed; he doesn't care whom he tramples in his pursuit of supremacy. In contrast, God's passion is always for our well-being. Enter into the New Covenant with God and He will bless you; make a pact with the devil and you will get burnt.

Integral to our well-being is the transformation of our hearts from a self-centered "I will" agenda to an other-centered "I will" agenda of love. The gospel is not merely about self-improvement or behavior modification. Becoming a new creature in Christ involves a total heart makeover. We receive a New Covenant identity through faith in Jesus Christ, and then live out that reality through the power of grace.

When I was in high school, I had a buddy, Chris, who often got in trouble. Chris always seemed to be hatching one mischievous plan or another. Frustrated by the weight of his self-inflicted grief, my friend decided to amend his ways. One day, as we sat in chemistry lab, Chris boldly announced to the class, "I am turning over a new leaf! From here on out, I will no longer be getting into trouble." I don't think he made it a week. Before we knew it, Chris was in hot water (again) with the school administration.

Attempting to modify our behavior while still living out of our old, fallen natures amounts to little more than a lesson in futility. Most people fail miserably, only to wallow in their dysfunction under a cloud of hopelessness. Those who manage to make favorable changes often trade one form of dysfunction for another. They quit smoking but start over-eating. They stop stealing but become compulsive shoppers. In the rare instance that someone actually breaks free from a vice, his or her heart then brims with a sense of personal pride that morphs into a judgmental attitude. "If I was able to change my life, there is no reason you shouldn't be able to as well!" might be a typical statement from someone who has managed to overcome a personal struggle.

Humanity's fallen nature is why mere religious activity will never suffice. Reading the Bible, praying, and going to church will lead only to a sense of pious superiority if these things don't flow out of a new heart in Christ. The essence of being "born again" (John 3:3)—or "born from above"—is not about trying to be a better person, but rather living with a new heart. No longer do we attempt to live up to Heaven's standards by our own law-based efforts; the blood of Jesus cleanses our hearts from all of our sins so that the Holy Spirit can take up residence. Victory over the dominion of sin is achieved not by trying harder, but by trusting, yielding, and subsequently obeying. How ironic it is that true freedom flows from obedience!

EXPLORING GOD'S COMMANDMENTS

Dealing with the issue of obedience is where Christianity appears to get terribly complicated. Legalists demand that we obey long lists of rules. Those who proclaim a one-dimensional view of grace would prefer to erase the word *obey* from the entire New Testament text. On one hand, we struggle under the burden of unattainable standards; on the other hand, we are ruled by our inner passions. Therefore, we must ask, "How does grace relate to obedience?"

Under the New Covenant, the laws of God are written on warm, pliable hearts (Jeremiah 31:33 and Hebrews 8:10) rather than being etched on cold, hard stone as were the Ten Commandments. The gospel of grace does not eliminate all laws. Instead, our motivation goes from being *external* to *internal*. God's laws create an *inside-out* transformation. Check out the following verses from the first and last chapters of the apostle Paul's letter to the Romans:

*. . . Jesus Christ our Lord, through whom we have received grace and apostleship to bring about the **obedience of faith** among all the Gentiles for His name's sake . . . Romans 1:4b-5 (emphasis added)*

*. . . but now is manifested, and by the Scriptures of the prophets, according to the commandment of the eternal God, has been made known to all the nations, leading to **obedience of faith** . . . Romans 16:26 (emphasis added)*

Do you see it? Romans—the one book of the Bible that lays out the gospel better than any other—begins and ends with references to "obedience of faith." This is where our perspective of the gospel looms large. If the good news is nothing more than an "Accept Jesus so you can go to Heaven." message, then obedience means little. But if the gospel is "the word of the kingdom" (Matthew 3:19), then obedience to the law of the kingdom means everything. The importance of obedience becomes even clearer as we return to our vine/branches passage in John 15:

"If you keep My commandments, you will abide in My love; just as I have kept My Father's commandments and abide in His love." John 15:10

We abide in God's love and stay connected to the flow of His transformational grace by keeping His commandments. *Abiding in Christ is not automatic; it depends upon our obedience to His commands.*

We're not referring to the message of a legalist; Jesus, the Son of God, spoke this to His followers. Some people might argue that Jesus admonished His disciples under the Mosaic Law—i.e. before the New Covenant of grace was established. Take note, however, that Jesus spoke these words just prior to His sacrificial death. Do we honestly think that His call to obedience was intended to apply only for a few hours? Clearly, the Christ was referring to the time *after* His departure from earth, and the message is intended for all who seek to be His disciples.

Alas, we now have a new problem—exactly what commandments was Jesus speaking about? The Ten Commandments? The 613 laws contained in the Mosaic Law? Or maybe some of our church rules such as "Don't drink, spit, or kick your neighbor's cat!" What about all of the other things we should be doing to make the Christian grade?

Will reading our Bibles every day, praying for 30 minutes or more, and giving ten percent of our income (plus offerings) put us on solid ground with the Lord? We need a way to make sense of what God expects of His children. The answer can be found by incorporating the broader New Testament context. By reading just a little further in John, we can find the primary command that Jesus emphasized just prior to the cross:

> *"This is My commandment, that you love one another, just as I have loved you. Greater love has no one than this, that one lay down his life for his friends. You are My friends if you do what I command you." John 15:12-14*

The commandment to love God wasn't new; love for God and others was intended to be the foundation of the Mosaic Law (Matthew 22:34-40). With the gospel, however, we find a new, simplified law—the law of love—that begins on the inside and works its way out. The gospel of grace facilitates a transformation of our inner core. We can't simply wave a magic wand and make ourselves more loving. While every fiber of our being seems to long for freedom, true liberty flows only from a new heart.

Those who like to quote Hebrews 8:12—"For I will be merciful to their iniquities, and I will remember their sins no more"—must apply the passage within its context. This means that experiencing the fullness of God's New Covenant promises is dependent on His laws being written on our hearts.

SEPARATING LAW FROM LAW

Christians are free from condemnation because the law of the Spirit of life in Christ Jesus has set us free from the law of sin and death (Romans 8:1-2). Life by the Spirit of grace is characterized by the free law of love, which governs our new hearts in Christ. A law-based existence is embodied by the tree of the knowledge of good and evil, which defines our old fleshly nature.

Galatians was a letter of correction written by Paul to Gentile believers whom he had introduced to the gospel. Paul was distraught to hear that their faith had been corrupted by the influence of law-breathing *Judaizers*—a group of Jews who professed Christ, but felt that adhering to the Mosaic Law was as vital to their existence as breathing. A Judaizer would be considered the ultimate "Christian legalist"—if such a creature could even exist. Paul's response was adamant:

> *Plant your feet firmly therefore within the freedom that Christ has won for us, and do not let yourselves be caught again in the shackles of slavery. Listen! I, Paul, say this to you as solemnly as I can: if you consent to be circumcised then Christ will be of no use to you at all. I will say it again: every man who consents to be circumcised is bound to obey all the rest of the Law! If you try to be justified by the Law you automatically cut yourself off from the power of Christ, you put yourself outside the range of his grace. For it is by faith that we await in his Spirit the righteousness we hope to see. In Jesus Christ there is no validity in either circumcision or uncircumcision; it is a matter of faith, faith which expresses itself in love. Galatians 5:1-6 (Phillips)*

What a powerful, albeit difficult, passage! How do we reconcile Paul's hard words with our one-dimensional definition of grace? We can't. Allow me to make two observations:

1. **Paul was writing to Gentile Christians who were being pressured by the Judaizers to adopt certain tenets of the Mosaic Law—the practice of circumcision in particular—in order to maintain an ongoing relationship with God.**

2. **The primary context of Paul's letter deals with *living under law*—that is utilizing obedience to the Mosaic Law as a means of attaining approval and acceptance in the eyes of God.** To be justified by law, in the eyes of Paul, was to nullify Christ's sacrificial death on the cross by establishing one's own kingdom righteousness through self-effort. God is offended—not pleased—by such efforts.

Galatians 5:4 clearly states that living under law *excludes* us from abiding in grace:

> *You are severed from Christ, you who would be justified by the law; you have fallen away from grace. Galatians 5:4 (ESV)*

Translated here as "severed," the Greek word, *katargeo*, can also mean "to render ineffective."[28] Was Paul saying that it's possible for a Christian to lose his or her salvation? In all honesty, I prefer to avoid the eternal security issue. I have my opinion on the matter, but discussions regarding this topic always seem to degrade into useless bickering. We can all agree, however, that Paul is describing a highly undesirable scenario.

How can a Christian be severed from Christ and fall away from God's unmerited favor—especially when he or she has done nothing to earn that favor in the first place? This passage seems very confusing until we consider the multidimensional nature of grace. When we try to gain God's approval by self-effort, we put ourselves outside the range of His *transformational* grace. This is the *opposite* of abiding in Christ. Those who live under law in this sense become mired in spiritual slavery—or *bondage to sin*, if you will. Becoming righteous through self-effort stands diametrically opposed to living by faith and abiding in grace. Three terrible things happen when we seek to live by law as a means of righteousness:

1. **We awaken, arouse, and empower the sinful nature (Romans 7:5 and 1 Corinthians 15:56).**

2. **We are alienated from the place of abiding in Christ (Galatians 5:6).**

3. **We disconnect ourselves from the flow of God's transformational grace (Galatians 5:6).**

Have any of us *not* been there?—that pit of frustration where the harder you try the *worse* you do.

I grew up near a main railroad line. It's illegal now, but as teenagers my friends and I would often walk the tracks to go fishing in an old refuse area we called "Swampy Doodle." Along the way, we would sometimes challenge one another to see who could walk the farthest without falling off of a steel track. A half-mile is a long way to walk such a fine line, and so what began as fun would soon become exhausting.

---

28. Barclay M. Newman Jr., *A Concise Greek-English Dictionary of the New Testament* (Stuttgart, Germany: Deutsche Bibelgesellschaft; United Bible Societies, 1993), 95.

Sometimes, moral living feels like being bound to a "railroad track" existence. We feel as though we will draw Heaven's ire if we take even one step off of the straight and narrow. Life quickly becomes joyless and constrained, and the harder we try to stay on that track, the more we fall off. How can a person possibly live in a way that honors God when he or she empowers sin, is severed from abiding in Christ, and is removed from the range of His grace? Living free from the dominion of sin becomes *impossible*. The law of the Spirit of life frees, enlivens, and strengthens us; the law of sin and death constrains, frustrates, and exhausts us.

ISN'T SIN DEAD?

But wait! Didn't the apostle Paul teach that the sinful nature has been put to death through Christ's work on the cross—that Christians are free from the power of sin? He most certainly did. However, our freedom from sin must take into account the original language of Paul's letter to the Romans along with its overall context. Space does not permit me to explore this issue thoroughly, but I will draw from a couple of passages in Romans to help provide context:

> *Therefore we have been buried with Him through baptism into death, so that as Christ was raised from the dead through the glory of the Father, so we too might walk in newness of life. For if we have become united with Him in the likeness of His death, certainly we shall also be in the likeness of His resurrection, knowing this, that our old self was crucified with Him, in order that our body of sin might be done away with, so that we would no longer be slaves to sin; for he who has died is freed from sin. Romans 6:4-7*

As much as I appreciate the New American Standard Bible, I think that its rendering of "might be done away with" in verse six is slightly off base. This is actually the same Greek word, *katargeo*, that we just highlighted from Galatians 5:6. While *katargeo* can mean "destroyed" or "done away with," a better translation for this passage would be "rendered ineffective" or "rendered powerless."

You can relax; I am not claiming to rewrite the meaning of *katargeo*. My position is well in line with several of the newer Bible versions:

- ... in order that the body of sin might be brought to nothing (ESV).

- ... in order that sin's dominion over the body may be abolished (HCSB).

- ... so that sin might lose its power in our lives (NLT).

If we consider the entire context of Paul's writings, we see that he never claimed that the sin nature is totally destroyed when a person becomes a Christian, but that the power of sin is *disarmed* when we live by faith (as opposed to being under law). Paul used the word *dead* as a metaphor to help explain the state to which sin is rendered. How do we know this? Throughout Romans, Paul employed three Greek words which can all refer to being dead in a *figurative* sense. One such use is in Romans 4:19:

> *Without becoming weak in faith he contemplated his own body, now as good as dead since he was about a hundred years old, and the **deadness** of Sarah's womb . . . (emphasis added)*

Was Sarah's womb literally dead? If so, she would have been a very sick woman. Sarah's womb was dead for its intended purpose of bearing children, or, to better align with our discussion of sin, Sarah's womb was *rendered powerless* to bear children. Through faith, Sarah's womb was returned to its "living state" and so Isaac was born. With sin, the same principle applies, but from the opposite perspective. Sin is disarmed—i.e. rendered powerless—when we live by faith, but sin is *empowered* when we cease to live by faith and return to living under law as a means of righteousness. Thus, we are to consider ourselves as being "dead" to sin (Romans 6:11).

Empowering sin, alienating ourselves from abiding in Christ, and falling away from the transforming power of grace—can we think of a worse scenario? The end result—even for the person who valiantly tries to conquer sin—can be nothing short of failure. Self can never defeat self. The harder we try in our own strength to be good Christians, the worse we will become. It can seem difficult enough to live in victory over sin when we draw upon God's abundant grace, but living in freedom is impossible when we put ourselves outside of the range of His transformational grace. This is why Paul adamantly opposed the law-breathing Jews—to live under law as a means for self-validation is to live in bondage to sin. Freedom comes only as we let go of our self-effort and learn to live by faith, resting in the shadow of the cross.

As deadly as this problem of living under law may be, it is a difficult concept for us to grasp. Living under law is entirely natural for us. From an early age, we enter a sphere of comparisons and judgments. Many of us grow to hate this type of existence, but it is the world into which we are born. Living by grace is unnatural. We must cry out to God for the light of revelation if we are to live in a spirit of true freedom.

I've taught this material to many people over the years and a blank stare is a common response. I begin to think, "Maybe the person is tuning me out—perhaps thinking about what to eat for dinner." Thankfully, that "cow-at-a-new-gate" look often gives way to an exclamation of delight: "I get it! Now I understand!" I can almost see a light bulb switching on above the person's head. Dealing with the issue of law-based living is never easy—I'm even hesitant even to write about it—but it is profitable.

IDENTITY BY LAW?

If you remember *The Humanistic Progression of Sin* diagram from page 110, we addressed two primary dimensions of righteousness: *kingdom righteousness* and *social righteousness*. Kingdom righteousness deals with our right standing before God, while social righteousness involves being seen in a condition acceptable to our contemporaries.

When it comes to kingdom righteousness, most evangelicals seem to understand that Jesus Christ is our only means of eternal salvation. What we don't seem to comprehend, though, is the fact that a person can trust Christ for salvation (i.e. with regard to kingdom righteousness), but live by law in pursuit of social acceptance (i.e. social righteousness). In other words, an individual can live by faith to be eternally saved, but use law-based efforts to obtain a favorable identity. A person may discover acceptance with God through the cross of Christ, but try to establish a sense of identity based on what he or she perceives to be the accepted standards of Christian behavior. All the while, something insidious is happening—the power of sin is being fueled.

Why is there so much roadkill fruit in so many of our churches? All too often, we constantly compare our spiritual "performance" to that of others. Our hearts swell with pride when we think we've succeeded, and so we look with contempt on those who fail to meet our lofty standards. When we fail, self-condemnation becomes the order of the day.

Pursuing a favorable identity through law breeds the fruit of death—even in the life of a Christian. For the first several years of my Christian walk, I merely transferred my pre-Christian law-based mentality into a different social environment. It didn't work very well.

Having become attuned to this issue, I now realize its prevalence in practically every sphere of the church. Christian practice—even in evangelical circles—is plagued by a never-ending quest for social righteousness. The result is a staggering amount of roadkill fruit that both nauseates and alienates sincere seekers. Whether we fear criticism from outside our circle of relationships, feel the crushing weight of peer pressure, or seek a sense of significance through performance, all too often, we value the opinions of people more than we do the favor of God. Those who live by peer—or is it *fear*?—pressure are by no means free.

TOXIC CHURCH?

If we as Christians live by faith for kingdom righteousness, but live by law in pursuit of social righteousness, we still alienate ourselves from abiding in God's transformational grace. When this type of existence becomes corporate—that is when it begins to characterize a significant portion of a church—the environment becomes spiritually toxic. Church members will then lead dual lives for fear of being "found out"—and judged—by other church members.

Rather than seeking to lift one another to new heights in Christ, we become pouncers. Peering from our pious heights, we look down our noses and heap contempt on those we feel are below our exacting standards. When they inevitably fail, we pounce—attacking their ungodly behavior in the name of "righteousness." When the people of God are characterized by this type of a law-based mindset, their practical expressions of grace will be found wanting.

We make our judgments in the name of Christ, but a judgmental attitude is spiritually rotten to its core, any vestige of life undermined by inner decay. Judgmental attitudes harden our hearts. A hardened heart, then, blinds us from recognizing the error of our own ways. Sadly, those on the outside looking in—especially our young people—are well aware of the roadkill stench. Living by law as a means of social righteousness may not keep a person out of Heaven, but the resulting bad fruit will surely drive others away from Christ.

Living by law in pursuit of social righteousness is a *massive* problem in the church. We fail to realize that the gospel is a message of identity as much as one of eternal salvation. Only by receiving a real and personal revelation of one's identity in the eyes of the Father and the Son can a person be freed from the constant compulsion to live up to human standards.

Social righteousness means nothing to God. He does not value our peer-driven standards and cares even less about human approval. In fact, any genuine effort to walk with God will put us at odds with other humans who demand that we too conform to their standards of social righteousness. If our pursuit of human favor compels us to sacrifice our devotion to God on the altar of self-significance, we have a serious problem (Galatians 1:6-10). This is a primary reason the Scriptures encourage us to be bold and stand strong in the faith.

THE ESSENCE OF THE GOSPEL

We now see that staying connected to God's flow of grace is not automatic. We can be children of God by our standing, but fail to abide in an intimate relationship with Christ. As painful as it may be to come to such a realization, we also find a bright ray of hope. There are valid reasons many of us flounder as we try to live out our Christian faith.

As previously presented, the way to remedy this problem is *not* to try harder. Instead, the answer lies in making the *essence of the gospel* central to our existence. The heart of this essence can be found in Galatians 5:1-6—a passage that we've already highlighted. The following paraphrase of the last two verses will help us better grasp God's expectations:

> *For we through the Spirit [of grace], by faith in Christ's sacrificial death and resurrection, are waiting for the hope of righteousness. For in Christ Jesus neither law, nor lawlessness, renders us in a condition acceptable to God, but the Christian life flourishes as **faith expresses itself through love.** Galatians 5:5-6 (BOBS; emphasis added)*

The essence of the gospel—and all of life for that matter—is *faith expressing itself through love*, or *faith working through love*. When we become part of the family of God, all that our heavenly Father expects is for us to trust Him in everything, and to live out that trust in the form of obedient love. This is the profoundly simple law of the kingdom! The apostle John penned something similar:

> *This is His commandment, that we **believe** in the name of His Son Jesus Christ, and **love** one another, just as He commanded us. The one who keeps His commandments abides in Him, and He in him. We know by this that He abides in us, by the Spirit whom He has given us. 1 John 3:23-24 (emphasis added)*

Our right standing in the eyes of God comes as we exercise faith in Christ's saving work on the cross, and, as faith permeates every aspect of our lives, we abide in his transformational grace. Grace, in turn, produces the very active fruit of love. *Faith expressing itself through love really is the sum total of what God expects from us. If we have the essence right, everything else will follow in its time. If we don't have the essence right, we'll be plagued by a malodorous harvest of roadkill fruit.

We stray from the essence of the gospel when we try to establish righteousness as a stand-alone concept. Righteousness and love should never be two separate issues. Isn't this the point that Jesus was making with the parable of the Good Samaritan (Luke 10:25-37)? The ancient Hebrew understanding of righteousness—which was often viewed as a relational concept—contained a strong ethical element.[29]

When we live by faith in Christ, we are clothed in His righteousness and made acceptable in the eyes of Heaven. As love becomes the core

---

29. Harold G. Stigers, "1879 צדק," ed. R. Laird Harris, Gleason L. Archer Jr., and Bruce K. Waltke, *Theological Wordbook of the Old Testament* (Chicago: Moody Press, 1999), 752.

motivation of our hearts, we begin to act righteously—that is, we do right by others. God's internal work of grace produces the fruit of love which is then manifested in our external behavior. As we grow into spiritual maturity, the gap between our kingdom righteousness in Christ and our actual behavior will narrow.

Faith expressing itself through love—God's expectations really are that simple! Establish this essence firmly in your heart because you will need to draw upon its profound simplicity during difficult times. My spiritual struggles always seem to boil down to three primary issues: a lack of faith, the unwillingness to love, or insufficient wisdom to know how faith and/or love should be applied in a given situation. *Faith expressing itself through love*—the essence of the gospel—is the path that all who seek to be spiritually fruitful must traverse as they blaze a trail for others to follow.

RENEWING OUR MINDS

The essence of the gospel is simple. Human nature is complicated. It is also deceptive, elusive, and evasive. One danger of exposing internal motives is that of "spiritual navel gazing." When we highlight issues such as pride and living under law, we can become self-focused—and sometimes even panic—as we realize that our hearts are overrun with selfish, prideful, and judgmental attitudes. Our natural tendency, then, is to either fall into the trap of self-condemnation, or to begin wrestling with our inner selves (as though we can somehow make our motives pure). Neither option is desirable.

Most of us can relate to Chapter Seven of Paul's letter to the Romans as he confesses his internal struggles against sin. Paul concludes his train of thought with a statement that has huge ramifications for every believer:

> *Therefore there is now no condemnation for those who are in Christ Jesus. For the law of the Spirit of life in Christ Jesus has set you free from the law of sin and of death. Romans 8:1-2*

Our sufficiency is *always* to be in Christ, never within ourselves. No matter how undesirable our personal state may be at any given moment, the path to freedom is one of learning to rest in the shadow of the cross.

When I am resting, I am not constantly questioning myself. I am not second-guessing everything that I do. I am not trying to be the perfect Christian. I am simply trusting in what He has done for me. How freeing!

Self cannot be overcome by self, but when we rest in the sufficiency of Christ we begin to disengage the flesh and engage the Holy Spirit of grace. Only then can our spiritual lives flourish. Do you see the irony of it all? We move forward spiritually when we rest in the shadow of the cross. Why? Because in resting from our self-sufficiency, we access the flow of God's life-giving grace that produces spiritual growth.

The essence of the gospel is profoundly simple, yet living it out can prove intensely difficult. In part, that is because spiritual rest does not come naturally to any of us. Only as we learn to *renew* our minds (Romans 12:1-2) with the truth of God's word can spiritual rest become a way of life.

There was never an official announcement, but I have my own chair at our dinner table. I've been sitting in that same seat for the twenty-seven plus years that we've been in our house. When our kids were at home, the after-dinner cleanup involved pushing all of our chairs in toward the table. After the kids moved out, however, I developed the bad habit of leaving my chair out—problematic behavior in our small dining room.

One day, while walking past the table, Debi tripped over the chair leg and almost broke her toe. I felt terrible, so I determined to always push my chair in after eating. It was a great idea in principle, but changing my bad habit has not come easily. I commonly read when eating breakfast or lunch by myself, so I often rise from the table engrossed in thought while the chair continues to protrude into Debi's path. So much for good intentions!

I am getting better with remembering to push in my chair, but I still forget on occasion. There are even times when I think about it as I sit down to eat, but my mind is in another world by the time I've finished my meal. Old, ingrained habits are the most difficult to break. In a similar vein, many of us have spent our entire lives living under law as the normal expression of our inner selves. To us, the comparison game is as natural as home-grown lettuce. The painful result is that judgmental attitudes flow like water in a stream. Training ourselves to rest in the shadow of the cross is not something that happens quickly or easily, but change will come if we will stay with the process of renewing our minds.

Once again, the importance of confessing our sins comes into play. Confession allows us to bring closure to our failures—even when we fail repeatedly—and get a fresh start so that we can effectively renew our minds. Through confession, we humble our hearts and draw upon His transformational grace. We confess our failures to God, we believe we are forgiven, we rest in the sufficiency of Christ, and we move on in our devotion to God. Profoundly simple! Profoundly powerful!

THE ESSENCE IS DELIGHTFUL!

Because of the Old Testament emphasis on law and judgment, and because the God of Heaven is wrathful toward the unrighteous, it's easy to develop the mindset that He is an eternally angry patriarch whose collar is buttoned much too tight. But if we wish to know God and understand His ways, we must, through the eye of faith, learn to see Him as He is.

Three primary issues come into play. First, I've already explained that Genesis 1 and 2 provide us with a clearer picture of God before sin entered the picture. The garden of Eden—garden of delights—was His idea. Second, as important as humanity is to God, we live in a *big* universe. There is much more to God's existence than His interaction with wayward humans. As much as we are prone to think otherwise, it isn't all about us. Finally, God's wrath is directed toward those who are *outside* of the New Covenant. Jesus died on the cross so that the barrier of sin might be removed, and so that we might draw near as intimate friends of God.

Those who have tasted of God's presence understand that, at the core of His personhood, God is a delightful being. Through the simplicity of the gospel and the unmerited favor of His grace, God's covenant children are able to experience His delight. My primary focus has been on the fruit of love, but there is so much more to the story. Joy and peace are also vital fruits of the Spirit and marks of God's eternal kingdom. God doesn't expect us to be fruitful because He is a stingy farmer trying to multiply profits; God expects us to be fruitful because spiritual fruit is delightful—just like God Himself.

Throughout the Scriptures—including the Old Testament—we find commands to be thankful, to give praise, and to rejoice. Are those things that a drill sergeant type of god would command? I don't think so. Our God took delight in creating our world and especially humanity (Genesis 1:31 and Proverbs 8:22-31). Pride and the resulting human condition have marred the beauty of God's creation, but they haven't changed who He is. Because of Christ's sacrificial death on the cross, and through the unmerited favor of grace, the King of the Universe welcomes us into His delightful existence. Is this not the heart of true liberty? Christianity isn't about the *have* to; it's about the *get* to!

BLAZING A TRAIL TO FRUITFUL LIVING

We find freedom on the path of life as we begin to grasp the profound essence of the gospel—*faith expressing itself through love.*

CHAPTER THIRTEEN
A FAITH TO DIE FOR

Now faith means putting our full confidence in the things we hope for, it means being certain of things we cannot see. It was this kind of faith that won their reputation for the saints of old. And it is after all only by faith that our minds accept as fact that the whole scheme of time and space was created by God's command—that the world which we can see has come into being through principles which are invisible.

Hebrews 11:1-3 (Phillips)

Faith is a living, daring confidence in God's grace, so sure and certain that a man could stake his life on it a thousand times.
—Martin Luther

We live in a world that is governed by law, but of what benefit are the laws of a nation if the people of that nation do not understand those laws? James Madison—the "Father of the [U.S.] Constitution"—once wrote, "It will be of little avail to the people that the laws are made by men of their own choice if the laws be so voluminous that they cannot be read, or so incoherent that they cannot be understood."[30] Consider also the following quote from forbes.com:

> There's probably nothing more dangerous to individual rights than vaguely written laws. They give prosecutors and judges undue power to decide whether or not to punish conduct that people did not know was illegal at the time. Vagueness turns the law into a sword

---

30. James Madison, *Federalist* no. 62, February 27, 1788.

dangling over citizens' heads–and because government officials can choose when and how to enforce their own interpretations of the law, vagueness gives them power to make their decisions from unfair or discriminatory motives.[31]

Whether we speak of federal anti-discrimination laws, state business requirements, or local building codes, vague wording can easily be used to manipulate and control people. Sometimes a lack of clarity is simply a matter of oversight—no one anticipates a particular outcome. There are times, however, when laws are crafted to be *intentionally* vague in order to gain popular support. After all, why should anybody complain about a "good" law being passed for a worthy cause? The use of these laws turns sinister as they are leveraged for unjust or controlling purposes.

A similar principle applies to religious doctrine. Enemies of truth are often intentionally vague because there can be no clear understanding without clear definitions. In fact, it's quite common for false teachers to use biblical words such as *faith* and *love*, but with meanings in conflict with the intent of the Scriptures. The message may sound Christian even though it is actually *anti*-Christian.

Some mysteries—such as the line between God's sovereignty and human free will—are nearly impossible to fully explain and need to be accepted as such. But there is much more that can—and should—be clearly defined. So it is with the essence of the gospel. In principle, living out the essence of *faith expressing itself through love* is both freeing and transforming. In practice, however, the simplicity of the gospel can be perverted to promote all sorts of selfish behavior if faith and love are not accurately defined.

ESTABLISHING CONTEXT

I have a good friend, Ted, who is a retired Methodist minister. Ted has impacted the lives of many people through the years and I've always respected his opinion. Because of his established track record and keen eye for truth, I often use Ted as a resource when I develop my teaching materials. Ted is clearly troubled when Christian communicators try

---

31. http://www.forbes.com/2010/03/30/vague-laws-economy-government-opinions-contributors-timothy-sandefur.html

to explain biblical terms—such as faith and love—using a modern language dictionary. Ted will say something like, "You can't do that and expect it to be right! A term in the Bible doesn't necessarily mean what it does in the latest edition of the dictionary." Ted is right, of course.

Once again, cultural relevance has its limits. The mindsets, languages, and cultures of our modern world are far from the context of the Bible. If we are to avoid error and genuinely live out Christianity in a way that honors God, we must seek to comprehend the concepts of faith and love as they were understood in the original context of the New Testament church.

The Bible was written in three languages (Hebrew, Aramaic, and Greek), on three continents (Africa, Asia, and Europe), and over a span of 1500 years. Consider how much your own culture has changed over only 200-300 years and then factor in the geographical and cultural differences between continents. Do you think that your perspective might differ somewhat from the mindsets of those who penned the Scriptures?

It's no big deal for an American man to cross his legs while sitting. To expose the sole of one's shoe to an Arab, however, is a terrible insult. Former U.S. Congressman Bill Richardson once insulted Saddam Hussein during a diplomatic mission by inadvertently crossing his legs. The Iraqi dictator walked out of the room in a huff, and the effort to secure the release of two employees of an American defense contractor was almost ruined.[32] If something as simple as showing the sole of one's shoe can create conflict between two contemporary cultures, how much more would the difference of 1500 years tend to confuse things?

The New Testament has come to us in the Koine Greek language, although parts may have initially been recorded in Aramaic. Regardless of the language, it is essential to understand that most of what was written in the Old and New Testaments flows out of *Jewish* culture. Ideas that now have almost universal acceptance may have been radical—if not scandalous—during ancient times. For example, government leaders in the ancient world were not thought of as servants—they were *lords* who

---

32. http://www.washingtonpost.com/wp-srv/inatl/longterm/iraq/keyplayers/rich121396.htm

often oppressed and exploited the powerless. Most Western cultures at least recognize the ideal of politicians as public servants even though it may not always play out that way in actual practice.

Faith and love, in the Hebrew context of New Testament times, were not tied to an individualistic pursuit of happiness, nor were they merely mental concepts. Both faith and love were virtues with *substance*—as evidenced by the way they were lived out in the covenant community of God's people. The early advance of Christianity almost always took place through the establishment and growth of local churches. As the core element of the Christian faith, the essence of the gospel, then, must be defined within the context of the New Testament church. To do otherwise is to risk dashing our "spiritual ships" upon the rocks.

Further, as much as we hate to admit it, we don't always know what faith and love look like in a given situation. Nor do we always understand how the simplicity of the gospel should be applied to the circumstances of a particular relationship. The gospel is not complicated, but people can be. If I see a friend exercising destructive behavior, for example, would it be more loving to speak out or to silently pray? Sometimes we don't know what love should look like. How we need to draw upon the wisdom of God and the guidance of the Holy Spirit!

DEFINING FAITH

Faith, in many Western cultures, is considered to be something of a *mental exercise*. It's considered normal for a person to express a "belief" in the existence of God without that belief having any real influence on the person's life. Not so in a Hebrew context! According to the *Theological Wordbook of the Old Testament*:

> This very important concept in biblical doctrine gives clear evidence of the biblical meaning of "faith" in contradistinction to the many popular concepts of the term. At the heart of the meaning of the root is the idea of *certainty*.[33] (emphasis added).

To the ancient Jewish mind, faith wasn't simply an idea—it involved a certainty about the existence of God and His faithful character as known

---

33. Jack B. Scott, "116 אָמַן," ed. R. Laird Harris, Gleason L. Archer Jr., and Bruce K. Waltke, *Theological Wordbook of the Old Testament* (Chicago: Moody Press, 1999), 51.

through a covenant relationship. Such a certainty was expected to impact the way that a person lived. Faith was a firmness or steadfastness of belief that resulted in devotion to the commandments of God. Thus, the words "faith" and "faithfulness" can often be used interchangeably to translate the concept of *faith* from a Hebrew context.[34] This sense of certainty is borne out in the New Testament letter to the Hebrews:

> *Now faith is the assurance of things hoped for, the conviction of things not seen. Hebrews 11:1*

From a biblical perspective, faith must have *God* as its object. Thus, we can define *faith* as "unwavering confidence in the unseen—but very real—Creator of the Universe." This type of "God-confidence" was expected to impact every dimension of a person's life.

I purchased a Pittsburgh Penguins T-shirt from a clearance rack after the 2012-2013 hockey season. The word "BELIEVE" is printed across the shirt in large letters. That was the year that everyone in Pittsburgh "believed" that the Penguins would win the coveted Stanley Cup trophy. The team was so good that it finished the strike-shortened season with a record of 36-12. Sadly, they scored only two goals while losing four straight games to Boston in the Eastern Conference finals. Good-bye, Lord Stanley! Penguins fans had passion, desire, devotion, and hopeful anticipation, but they didn't have faith in the biblical sense of the word because God was not the focus of their trust. Finite, imperfect humans are bound to let us down from time to time.

The sense of certainty inherent to biblical faith flows from the unchangeable reality of God's personhood. Our faith is not a matter of presumption or wishful thinking, but of complete confidence based on the knowledge of God's character. Being anything but blind, faith grows strong through the investigation of God's word *and* its application in daily life. In the end, faith is much more about the unveiling of God's faithfulness than it is about making ourselves believe.

Pseudo-faith has always marred the religious landscape (John 6:60-66). For some, faith is nothing more than a mental assertion. Others attempt to use belief in God as a means to pacify their conscience or

---

34. Ibid., 51-52.

to fulfill selfish lusts. I have a friend who used to share his Christian faith with others when he got drunk at parties. It took an offhanded comment from a non-Christian for him to realize the error of his ways. In ecumenical circles, we may speak of "many faiths" while referring to various religions. The use of *faith* in this context makes sense, but it is not biblical by any stretch of the imagination.

THE IMPORTANCE OF FAITH

Faith is one of the primary battlegrounds on which the war between the kingdoms of darkness and light is fought. Just as the serpent sought to instill doubt in the hearts of Adam and Eve, so too, he seeks to undermine the vitality of faith in the people of God. Dark forces pressure us to doubt the validity of the Bible, to doubt the work of the Holy Spirit, and to doubt the integrity—and even the existence—of God. In exchange, we are encouraged to put the full weight of our confidence in human reason and to find our security in human institutions—not a very good course of action if you ask me!

It should come as no surprise that faith is emphasized throughout the Bible. Abraham was justified by faith (Genesis 15:6). The entire Jewish system of Sabbath days—and even years—of rest was founded upon faith. The prophets continually challenged God's people to trust Him. When Jesus identified a person, it was often by his or her measure of faith (Matthew 8:10 and 26). "Oh you of tall stature," is not a statement you'll ever find attributed to Jesus. The Son of God cared nothing about height, weight, material wealth, or social status; it was the evidence of faith in human lives that made His heart leap with excitement.

In some Christian circles, the importance of faith has been minimalized in backlash against erroneous teachings that proclaim faith as a means to fulfill selfish desires. While concern over such false doctrine is justified, trying to lessen the biblical emphasis on faith is a major error in its own right. Without faith it is *impossible* to please God (Hebrews 11:6). We dare never forget the critical role that faith plays in every aspect of our relationship with God.

Two particular Old Testament passages played a major role in helping to cement the importance of faith into the fabric of New

Testament thought. Both passages are repeated more than once in the context of New Covenant doctrine.

> *Then he [Abram] believed in the LORD; and He reckoned it to him as righteousness. Genesis 15:6 (see Romans 4:3; Galatians 3:6; and James 2:23)*

> *"Behold, as for the proud one,*
> *His soul is not right within him;*
> *but the righteous will live by his faith." Habakkuk 2:4 (see Romans 1:17; Galatians 3:11; and Hebrews 10:38)*

In each passage, we can see the necessary relationship between faith and righteousness, between trusting God and becoming acceptable to Heaven. This is where the context of a covenant relationship looms large. Remember, a covenant is a sacred and binding relationship that is defined by the faithfulness of each party. How would a man do right by his covenant brother? By being faithful to the terms of their covenant.

In a similar sense, faith in a New Covenant context translates into doing right by God and others. Generally, we bare the deepest parts of our souls only to those whom we trust. Without faith and its necessary fruit of faithfulness, relational intimacy becomes impossible. Put your trust in someone who is untrustworthy and you are sure to be burned.

This brings us to another friction point of Christian living—a truly wise person will not superimpose human unfaithfulness on his or her image of God. I really enjoyed Greek mythology when I was in junior high; the Greek gods seemed to be the fulfillment of every young boy's imagination. In many ways, they can be equated to today's superheroes—characters with superhuman powers but intense personal struggles. The gods of Greek mythology often mimicked the attitudes and character (or lack thereof) seen in humans. Why? The ancient Greeks reversed the divine order by creating gods in their *own image.* Until we learn to see God for His real person, faith—and therefore intimacy with our heavenly Father—will elude us.

SALVATION BY FAITH

We are *saved* by faith, enabling us to be at peace with God (Romans 5:1). The Creator of our Universe could have made salvation by any means imaginable, but He chose faith. He didn't pick social standing, having looks to die for, possessing a boatload of money, living a moral life, or even making huge sacrifices to honor His name. No, God chose *faith*. What does the King of kings and Lord of lords ask of us? That we trust Him with every aspect of our lives (Matthew 6:19-34 and John 14:1).

Saving faith not only initiates us into the New Covenant, it also provides the opportunity to receive a free "heart transplant" so that we are capable of abiding in God's love. Those who live under law put their confidence in the flesh; those who live by faith put their confidence in Christ. Living under law fuels the flames of selfish pride. Living by faith in Christ disarms pride and the power of sin.

When I justify myself by measuring up to a set of given standards, my heart can't help but boast. But when I find acceptance with God through the unmerited favor of His grace, my heart can find no reason to boast. The self-sufficient heart knows only self-glorification. The Christ-sufficient heart knows only humility. Authentic biblical faith rooted in the person of Jesus Christ is the only truly effective antidote for human pride. Only through faith in Christ can the painful reality of the human condition be remedied.

There was a time when I struggled to understand the relationship between faith and repentance. Some Christians contend that repentance is "a work" and, therefore, is unnecessary for salvation. How excited I was to finally realize that the gospel is not a message of repentance *and* faith but of repentance *to* faith. God is calling us to turn away from idolatry and self-reliance to dependence on Him.

The ability to believe is a gift from God, but we must still choose to *exercise* faith in all aspects of life—provision, guidance, identity, etc. Living by this type of functional faith allows us to continually draw upon God's transformational grace, and the results can be staggering! First and foremost, our hearts are transformed to produce the fruit of the Holy Spirit. Faith also enables us to draw upon God's empowering grace, which gives us the supernatural ability to advance His kingdom on earth. Ordinary people can dramatically impact our world in ways far beyond natural human capacity (Romans 12:6-8; 1 Corinthians 12:1-11, 15:10; and 2 Corinthians 8:1-21).

If you live by pride for long, your life will sink into lifelessness. Selfishness will leave you feeling empty, the need to be in control will steal your joy, and the compulsion to measure up will consume your vitality. But learn to live by faith and you will soon discover just how delightful God can be and how much He delights in His children. How important is faith? The list goes on and on.

YOUR NEW CAREER

Faith is not optional—Christ *commands* that we believe:

> *"Do not work for the food which perishes, but for the food which endures to eternal life, which the Son of Man will give to you, for on Him the Father, God, has set His seal." Therefore they said to Him, "What shall we do, so that we may work the works of God?" Jesus answered and said to them, "This is the work of God, that you believe in Him whom He has sent." John 6:27-29*

Do we grasp what Jesus was (is) communicating? Trusting God is to become our "career" of sorts. Humanity is constantly preoccupied with all things physical. Our thoughts are consumed by what we'll eat and drink, where we'll live, how we'll get places, and what we'll purchase next. A material world is where we live. Jesus, however, radically challenged the status quo. He called His followers to devote their core energies to believing in Him. That doesn't mean that we all run off and quit our jobs, but that we elevate trusting God to a level of priority that exceeds our emphasis on material provision. Why did Jesus call His followers to pursue "new careers"? Faith serves as the foundation for all that is to follow.

Jesus didn't give lists of rules to obey, He didn't tell His disciples to go serve in the temple nursery, and He didn't constantly prod them to donate money to the cause. Why not? As we come to understand *The Divine Progression of Grace*, we realize that faith in God is the gateway to all truly good behavior. What begins with faith ends with joyful giving and sacrificial love. If the people of God exercise genuine faith, everything else will follow in its appropriate season.

It is here that far too many Christian leaders make a critical error. Feeling the very real weight of pressing needs, they prompt, prod, and persuade people to serve in various ways. Too often, this is done while teaching an incomplete understanding of faith and grace. The unhappy result is that the hearts of the people are not transformed, and so they must be constantly pressured to take action.

Jesus took a very different approach. He challenged His followers to believe and then encouraged them to seek God and wait for the empowerment of the Holy Spirit. When grace has its way in a heart, the primary focus of the leader will shift from prompting action to imparting wisdom. This is not to say that pastors should wait for their people to fully mature in faith before encouraging church involvement; we all need to be nudged forward as part of the growth process. Pushing service apart from an accurate understanding of grace, however, is like piling heavy weights on a person's shoulders. Sooner or later, something is going to give. Equally problematic, we end up putting people in positions of responsibility they are not prepared to handle.

If my emphasis on the importance of faith is accurate, it stands to reason that a loving God would more than desire that we grow in faith; He would seek to train us in faith. If faith is central to our growth, and if God really wants the very best for our lives, wouldn't He go to great lengths to establish us as people of faith? Absolutely!

We all follow a path of trust which Abraham pioneered and many others have traversed. We are not lone individuals, but rather integral parts of the body of Christ formed by God over the ages. Therefore, our paradigm should go well beyond our current generation, reaching both backward and forward in time. In light of those who have given—and will give—so much, we dare not be content to give so little. How we need to grow in faith! The author of Hebrews provided us with some much-needed perspective when he penned the following:

> *Therefore, since we have so great a cloud of witnesses surrounding us, let us also lay aside every encumbrance and the sin which so easily entangles us, and let us run with endurance the race that is set before us, fixing our eyes on Jesus, the author and perfecter of faith, who for the joy set before Him endured the cross, despising the shame, and has sat down at the right hand of the throne of God. Hebrews 12:1-2*

GOD'S AGENDA OR OURS?

Believing God is one of the core requirements for abiding in Christ and bearing the sweet, abundant fruit of the Holy Spirit. However, the fact that we have faith in Christ for salvation does not guarantee that we trust God in every area of our lives. Accordingly, Christ's goal is to bring our faith to full maturity so that it will become both fully functional and fully fruitful. It is here that many of us get stuck. Living by faith appeals to comfort-seeking souls about as much as eating a liver and onions ice cream cone.

Years ago I heard a pastor wax nostalgic as he told of his early days in ministry. It was a season when he and his wife seemed to just barely survive financially. "Those were such exciting times," he reminisced. "We saw God provide for us so many times and in such dramatic fashion." The pastor grew quiet for a few seconds and, gathering his thoughts, went on to proclaim, "I never want to live that way again!"

I laugh every time I think about that story. Is this not the internal conflict that we all face? We want to know God and walk with Him, but we don't want to live by faith. Comfort and security are high on our agenda; faith not so much. This brings us back to Romans 1:16-17:

> *For I am not ashamed of the gospel, for it is the power of God for salvation to everyone who believes, to the Jew first and also to the Greek. For in it the righteousness of God is revealed from faith to faith; as it is written, "BUT THE RIGHTEOUS man SHALL LIVE BY FAITH."*

The Bible doesn't teach that Christians shall merely *possess* faith, but that they shall *live by* faith. Faith is a confident trust in God that impacts every dimension of our existence. To live by faith is to exercise faith, but faith will only be exercised if there is a need to trust God. If we have no needs, we have no reason to trust.

This may be why Christians who live in prosperous societies tend toward shallow faith. Those who are self-sufficient will sense little reason to develop a Christ-sufficiency. Make comfort and security top priorities if you like, but realize that you do so at the expense of knowing Christ better. In the end, isn't knowing Him what faith is all about?

I grew up knowing want. We lived in a government housing project and on government assistance. In addition, we often spent money unwisely. In many ways, our existence revolved around what we wanted, but didn't have. Even relatively simple issues became magnified. Finding a couple of dollars to pay for my bowling league, for example, would often involve a painful ordeal. Affording a decent pair of boots to go hunting? Forget it! The American Dream, then, became my life's goal. I would attend college, get out of the projects, establish myself in a well-paying career, and then live comfortably for the rest of my days. I needed only to add a lovely wife, 2.1 kids, a nice house in the suburbs, and a yearly beach vacation to make my agenda complete.

Should I be surprised that God would call me away from my comfortable career path to a ministry that requires me to live by faith for financial provision? I'm a slow learner so it has taken a long time for me to see my heavenly Father as my faithful provider and to get over my fear of want. My voluntary faith walk has, in a sense, "forced" me to seek to know Him better. The more I come to know Him, the less I fear lack and loss. More importantly, as I grow older, the more I understand it is in Him that my reason for existing and my purpose for serving both lie.

This would be a great opportunity for me to suggest that you send a sizeable check to our ministry so that you, too, can learn to live by faith, but I won't let you off so easy. The sovereign King of the Universe knows well the areas in which your faith needs to be perfected. He is the One to guide your footsteps and challenge your unbelief. If you want to grow in faith, sensitize yourself to the leading of the Holy Spirit. He will put His loving finger where it needs to be put, He will nudge you where you need to be nudged, and He will challenge you to step out of your comfort zone into new, adventurous territory. Genuine life is realized where faith flourishes.

Fear is in many ways the antithesis of faith. Fear is a fruit of spiritual death, and death, in its many dimensions, is about *loss*. Our hearts tremble with fear as we contemplate the loss of reputation, loss of friends, loss of material possessions, and loss of health, among other things. Thus, we are led to believe that life and loss are *always* functional opposites. Not so! In God's paradigm, to lose is to win; to die is to live.

Only by fully surrendering our agendas can we come to know His fullness. If our faith in God isn't worth dying for, it will be devoid of true life.

FROM FAITH TO FAITH

"The righteousness of God is revealed from faith to faith . . ." The measure of faith that a person begins with as a new Christian should be surpassed by the measure of faith that he or she ends with when it comes time to advance to eternal glory. We start at one place of faith and grow into another through the course of our time on this earthen globe.

With regard to the righteousness of God being revealed, I see a possible two-fold meaning. First, the righteousness of God is revealed in and through us. As our faith matures, the fruit of our lives increases. The invisible Christ is then made visible through us—His children. Second, we begin to see God's righteousness in ways that we never imagined. Through this journey of grand discovery, our loving God reveals the intricate facets of His amazing nature—things that the unbelieving can never see. In particular, we begin to understand that the Creator of the Universe will always do right by us. His character knows no injustice or unfaithfulness. He cannot lie, and He will always be true to His word. To see Him as He is will change the meaning of our existence!

Are you struggling with finances? The end goal is to see God as your provider. Are you wrestling with anxiety? Learn to see Him as your rock of stability. Are you overrun by discouragement? Fully realize Christ as your eternal hope. Do you see it? The perfection of our faith through various trials enables us to intimately know our Creator in ways that go far beyond the words on a page. Don't be duped into thinking that real faith will always result in happy times. No, it is through dark circumstances—through the fires of adversity—that genuine faith must be forged. Those pursuing the joy-filled goal of knowing God better cannot help but have their faith rigorously tested and proven.

For years I fought against God's attempts to perfect His faith in my life because I was too proud to admit my weaknesses—and because I failed to understand what He wanted to accomplish in and through me.

Everything—the quality of my life, my ability to overcome sin, the depth of my love, the fruit of my ministry efforts, etc.—began to gradually, but steadily change after I got on board with God's "faith building program." With the growth of my faith has come an increased realization that my Savior has so much more planned for me than I could have ever imagined. My flesh still longs for a comfortable existence, but that goal now appears both foolish and pitiful.

Growing in faith is, without question, an ongoing process for me. I think I was several hundred meters behind the starting line when the race of faith began; it took me a long time just to admit my unbelief, and then even longer, to catch up to the rest of the pack. Even though I may still struggle to trust in various situations, thankfully, I am now aligned with God's plan. At the very least, life is less confusing because I know what He seeks to accomplish in me during adverse circumstances.

Also, because I now understand that challenges to my faith are a means of coming to know my heavenly Father better, I have come to see that *questioning* and *doubting* can be two very different issues. It really bothers me when Christian leaders tell people not to ask questions about their faith—as though there were something inherently wrong with asking. I think that there is something wrong with *not* asking. A question in a human heart is a question in a human heart. No matter how hard we try, we can't simply wish away our questions. Discouraging an honest exploration of God's truth and personhood is rarely a good idea. When unanswered, questions about the character of God and the validity of the Bible will grow into tangling roots of doubt. I realize that human reason alone will not lead us to an accurate understanding of our Creator, but that doesn't mean that we shouldn't ask our questions.

It is here—in the pursuit of knowing God and understanding His ways—that the importance of seeking wisdom comes into play. When something bothers me about the Scriptures, I pray, asking Him to open my eyes to His reality. It's not necessarily an easy process, but it is a powerful one as I allow the Holy Spirit to become my primary teacher. I can't say that I've had all my questions answered, but most of the major issues have been settled in my heart. Faith and an understanding of God's ways often go hand-in-hand; faith leads to further understanding, and understanding leads to stronger faith. Even when I don't fully comprehend my circumstances, I can still trust that my heavenly Father will work things for my good. In the end, He always does—as long as I keep moving forward. The key is for me to grow from faith to faith so that I can give Him the freedom to write the end of my story.

God is the author and perfecter of our faith (Hebrews 12:2), but we still play an integral role in the faith building process. Apart from Him, any amount of effort is fruitless. Through His grace, however, our faith will grow stronger over time. This may sometimes seem like a slow and agonizing process, but the transformation will take place nonetheless.

BLAZING A TRAIL TO FRUITFUL LIVING

Merely *possessing* faith is insufficient to produce a fruitful life; we must learn to *live* by faith in our loving and faithful God as we navigate the circumstances of life. The following is a short list of things that have helped me cultivate faith through the years:

- Praying for God to reveal Himself to me.
- Studying and meditating on the character of God.[35]
- Confessing my unbelief to God; asking Him to cleanse that unbelief and perfect His faith in my heart.
- Surrendering all that I am and have to my heavenly Father.
- Memorizing Scriptures that are relevant to my needs and standing on them.
- Sharing my faith struggles with a friend(s) and asking for prayer.
- Reading biographies about heroes of the faith.[36]
- Reading testimonies of God's miraculous work.
- Studying the concept of covenant.

---

35. A.W. Tozer's small book, *Knowledge of the Holy*, has been particularly helpful so I try to read it every few years.
36. George Muller and Hudson Taylor are two of my favorites.

CHAPTER FOURTEEN
DEFINING LOVE

The one who does not love does not know God, for God is love.
1 John 4:8

I have found the paradox, that if you love until it hurts, there can be no more hurt, only more love.

—Mother Teresa

It was the moment that Maria had been waiting for all of her teenage life. "I love you more than you can imagine," whispered David gently in her ear. Just the thought of it sent her heart into orbit! After years of longing, her dream was finally being filled—a man whom Maria deeply loved, now loved her in return. What happened next, however, threatened to implode the moment as David reached his hand under her blouse. Instantly, Maria pulled back, conflicted. She really cared about David and wanted to be with him, but she didn't know about this next step. Years before, Maria had promised herself that she would not have sex until her wedding day.

Sensing Maria's hesitation, David drew back and gently asked a series of well-worn questions. "We love each other, don't we? We want to be together all of our lives, don't we? What difference does a piece of paper make? As long as we're married in the eyes of God, who cares what the state thinks?" In the end, David's argument echoed one that has been used untold times over the years. "We love each other. That's all that matters." Still feeling uncertain, Maria reluctantly acquiesced. Six months later, David was dating another girl.

THE ESSENCE OF LOVE

If we struggle to comprehend biblical faith, we wrestle even more to grasp a thorough understanding of biblical love. Listen to a few contemporary songs or watch a couple of romantic movies, and you'll soon see that love is seen mostly as a *highly desired feeling*. Sure, we want love to be faithful and long-term, but at its core, our idea of love centers on romantic notions. Christ's short description of love is very different from our often self-centered romantic images:

> *"Greater love has no one than this, that one lay down his life for his friends." John 15:13*

All too often, our idea of love centers on what others can do for us. That, my friends, is *selfishness*, not love. On the contrary, Jesus spoke of a *sacrificial* love. By its actions, this type of love makes a clear statement: "I value you more than I value myself." This was the love both taught and modeled by the Christ. Biblical love is not self-centered, nor is it passive. Love that costs a person nothing means nothing. The emotional passion that accompanies true love will produce a willingness to make personal sacrifices for the sake of the loved one. In the case of David and Maria, true love would have been willing to wait.

The Scriptures make it clear that love is at the top of God's priority list. As important as faith may be, it is not our ultimate goal. Faith forms the foundation of intimate relationships, but it is not a substitute for them. Our faith can and must bear the fruit of love. If our faith does not ultimately express itself through love, then it really isn't biblical faith.

> *If I speak with the tongues of men and of angels, but do not have love, I have become a noisy gong or a clanging cymbal. If I have the gift of prophecy, and know all mysteries and all knowledge; and if I have all faith, so as to remove mountains, but do not have love, I am nothing. And if I give all my possessions to feed the poor, and if I surrender my body to be burned, but do not have love, it profits me nothing. 1 Corinthians 13:1-3*

This passage reminds me of Matthew 7:15-21 in which Jesus talked about those who performed miraculous deeds without really knowing Him. Whether they come by positive thinking, a winning attitude, or genuine belief, the greatest feats in the world mean nothing in the eyes of Heaven if they are not motivated by love. It is here that the possibility for deception looms large because faith-minded people can sometimes accomplish great things without actually walking with God.

THE CONTEXT OF LOVE

Unlike biblical Greek which uses four different words—*eros, philos, storgy*, and *agapeo*—for love, the English language employs only one word to cover multiple meanings. The Greek noun used by Jesus in John 15:13 is *agape*, which can speak of "affectionate regard."[37] *Agape* is often interpreted to mean "unconditional love." It is the verb form of this word—*agapeo*—that we see in the now famous John 3:16:

> *"For God so loved the world, that He gave His only begotten Son, that whoever believes in Him shall not perish, but have eternal life."*

In a very real sense, this passage tells us that God had such an affectionate regard for the human race that He sent Jesus to die a horrible death as the sacrificial Lamb of God so that we might have the potential to be forgiven, cleansed, and redeemed from our sins. Our value in this sense has nothing to do with how we feel about ourselves or how others may feel about us. Such amazing love flows from who God is because God is love (1 John 4:8).

God's love for us does not change *no matter what we do*. The One who is characterized by perfect love cares every bit as much about those who, from a human perspective, are unlovable as those who are seen as desirable. Experiencing the depths of God's unconditional love stretches the limits of our human comprehension. It is one thing to be loved when you believe that you have something significant to offer; it is an entirely different matter to be fully loved when you feel that you are lower than low.

I can recall a time when the Holy Spirit prompted me to do something, but I failed to respond because of my own stubborn pride. What I deserved at that moment—and I knew it—was to be cracked over the head with a wooden board. Instead, what I experienced was

37. Spiros Zodhiates, *The Complete Word Study Dictionary: New Testament* (Chattanooga, TN: AMG Publishers, 2000).

God's presence warmly pouring down over my head and melting my hard heart. What I expected to hear was, "Repent, you self-absorbed fool!" Instead, the Holy Spirit spoke to my heart, "I just want you to know that even at your worst, I still love you." Even at our worst, God loves us the most.

As awesome as the idea of God's unconditional love may be, not everyone experiences its full benefits. Why? We tend to view love through self-centered, individualistic eyes. The love of which Jesus spoke was lived out in a Jewish culture by the *people of the covenant*. In other words, the ideal of love was viewed and expressed through a covenant context in which love was faithfully given and received. If we attempt to separate our understanding of biblical love from a covenant context, we make a mistake of massive proportions! Apart from covenant, we may catch glimpses of God's unconditional love, but we won't abide in it.

The apostle John is widely recognized as the "Apostle of Love." John had an especially close relationship with Jesus and his first epistle is all about Christian love in the context of the New Covenant:

> *Beloved, let us love one another, for love is from God; and everyone who loves is born of God and knows God. The one who does not love does not know God, for God is love. By this the love of God was manifested in us, that God has sent His only begotten Son into the world so that we might live through Him. In this is love, not that we loved God, but that He loved us and sent His Son to be the propitiation for our sins. Beloved, if God so loved us, we also ought to love one another. No one has seen God at any time; if we love one another, God abides in us, and His love is perfected in us. 1 John 4:7-12*

In verse eight, John communicates the life-giving message that "God is love." Notice, however, that this passage does not read "love is God." Does the difference really matter? Absolutely! If *God is love*, then love is defined by God; but if *love is God*, then God is defined by our human understanding of love.

We open ourselves to deadly deception when we begin to think that God is present and approving any time human love is present. If the expression of our love does not align with His divine design, we stray into humanism. Our hearts can be corrupted by selfish and prideful motives even when adorned with altruistic desires. Furthermore, the fruit of love that God wants us to manifest is grown and perfected in the context of covenant relationships. Love and faithfulness should go hand in hand.

The Hebrew word *chesed* (or *hesed*) was especially meaningful to ancient Jewish society. The limitations of the English language do not allow for a single word which embodies this rich concept. Consider the following ways in which several modern versions of the Bible translate *chesed*:

- *Mercy and steadfast love* (Amplified Bible)
- *Grace* (Complete Jewish Bible)
- *Steadfast love* (English Standard Version)
- *Faithful love* (Holman Christian Standard Bible)
- *Mercy* (King James Version)
- *Lovingkindness* (New American Standard Bible)
- *Covenant faithfulness* (New English Translation)
- *Love* (New International Version)
- *Unfailing Love* (New Living Translation)
- *Loyal love* (The Voice)
- *Kindness* (Young's Literal Translation)

If we could put all of these translations into a blender and mix their meanings together, we might hone in on the general idea that *chesed* speaks of "love freely given and faithfully exercised, while overflowing the boundaries of what might otherwise be expected." We refer to an intensity of love that is not limited to a covenant relationship, but is certainly a willing expression of one.

The point is—and it's an important one—that the covenants created by God (including the marriage covenant) aren't just about stone cold commitment; they are defined by an intensely faithful and devoted love that flows from a generous and willing heart.

Kind and generous love combined with unwavering devotion make a covenant to be a truly wonderful relationship. This is to be the nature of *the church*—the covenant body of Christ. We are the people of God bound together by love through the New Covenant in Christ.

God does not value any particular gender, race, nationality, or denomination above another. Our heavenly Father is filled with passion for all who join His royal family through faith in Jesus Christ. Through the context of the New Covenant, God calls us to faithfully respond to His sacrificial love with sacrificial love of our own. Our devotion to our Savior then flavors the manner in which we treat all others, but especially the members of Christ's body. Love, from a biblical perspective, was never intended to be a stand-alone virtue.

BAPTIZED INTO CHRIST

A *sacrament* can be defined as "a religious act that serves as a visible indicator or reminder of a significant spiritual truth." The two primary sacraments practiced by the Christian church are *water baptism* and *communion*. I see both as covenant acts. Ironically, even though these sacraments are widely practiced, their fuller meaning eludes those who fail to understand that the New Covenant is cast in the nature of the ancient covenants.

As Peter was preaching the gospel to the household of Cornelius (Acts 10:34-48), the Holy Spirit fell upon all who had gathered to hear the message. Amazingly (to Peter and his companions), Gentiles began speaking in tongues and exalting God just as Jews had done on the day of Pentecost. Peter then had what some call an "aha" moment. His supernatural vision wasn't simply about unclean animals—the blood of Jesus was able to render all people—regardless of descent—clean in the eyes of God. How did Peter respond? "He ordered them to be baptized in the name of Jesus Christ."

While not required for entry into Heaven—Peter's command to baptize the Gentile believers in water came *after* God had already baptized them with His Spirit—for the early church, water baptism was integral to the salvation process. Accordingly, baptism was not seen as an optional step to be taken according to one's own discretion. Water baptism had covenant connotations. Similar to the way a wedding ceremony marks the entry into a marriage covenant, so too, water baptism was a somewhat public (due to persecution, water baptisms may be done secretly) ceremony proclaiming a person's entry into the New Covenant in Christ.

In the time of Christ (and in some Middle Eastern countries today), marriage was done differently than it is in contemporary Western culture. When two people get engaged in the United States, for example, they are more or less deepening their commitment as a next step in their relationship. Engagement generally leads to marriage, but it can be broken off with no legal repercussions—even if the overall result is two unhappy people. In New Testament times, an engaged (betrothed) couple was seen as being legally married; however, they were not permitted to have sexual relations until their actual wedding day.[38] This is why Mary's pregnancy with the Messiah was scandalous; in the eyes of the culture, she should have been a *married virgin*.

In a similar sense, water baptism can be seen as a "betrothal" service for someone entering into the New Covenant with Christ. The Bible doesn't spell it out as such, but I see water baptism as a *covenant* ceremony. The individual is immersed under water, symbolizing both the cleansing of sins and death to the old, selfish life. Someone then lifts the person from the water to indicate a sharing in Christ's resurrection life. The symbolism is rich, but what takes place is more than symbolic. Through water baptism, a person's inward faith is outwardly manifested in the form of a covenant ceremony.

It's not uncommon for a newly-born Christian in the United States to wonder if he or she is truly saved. Interestingly, I've never met a newly married couple who doubted if they were really married. Why? They had a covenant ceremony to establish their union. I can't help but wonder how many young believers would get a much better start with their Christian walks if their salvation were linked to water baptism in light of a covenant context. Wouldn't they have a much better sense of who they are and what their lives are to be about?

---

38. Alfred Edersheim, *The Life and Times of Jesus the Messiah: New Updated Edition* (Peabody, MA: Hendrickson Publishers, 1993), 245.

We should also note that water baptism wasn't an individual act; the Gentile believers that Peter initiated into the Christian faith didn't baptize themselves. Love as expressed in and through the New Covenant was never individualistic. Water baptism marked entry into a mystical union with the entire covenant body of Christ—the church universal. Their love was then lived out in the context of a local body of believers.

THE GREATEST COMMANDMENTS

Not only must we establish the context of love in the New Testament, we also should recognize the *depth* of New Covenant love. The two greatest commandments identified in the Bible—both of which transcend all of the Old Testament covenants between God and man—are centered on love:

> But when the Pharisees heard that Jesus had silenced the Sadducees, they gathered themselves together. One of them, a lawyer, asked Him a question, testing Him, "Teacher, which is the great commandment in the Law?" And He said to him, "'YOU SHALL LOVE THE LORD YOUR GOD WITH ALL YOUR HEART, AND WITH ALL YOUR SOUL, AND WITH ALL YOUR MIND.' This is the great and foremost commandment. The second is like it, 'YOU SHALL LOVE YOUR NEIGHBOR AS YOURSELF.' On these two commandments depend the whole Law and the Prophets." Matthew 22:34-40

Take a Bible and pinch the entire Old Testament—from Genesis to Malachi—between your thumb and your index finger. Everything—including the Ten Commandments—contained within those pages rests upon two primary commandments: to love God with your entire being and to love others as a result of your love for Him (Romans 13:8-10 and Galatians 5:13-14).

LOVING GOD

What does it mean to love God with all of your heart, soul, and mind? If love means laying down your life for someone, this can only mean that you lay *everything* down for God. A one-dimensional perspective of grace may allow us to live selfishly as Christians, but a fuller understanding will never allow for such a twisted perspective. I don't see a way around this. Any "version" of Christianity that proclaims grace and freedom apart from total devotion to God is nothing more than a cheap and ineffective substitute.

We may have warm feelings toward God, but if our Christianity is passive, and if our relationship with God is primarily about what He can do for us, is our "love" actually love? Where would we be if God loved us with the same measure of devotion that we show toward Him? How thankful I am that I will never hear God say, "Bob, I'm sorry I couldn't meet with you this week. The angels had their annual fly-off on Alpha Centauri, and I couldn't stand to miss it."

I fully understand that our love is often shallow and imperfect, but when we are betrothed to Christ through water baptism, we enter into a sacred and binding covenant with our Creator. He becomes our *first love* above all other loves (Luke 14:25-33). Above our careers. Above our possessions. Above our hobbies. Above our earthly loved ones. Above even our own bodies. There can be no such thing as being *partly* married to God; the idea of a half-hearted covenant makes for a contradiction in terms.

> *The very spring of our actions is the love of Christ. We look at it like this: if one died for all men then, in a sense, they all died, and his purpose in dying for them is that their lives should now be no longer lived for themselves but for him who died and rose again for them.*
> *2 Corinthians 5:14-15 (Phillips)*

The New Covenant will not work as intended without deep, devoted love. God is not a giant Santa Claus in the sky who winks at human selfishness. Our heavenly Father loves His covenant children with absolute devotion. Is it unreasonable for Him to ask the same in return? Authentic faith will always lead to faithful love. Those who attempt to manipulate faith toward selfish gain will find that, in the end, they have lost much and gained little.

THE LAW OF LOVE

Grace was never intended to promote lawless living and shallow love. The ethical emphasis of the Old Covenant is carried into the New not as a means of righteousness, but as the necessary expression of love.

Life is no longer about right and wrong but about loving versus not loving. Grace does not remove all standards, but provides us with a new standard of unselfish love that aligns with the dynamics of God's eternal kingdom. And we must never forget that the progressive work of grace produces the fruit of that love in our hearts.

Grace doesn't give us a license to do whatever we want; it empowers us to live according to God's design. Through grace, we are freed from being controlled by internal passions and external rules. Through grace, *love* becomes the law that governs our lives. This is the *royal law* (James 2:8), or the *law of liberty* (James 1:25 and 2:12) that God intends to govern all that we do. Authentic love is the most powerful motivating factor on this earth. It is easier to fight against a well-trained mercenary than to confront a man fighting for his homeland and the family he loves. Love will take us so much farther than pride or greed ever can.

Do we want to see God's kingdom advance on this earth? The royal law—the law of liberty—that governs the kingdom must also rule in our hearts. *The Divine Progression of Grace* frees us from a legalistic existence, imparts to us a new heart, produces within us the fruit of love, and empowers us to advance God's kingdom on this earth. Only as we come together in love is the life of God released and the human condition eradicated.

BLAZING A TRAIL TO FRUITFUL LIVING

We tread on deadly ground when we attempt to redefine love according to human reason. If we are to move forward in our spiritual growth, we must allow God's love to define us and the nature of our relationship with Him.

CHAPTER FIFTEEN
LOVING OUR BROTHERS AND SISTERS IN CHRIST

"And as you wish that others would do to you, do so to them."
Luke 6:31 (ESV)

Truth and love are two of the most powerful things in the world; and when they both go together they cannot easily be withstood.
—Ralph Cudworth

I spent a lot of time doing lab experiments when I majored in chemistry. A four-credit science class usually meant four hours in the lab—in addition to three hours in the classroom—each week. When conducting an experiment, we commonly used an *indicator* that would turn a distinct color to show that a reaction had reached a particular point. When the solution turned blue, for example, we immediately knew that we had achieved the desired threshold. Faith finds its fulfillment as grace generates the fruit of authentic love in our hearts. We see then that love—especially love for our fellow Christians—serves as the primary indicator to confirm the presence of genuine faith:

> *"A new commandment I give to you, that you love one another, even as I have loved you, that you also love one another. By this all men will know that you are My disciples, **if** you have love for one another." John 13:34-35 (emphasis added)*

According to no less of an authority than Jesus Himself, our love for one another becomes the defining marker to show whether or not we are truly walking with God. If love isn't present between Christians, people—especially those in the world—have every right to question the depth of our devotion to Christ. Ouch!

The truth of John 13:35 was never more real to me than when Debi and I participated in a host program for internationals. When a student was new to the university, we would always give our five-minute (that's about all it took) tour of the Indiana, Pennsylvania community. As we drove down Church Street with its nine church buildings, a student unfamiliar with Christianity would inevitably ask, "Why are there so many different Christian churches?" Answering that sincere question was always awkward. On one hand, it is understandable that we would have many different "flavors" of churches due to personal preferences (as it is with ice cream). Even so, far too many churches and denominations have been born out of strife rather than mere preference.

The division that separates professing Christians isn't simply unfortunate—it is tragic. Not only do we betray the shallowness of our devotion to Christ, we also undermine the strength of our mission and alienate those who don't know our awesome Lord and Savior. A divided church is a defeated church; it cannot possibly fulfill Christ's call to the Great Commission.

RIGHTEOUS AND UNRIGHTEOUS JUDGMENTS

We all encounter the tension that can exist between covenant love and God's eternal truth. Unfortunately, our Lord doesn't magically engrave a cross on every Christian's forehead so we know who is a genuine believer and who isn't. We also face the very real—and dangerous—problem of false doctrine. There are times when we need to speak out publicly against false teaching; we dare not yield to deception in the name of love. Wield the sword wildly, however, and innocent people will be unjustly harmed. More than once, I have seen people with "corrective" ministries get it wrong by unrighteously attacking sincere and devoted servants of Christ.

None of us knows the depths of another person's heart, and so we are not in a place to determine exactly who is and who isn't a genuine Christian. However, we can—and should—make reasonable judgments about the doctrines, fruits, and the actions of some professing Christians—especially those who exert significant measures of influence. It all comes down to making *righteous*—as opposed to *unrighteous*—judgments.

A pouncer is characterized by a *judgmental spirit*. He or she lies in wait, constantly watching for an opportunity to malign those who don't meet a particular standard. A harsh, negative attitude permeates the whole process. Jesus adamantly opposed this type of unrighteous judgment:

> *"Do not judge so that you will not be judged. For in the way you judge, you will be judged; and by your standard of measure, it will be measured to you. Why do you look at the speck that is in your brother's eye, but do not notice the log that is in your own eye? Or how can you say to your brother, 'Let me take the speck out of your eye,' and behold, the log is in your own eye? You hypocrite, first take the log out of your own eye, and then you will see clearly to take the speck out of your brother's eye." Matthew 7:1-5*

We dare not delude ourselves. Looking with contempt on others while allowing pride to dominate and control our own lives is not something that God views favorably. This, however, doesn't mean that all judgments are bad. Christ's words against judging must be taken in context with other statements that He made about the subject:

> *"I can do nothing on My own initiative. As I hear, I judge; and My judgment is just, because I do not seek My own will, but the will of Him who sent Me." John 5:30*

> *"Do not judge according to appearance, but judge with righteous judgment." John 7:24*

The problem is that so many things taint our perspectives! That's why sales people are quick to buy lunch for prospective clients—and why lobbyists take politicians on trips. Envy can also skew our objectivity. If I get the opportunity to meet a highly successful author while my writing efforts have been a dismal failure, I may find myself saying something like, "Well, he really isn't all he's cracked up to be. I can see serious flaws in his writing style."

Ulterior motives may corrupt our judgments, but Christ's motivation always flows from a heart of *pure* love. Not one of His judgments was ever tainted by pride, envy, bitterness, greed, or anything of the sort. His goal was to always do the Father's will, which is to seek the well-being of those He loves. Because Jesus had no self-centered motives attached to His judgments, He could clearly see each situation for what it was.

Righteous judgments are *objective*. They refuse to bow to the emotions that come from personal gain, offense, or loss. They are also thoughtful and prayerful. The old adage that "appearances are deceiving" certainly contains an element of truth. Things aren't always what they seem to be; we tread on dangerous ground when we profess to know another person's motives.

Our ministry center sits adjacent to a secular university campus and so neighborhood drinking parties are commonplace. The house next to us is owned by a woman, Michelle, who lives about three hours away. When her sons attended school and lived in the house, they had parties, but usually within reason. The past year, however, was a different story—her renters ran wild! I thought about calling Michelle with my concerns, but I had never met her in the seven years that we shared neighboring properties. In my mind, she was a slumlord who cared only about milking the property for as much money as she could.

It turns out that Michelle was too trusting of the typical college student. Not knowing the guys personally, she assumed that they would respect the property. She was wrong—but so was I. My unrighteous judgment of Michelle was based on outward appearances. Had I made the effort to talk with her, I might have saved us both a lot of grief. When we finally met, I quickly realized that Michelle did care about the house and the neighborhood. I apologized for misjudging her, she apologized for allowing the mess, and we began working together to improve the situation.

LOVING CORRECTION

Making a righteous judgment can be the most loving thing to do if we are to correct the wayward and protect the vulnerable. For example, love may call us to gently confront a teenager who is seducing other youth in the church. In fact, it would be *unloving* to ignore such an issue. An offense, when appropriately given, may spare more long-term grief than we can imagine.

Brethren, even if anyone is caught in any trespass, you who are spiritual, restore such a one in a spirit of gentleness; each one looking to yourself, so that you too will not be tempted. Galatians 6:1

Our efforts to correct other Christians should always be redemptive and bathed in prayer. A truly mature child of God seeks to correct with a humble heart, fully understanding that we are all susceptible to the wiles of sin. In a Christian setting, behavioral change is best encouraged by appealing to a person's love for God. Obviously, there is no guarantee that the individual being corrected will receive our input as we intend. If there is resistance to loving correction, we might be compelled to take further action. Regardless of the response, it falls upon us to treat *every* person with honor and respect. A heart filled with contempt is love-deficient.

Many church leaders are hesitant to receive correction, in part, because they are accustomed to a steady barrage of unloving criticism. "Your sermon was boring! I don't like the music we sing! The color of the carpet is hideous!" Such treatment places an unreasonable standard of perfection upon a leader, which then forces the person into isolation. If we attempt to correct apart from a love-steeped environment, we will tear down the very lives that God seeks to build.

We so need the wisdom of Solomon as we relate to one another! God calls us to judge actions and fruit; we are not called to judge intentions. It is at times necessary to speak the truth in love, but to condemn or belittle another Christian—especially publicly— violates the heart of New Covenant love. The problem with maligning those who fail to meet our standards is that we may attack someone whom Heaven favors—something that, if we really understood the covenant nature of Christianity, would strike fear into our hearts.

WHEN WE DO IT TO OUR BROTHERS . . .

I don't completely understand how it works, but I do know that *we* bring condemnation on our own heads when we unrighteously judge a fellow Christian. This is not a claim I make lightly, nor do I lack a biblical foundation in doing so. By establishing the connection between several passages from the Bible—the very book we often use to justify our condemnation of others—we can develop a more accurate perspective of how seriously God takes this issue. We'll begin with God's covenant call to Abram (Abraham):

> *The Lord said to Abram:*
> *"Go out from your land,*
> *your relatives,*
> *and your father's house*
> *to the land that I will show you.*
> *I will make you into a great nation,*
> *I will bless you,*
> *I will make your name great,*
> *and you will be a blessing.*
> *I will bless those who bless you,*
> *I will **curse** those who **treat you with contempt**,*
> *and all the peoples on earth*
> *will be blessed through you."*
> *Genesis 12:1-3 (HCSB; emphasis added)*

Several versions of the Bible use the word *curse* twice in verse three ("I will curse those who curse you"), but the original Hebrew sheds a different light on the passage. God said that He would *bind with a curse* those who treat Abram *with contempt*. Great for Abram! Very bad for those who might treat him poorly!

Why would God curse those who treat Abram with contempt? God and Abram were entering into a sacred covenant through which they would become "blood brothers." Thus, Abram's well-being rocketed to the top of God's priority list. To malign one was to malign the other.

Many of us are familiar with the scenario in which Jesus portrays the contrast between the sheep and the goats (Matthew 25:31-46). The sheep look after the needs of the oppressed while the goats ignore them. From this passage, we can clearly see that Jesus takes the manner in which we treat His brothers personally:

> *The King will answer and say to them, "Truly I say to you, to the extent that you did it to one of these brothers of Mine, even the least of them, **you did it to Me.**" Matthew 25:40 (emphasis added)*

Such is the nature of a covenant relationship. If we do something for or against one of God's much-loved children, it's as though our actions are pointed directly at Christ. In the eyes of God, a covenant relationship isn't simply some nice sounding mumbo jumbo—it is a sacred brotherhood. That God takes the treatment of His children personally was a message also communicated to Saul (Paul) during his conversion experience:

> *But Saul, still breathing threats and murder against the disciples of the Lord, went to the high priest and asked him for letters to the synagogues at Damascus, so that if he found any belonging to the Way, men or women, he might bring them bound to Jerusalem. Now as he went on his way, he approached Damascus, and suddenly a light from heaven shone around him. And falling to the ground he heard a voice saying to him, "Saul, Saul, **why are you persecuting me?**" And he said, "Who are you, Lord?" And he said, **"I am Jesus, whom you are persecuting."** Acts 9:1-5 (ESV; emphasis added)*

Jesus didn't accuse Saul of persecuting innocent souls or even God's beloved servants. The King of Heaven took Saul's vicious attacks as *personal* assaults. Saul was—at least in his own mind—serving God. He was preserving the sacred covenants. He was standing against the erosion of truth. Saul may have seen himself as a valiant hero of truth. Jesus felt differently. Whose opinion carried the greater weight?

If you are a true believer in Christ, you can rest assured that God has your back. Perhaps that's why Jesus and Stephen pleaded for God to forgive their persecutors—they understood well the painful judgments that those men were bringing upon their own heads.

COMMUNION MATTERS

By now you should be grasping the seriousness of making unrighteous judgments against other Christians, but there is one more passage that we dare not ignore:

> *For I received from the Lord that which I also delivered to you, that the Lord Jesus in the night in which He was betrayed took bread; and when He had given thanks, He broke it and said, "This is My body, which is for you; do this in remembrance of Me." In the same way He took the cup also after supper, saying, "This cup is*

the new covenant in My blood; do this, as often as you drink it, in remembrance of Me." For as often as you eat this bread and drink the cup, you proclaim the Lord's death until He comes.

*Therefore whoever eats the bread or drinks the cup of the Lord in an unworthy manner, shall be guilty of the body and the blood of the Lord. But a man must examine himself, and in so doing he is to eat of the bread and drink of the cup. **For he who eats and drinks, eats and drinks judgment to himself if he does not judge the body rightly.** For this reason many among you are weak and sick, and a number sleep. But if we judged ourselves rightly, we would not be judged. But when we are judged, we are disciplined by the Lord so that we will not be condemned along with the world. 1 Corinthians 11:23-32 (emphasis added)*

I will be the first to admit that this passage stretches my comprehension of the gospel. At the same time, I cannot escape the connection with the other passages I've highlighted—especially Genesis 12:3.

The sacrament of communion was instituted by Jesus during the Last Supper as He established the New Covenant. A covenant ceremony is often celebrated with a meal and so early Christians often held *agapai* (love) feasts–meals similar to the Last Supper—to celebrate communion in conjunction with their worship services.[39] By sharing a meal—which included wine and bread—together, they were celebrating their *mutual communion* with God through the New Covenant in Christ.

Today, communion—symbolic of a covenant meal—is celebrated regularly by Christians to remind us of our joint participation in this sacred and binding relationship. Sadly, too few seem to understand the true depth of this covenant relationship. On a rare occasion, I will hear a pastor talk about the dangers of receiving communion in an unworthy manner, but it is even less common to hear this passage addressed within Paul's intended context of Christian relationships.

According to Paul's theology, God will use our self-induced judgment not to condemn us, but to discipline us toward change so

---

39. Spiros Zodhiates, *The Complete Word Study Dictionary: New Testament* (Chattanooga, TN: AMG Publishers, 2000).

that we might not be condemned. I'd prefer not to argue with Paul's theology. (Please note that Paul did not claim that taking communion in an unworthy manner is the cause of *all* sickness and death among Christians, but he did see it as a contributing factor.)

Although we are free from judgment when we live by faith in Christ, we put ourselves back under some degree of judgment when we choose to live by law rather than by grace. This is further accentuated when we direct unrighteous, law-based judgments toward our Christian brothers and sisters. Those who practice unrighteous judgment bring judgment upon themselves. Those who extend grace to others receive grace in return. How we treat other Christians really does matter. It is a fearful thing to scorn those whom Jesus sees as covenant brothers and sisters!

It is one thing to struggle with judgmental attitudes (as we all do); it is an entirely different matter to freely condemn someone who is the apple of our heavenly Father's eye. We all wrestle against judgmental attitudes, but God help the person who, with little or no remorse, belittles his or her fellow Christians.

BLAZING A TRAIL TO FRUITFUL LIVING

Are you tempted to unrighteously judge a fellow Christian? Sacrifice your feelings of contempt on the altar of love by praying a blessing over the person instead.

CHAPTER SIXTEEN
THE PERFECT BOND OF UNITY

Beyond all these things put on love, which is the perfect bond of unity.

Colossians 3:14

If I am in Christ and you are in Christ, and if He is in us, then we experience a profound unity in Christ.

—R.C. Sproul

The sense of betrayal mystified me. Being a hunter, I had just purchased a shotgun from an older member of the church we had just joined. The purchase was necessary because I couldn't seem to hit anything with the gun that I already owned. A new shotgun was undoubtedly the answer. Frank had been a gunsmith in his younger days, so I felt confident that he would steer me in the right direction. Instead, he sold me a gun with a flaw that a gunsmith could not have missed—a cracked stock. When I brought the problem to Frank's attention, he reluctantly agreed to replace the stock. It took several weeks and a little prodding until he finally returned the "repaired" gun.

There I stood, staring at the *replacement* stock with its own hairline crack. It's difficult to explain the sense of betrayal I felt at that moment. Frank was a faithful church attender who had been telling me stories about God's dynamic work in his life. Now, he was cheating me! Some things in this world simply should not be. Being scammed by a brother in Christ is one of them. I did my best to give Frank the benefit of the doubt, but it soon became all too obvious that several aspects of the man's life conflicted with his profession of faith.

My hunting and fishing budget was rather small, so it took a while until I could afford a decent replacement gun. Still, I determined not to do to someone else what Frank had done to me. When I eventually sold that shotgun—I couldn't hit anything with it either—I did so at a significant loss. Working through the pain of my experience with Frank took me a good bit longer.

Christian unity and spiritual maturity go hand in hand. Frank, the former gunsmith, was an immature Christian even though he had been in the church for more than forty years. The way he treated me was divisive, but I had a choice between forgiving and behaving immaturely in response. A loving confrontation with Frank would have been appropriate, but as a young, insecure Christian in a new church, I lacked the boldness. I never trusted Frank after that, but forgiveness and trust are two very different issues. I chose to forgive Frank and cried out to God for the grace to love him. Eventually my feelings followed. When Frank ended his last days on earth in a pitiful manner, it was a sense of sadness that filled my heart and not disdain.

I wish I could say that was the one and only time I found myself being unjustly treated by church people, but I would be lying. In the midst of some rich and highly-valued relationships, I've also experienced a lot of unnecessary—in my opinion—pain. While I never believed any of the harm to be malicious, it was all very hurtful nonetheless. Let's be honest; both in practice and in character, our working out of the Christian faith is often far from the biblical ideal.

Due partly—but not entirely—to church dysfunction, "lone ranger" Christianity is now trending in many places. I understand people's frustration. Debi and I have been a part of the same local body for over thirty years. More than once, I've wanted to walk away from it all. In the long run, however, I don't see how we can effectively abide in Christ's love if we are not living out our Christianity in some type of community with other believers. Human nature is messy, and we can't relate to people without sometimes getting messed on; some dark and disturbing experiences are unavoidable. It all becomes very discouraging, though, when what should be the exception becomes the general rule.

Love calls us to treat others with grace when they treat us with contempt. Love seeks to build others up even when we feel them tearing us down. Love forgives when self wants to go on the offensive. All too often, we leave a church for the very reason that *we should stay*—because of a personal offense. Yes, you read me correctly; relational struggles in the church provide opportunities for us to be conformed into the image of Christ, to grow toward spiritual maturity. What potential for the glory of God to be revealed in the midst of His people!

Do you want to see God's kingdom advance on earth? Extend love and grace toward those who have hurt you. Imperfect as we may be, we are still of one faith. We are to be, in the truest sense of family, brothers and sisters in Christ. Does this mean that a person should never leave a church? Not at all. Leaving, however, should be done for valid reasons and as graciously as possible.

THE UNITY OF THE CHURCH

The lack of a covenant worldview leads not only to a weak understanding of our oneness with God, but also the oneness of Christ's body—a central New Testament theme. Furthermore, our goal is not to build unity between Christians, but to preserve and build upon the unity that we already have in Christ.

Oneness is the essence of a covenant relationship. The Father, Son, and Holy Spirit are mystically One. Thus, various elements of relational oneness are indicative of being created (or re-created) in His image. Through Jesus' life, death, and resurrection, all who embrace salvation through faith enter into His oneness. When a person is born from above, the Holy Spirit enters into that individual's heart and mysteriously joins with his or her spirit, bringing it to life. The result is a "new creature" never before known to the Universe (2 Corinthians 5:17).

Please don't misconstrue my thoughts—I am not suggesting that a Christian becomes a god, but that we enter into a spiritual unity with God through the New Covenant in Christ. To think that a treasonous enemy of God can become one with his or her Creator! We refer to an intimate relationship unlike any other known to exist. This speaks not of our greatness, but of the magnificence of grace.

Too often, our church focus on unity is pragmatic. Division creates problems, so we seek peace in our local fellowships in order to make our lives less difficult. (I sometimes wonder how often church leaders emphasize the importance of unity to their congregations, only to treat members of neighboring churches with contempt.) Christian unity transcends our own needs and desires; we seek to live out biblical oneness not merely for our sakes, but for His. The apostle Paul continually emphasized the importance of church unity because his heartbeat was in sync with God's. Consider Paul's following words, most likely penned in a Roman prison cell:

> *Therefore I, the prisoner of the Lord, implore you to walk in a manner worthy of the calling with which you have been called, with all humility and gentleness, with patience, showing tolerance for one another in love, being diligent to preserve the unity of the Spirit in the bond of peace. There is one body and one Spirit, just as also you were called in one hope of your calling; one Lord, one faith, one baptism, one God and Father of all who is over all and through all and in all. Ephesians 4:1-6*

Paul's emphasis on "the unity of the Spirit" is characteristic of the entire New Testament. Jesus' followers spent enough time with their Lord to share His heart for His people. In Christ's high priestly prayer—the last recorded discourse between Jesus and the Father before the cross—Jesus expressed His burden for the unity of the church no less than *four* times (John 17:11, 21, 22, and 23). Part of that prayer reads as follows:

> *"I do not ask on behalf of these alone, but for those also who believe in Me through their word; **that they may all be one**; even as You, Father, are in Me and I in You, that they also may be in Us, so that the world may believe that You sent Me. The glory which You have given Me I have given to them, **that they may be one**, just as We are one; I in them and You in Me, **that they may be perfected in unity**, so that the world may know that You sent Me, and loved them, even as You have loved Me." John 17:20-23 (emphasis added)*

Jesus was nearing a torturous death on the cross and about to take upon Himself all of the sins of the human race. What was one of His most pressing concerns? *The covenant unity of His people.* If we don't highly value Christian unity, we are missing something of God's heart. How can we say that God really matters to us if we don't value what really matters to Him? The church is *one* body through the New Covenant in Jesus Christ, and the person who loves God will seek to preserve the unity that He has, at great cost, established.

UNITY IS NOT UNIFORMITY

One of the problems we have with preserving the unity of the church is that we often confuse *unity* with *uniformity*. Thus, we think that we can only respect and relate to those whose practices and beliefs are identical to ours. If we had a mantra, it would be, "Uniformity is the perfect bond of unity." How easily we ostracize those who don't fit our perspectives of religious doctrine and practice!

To a degree, I can understand how doctrinal differences create division. Truth matters. Too often, though, we confuse cultural practices with God's commands. There was a time when Christian missionaries compelled male converts to wear coats and ties—even in tropical climates. They treated their cultural norms as though they were Scriptural commands. A nineteenth century missionary named Hudson Taylor finally exercised the courage to break from established patterns by adopting native dress so that he could more effectively reach the Chinese people.

That we worship God is a command; which—if any—musical instruments we use are a matter of culture. That we instill God's word in our hearts is a command; which version of the Bible we use is cultural. That we make disciples for Christ is a command; how we go about fostering their growth can be cultural. I can't imagine a time when Christians should sacrifice their unity for the sake of cultural conformity.

I am always concerned when I encounter a church group with little or no diversity, one in which everyone emulates the leader(s) in speech, style, and dress. Unity must never be equated with uniformity. Christians can have very diverse practices—and even beliefs to a degree. The body of Christ consists of many different members with varying appearances, personalities, preferences, abilities, and languages. Most certainly, the day will come when people from every nation, race, and language worship together as one in Heaven. God desires to see Heaven's reality come to earth; He longs for a unified church in our era.

True unity must be *Christ-centered*. We don't sacrifice the integrity of the gospel in the name of unity. We don't overlook sin and divisiveness in the name of unity. We don't deny truth in the name of unity. And we don't relegate the Christian faith to a vague and spineless ecumenical existence in the name of unity. *Unity is established through saving faith in Jesus Christ;* this is non-negotiable.

Only those who enter into the New Covenant of grace become one body in Christ. Thus, we do not seek to preserve Christian unity at the expense of our core doctrines. The key lies in recognizing which truths are essential for salvation and which ones are to be cloaked with love. Augustine of Hippo is often credited as the source of a classic quote which stands as significant now as when it was penned hundreds of years ago: "In essentials, unity; in non-essentials, liberty; in all things, charity."[40]

Covenant unity is preserved by robust faith expressed through vibrant love. Our relational oneness is the consummate expression of abiding in God's love as we stay connected to God and to each other. Something powerful happens when people come together as one (Genesis 11:1-9). Something even more powerful takes place when this happens through a Christ-centered oneness (Matthew 18:20).

God has given me a gift to teach, and so I highly value doctrinal accuracy. Accurately expounding upon the Scriptures is never a task I take lightly. Through the years, I've worked hard to understand the dynamics of how to live in a way that honors God. At the same time, I have come to understand that my "perfect" doctrine is terribly imperfect if it leads to unrighteous judgments against others—especially Christians—who don't share my exact views. Through the intensity of my convictions, I must always be careful to guard my heart from unrighteous motives.

---

40. Some scholars believe that the quote originated with Marco Antonio de Dominis in the early 1600s. Regardless of the source, the quote stands as a classic.

ANTI-EVANGELISM?

During my college ministry days, we often set up outreach tables in the student union in an effort to engage students in "God talk." We tried to make the experience fun and low pressure. Those outreaches not only produced fruit; they sometimes led to memorable conversations.

One such discussion was with a young man who seemed reluctant to talk. With a little nudging, I learned that he didn't like to "talk religion" because his brother—a devoted Christian—would get angry every time they disagreed. I laughed and assured him that I wouldn't lose my cool. (I had no choice after making a statement like that!) We had an enjoyable and thoughtful discussion—after which he went on his way. That young man didn't fall to his knees and blurt out the sinner's prayer, but I'm confident that I helped to answer his brother's prayers by planting a few seeds for thought.

If we are secure in our faith, we need not be alarmed when others disagree with us. If we trust in the saving ability of God, we need not pressure people to adopt our points of view. If we love others, we can treat them with respect even when we don't see eye to eye. By setting the stage for healthy dialogue, we help to soften hearts to receive God's truth. Otherwise, we draw our battle lines and go to theological war, not caring if we break God's heart in the process. Is it personal pride that guides our outreach efforts, or is it Spirit-formed love?

I see tremendous value in the ministry of Christian apologetics— the task of providing a logical defense for the Christian faith. At the same time, we would do well to recognize that knowledge alone can easily puff up a person's heart with pride (1 Corinthians 8:1). Those who attempt to correct wayward souls apart from a sincere expression of Christ's love will do little in the long run to advance the cause of the gospel. What does it matter if we "win" arguments, but alienate hearts from Christ?

In spite of the occasional rift, the New Testament church was essentially of one heart (Acts 1:14, 2:46, 5:12, and 15:25). More than once, the apostles taught about, or made an appeal for, unity (Romans 12:4-12; 2 Corinthians 13:11-14; Galatians 3:26-28; Ephesians 4:3-6;

Philippians 2:2-5; and 1 Peter 3:8-12). The apostle Paul even went so far as to admonish the young overseer Titus to, "Reject a factious man after a first and second warning, knowing that such a man is perverted and sinning, being self-condemned" (Titus 3:10-11).

Christian unity—or lack thereof—influences people both inside and outside of the faith. In failing to recognize and value our oneness, we alienate many who don't yet know Christ and, in a very real sense, become guilty of *anti-evangelism*. The early church transformed both the Roman Empire and much of the Western world. How? In part, they did what Jesus commanded by actively loving one another and living out a unified faith. It should come as no surprise that the Holy Spirit moved so powerfully, as recorded in the book of Acts.

LIFE IMPARTED

The power of a unified church goes beyond the synergistic multiplication of resources. Our unity comes from being interconnected with God and with one another. When covenant unity is realized, the very *life* of God is released in our midst! What draws the unsaved to Christ? A divine impartation of life among God's people. Psalm 133 is another of my favorite passages, but not because it is short:

> *Behold, how good and how pleasant it is*
> *For brothers to dwell together in unity!*
> *It is like the precious oil upon the head,*
> *Coming down upon the beard,*
> *Even Aaron's beard,*
> *Coming down upon the edge of his robes.*
> *It is like the dew of Hermon*
> *Coming down upon the mountains of Zion;*
> *For there the LORD commanded the blessing—life forever.*

The psalmist was comparing covenant unity with the blessing of God that flowed down upon both the Jewish high priest and the Promised Land. God's heart is wonderfully blessed as His children came together as one.

In ancient Israel, the practice of *anointing* a person with oil was quite common. A king would be anointed to signify empowerment for his new position. Priests were anointed for the purpose of holy consecration—being set apart from the commonality of the world—in order to effectively serve God. In the ancient world, anointing oil was sometimes used as a part of a covenant ceremony. The Hebrew word *Messiah* literally means "the anointed one." The Greek translates it as "Christos."[41] Jesus was *the Christ*—the anointed one of God—who was set apart for the kingly purposes of God and empowered by the Holy Spirit to accomplish His mission. Our unity helps to further the Christ's purposes on this earth.

My experiences as a campus minister have helped cement the importance of unity into my heart. There were times when we'd have all of our "kids" together for some type of fellowship event. Often, I would just sit back and enjoy the moment. Watching them interact and enjoy each other warmed my heart like few other things could. Virtually every parent with more than one child understands this feeling. Still, more than feelings are involved—a supernatural impartation of life takes place when unique individuals come together in covenant unity.

We can pour tons of effort—and money—into our evangelistic outreaches and marketing campaigns, but it is the life of God through the anointing of the Holy Spirit that draws people into a genuine faith. When the life of God is absent, what choice do we have but to place the full weight of our outreach efforts on human means of influence that appeal primarily to the flesh?

A wise old pastor once said, "If it takes a hot dog to get a person to church, it will take a hot dog to keep him there." In the end, we make matters worse by drawing together people who are motivated by selfish desires rather than a sincere love for God. This is not to suggest that we avoid using the vast array of resources and natural talents at our disposal. The key lies in putting these resources in their proper place— as subservient to the life of God being poured out in our unified midst.

God's presence—as realized and expressed through His people— has always been the most powerful evangelistic force known to

---

41. Robert L. Thomas, *New American Standard Hebrew-Aramaic and Greek Dictionaries: Updated Edition* (Anaheim: Foundation Publications, Inc., 1998).

humanity. We don't *do witnessing*—we *are witnesses* by our love for one another and through the empowerment of His holy anointing.

UNITY MATTERS

God fully expects us to live out our unity in Christ, and it genuinely scares me that so few professing Christians seem to take the issue seriously. Not only do we grieve the heart of God, not only do we turn unbelievers away from Christ, not only do we damage the lives of others, but we also bring condemnation upon our own heads when we unjustly judge another brother or sister in Christ.

When we fail to recognize the unity of the body of Christ, the unsaved are not the only ones to pay a steep price. Christians can be mutually enriched by one another in untold ways. When one part of the body prospers, we all prosper. When one part of the body suffers, we all suffer. Both the saved and the unsaved suffer when Christians are divided, not to mention the pain that is brought upon our heavenly Father's heart. We find a powerful passage in Mark that makes little sense to me except in light of our New Covenant unity:

> Peter began to say to Him, "Behold, we have left everything and followed You." Jesus said, "Truly I say to you, there is no one who has left house or brothers or sisters or mother or father or children or farms, for My sake and for the gospel's sake, but that he will receive a hundred times as much now in the present age, houses and brothers and sisters and mothers and children and farms, along with persecutions; and in the age to come, eternal life." Mark 10:28-30

Some preachers distort this passage to say that God will give us a hundred dollars for every dollar that we give away. Point missed! How does a person receive a hundred brothers and sisters? He or she becomes a member of God's family.

What an encouraging message for those who have embraced Christ at a high personal cost! Has your family disowned you? You have a new, eternal family in Christ. Have you sacrificed material possessions? Your heavenly Father will meet your needs through His covenant children. This passage doesn't proclaim a message of prosperity but of covenant oneness. Christ's words reflect Christ's heart. To what degree do we allow God's law of love to govern our thoughts and our actions?

KILLING DEATH

As we abide in Christ, we abide in grace. As we abide in grace, we grow in spiritual maturity. As we grow in maturity, the fruit of love begins to manifest in our lives. As love manifests, we clothe ourselves with the perfect bond of unity. A truly spiritual church is unified, and truly mature Christians focus on *building up* other Christians (Ephesians 4:11-16). This applies not only to our local congregations but also to the church at large.

How many of us are truly diligent to preserve the unity of the Spirit in the bond of peace? All Christian denominations don't need to morph into one organization—that would mean *uniformity*—but we can honor and support one another as equal members of the body of Christ. There is only *one* church with many diverse and beautiful expressions.

Can we see why grace and law are on opposite ends of the spectrum? Grace produces love and, therefore, unity. Living by law as a means of righteousness creates animosity and, therefore, division. Those who are pouncers live by law; their hearts are filled with judgment, which in turn breeds animosity between brothers. They may profess to value Christ's sacrificial work on the cross, but their attitudes, words, and actions betray the true state of their hearts.

While emphasizing the mystical unity between Jew and Gentile that flows from the cross of Christ, the apostle Paul's letter to the Ephesians provides invaluable insight into the relationship between law and disunity:

> *But now in Christ Jesus you who once were far off have been brought near by the blood of Christ. For he himself is our peace, who has made us both one and has broken down in his flesh the dividing wall of hostility by abolishing the law of commandments expressed in ordinances, that he might create in himself one new man in place of the two, so making peace, and might reconcile us both to God in one body through the cross, thereby killing the hostility. And he came and preached peace to you who were far off and peace to those*

who were near. For through him we both have access in one Spirit to the Father. So then you are no longer strangers and aliens, but you are fellow citizens with the saints and members of the household of God, built on the foundation of the apostles and prophets, Christ Jesus himself being the cornerstone, in whom the whole structure, being joined together, grows into a holy temple in the Lord. In him you also are being built together into a dwelling place for God by the Spirit. Ephesians 2:13-22

Amen! This passage speaks specifically to Jews and Gentiles—two people-groups that held extreme contempt for one another. Christians from any background, race, or era can apply two universal principles drawn from Paul's message:

1. **Living by law creates animosity between people as we seek to draw a sense of significance from our efforts to promote flesh-based standards.** In the process, we then devalue those who fail to measure up. If the acceptable standard is a light skin color, those who live by the law (of racism) will proclaim the superiority of a light skin color and begin to look with contempt on anyone whose skin is dark. Those with dark skin will recoil at such treatment and respond with contempt of their own. Do you see it? Animosity is born out of law-based living. When law reigns, contention thrives.

   At its roots, hostility is the result of a glory deficiency. Those lacking in glory seek to find glory by living up to law-based standards. This is the reality of human nature. We desperately need hearts transformed from a state of "nakedness" by being clothed in the glory of Christ-significance. Only then can we be free from the need to measure up.

2. **The cross of Christ kills the hostility that kills unity.** In other words, His death kills our death and division. Those who become new creatures in Christ are freed from moral standards as a means of obtaining kingdom righteousness and flesh-based standards as a means of obtaining social righteousness. Not only did Paul proclaim us to be new creatures in Christ, he also communicated

that those who are in Christ "recognize no one according to the flesh" (2 Corinthians 5:16).

We can try all kinds of methods to create unity and breed peace on earth, but apart from the cross of Jesus Christ, our efforts will ultimately fall short. Peace, then, must be enforced through *control* and *uniformity*. They go hand in hand. A legalistic environment must be uniform in order to be unified. Even then, unity will remain elusive. Laws must be passed and freedoms restricted if humans are to become "one big happy family." Peace is forced and freedom lost. Rather than welcoming those who differ with open arms, legalists will drive away those who fail to conform to their expectations.

There are few experiences as beautiful as a joint worship service with men, women, and children from various races, nationalities, and Christian expressions. God's glory is revealed not only as we lift our praise to the heavens, but also as we worship together with unified hearts. The cross is the only viable means to achieve lasting peace. Diversity thrives when God's people are joined together by love.

How do we determine a person's value? Those who live by law will value and devalue people based on various standards of perfection. Those who live by love will value people because God values people. It has nothing to do with outward appearance, performance, material wealth, intelligence, or value to society. It really doesn't even matter if a person is a Christian or not. God created us each in His image and Christ died for all humans. Our value flows out of His love for us, not what we have to offer in return. How much more should we respect and honor those with whom we have been united through the precious blood of our Savior!

In a world inundated with information, it may be difficult for some people to realize the powerful link between Christian unity and fruitful living that exists on many levels. Our ability to be fully fruitful is integrally tied to our love for God's covenant children. We are called to build each other up, to sharpen one another, and to serve together as living stones in the temple of God. The grace we receive from God, we learn to extend to one another. In this, God is glorified as we display the power of the gospel through human relationships.

When we love other believers, we abide in God's love. However, we cannot fully abide in love when we constantly keep our covenant brothers and sisters at arm's length. Even worse, when we are divided, we are rendered powerless to confront the relentless assault of Hell against all that is good (Matthew 12:25). How I dread the thought of undermining the cause of the gospel at the same time that I am trying to promote it. On so many different levels, Christian unity matters—and it matters a lot!

BLAZING A TRAIL TO FRUITFUL LIVING

Brothers and sisters in Christ, let us cloak ourselves in God's love as we travel the road of life together. Love is the perfect bond of unity!

CHAPTER SEVENTEEN
LIVING OUT THE ESSENCE

This is His commandment, that we believe in the name of His Son Jesus Christ, and love one another, just as He commanded us. The one who keeps His commandments abides in Him, and He in him. We know by this that He abides in us, by the Spirit whom He has given us.

1 John 3:23-24

Logically, faith comes first, and love next; but in life they will spring up together in the soul; the interval which separates them is impalpable, and in every act of trust, love is present; and fundamental to every emotion of love to Christ is trust in Christ.
—Alexander MacLaren

Fruitfulness is a process that begins with *believing*, is facilitated in *receiving*, progresses through *abiding*, and finds fulfillment by *expressing*. This process is synonymous with living out the essence of *faith expressing itself through love* in a covenant context. The essence lived out fulfills the requirements of the Mosaic Law. The essence lived out brings the kingdom of heaven to earth. The essence lived out enables imperfect humans to abide in His love. The essence lived out unifies God's people. The essence lived out draws the unsaved to Christ. And the essence lived out reveals the glory of God like nothing else.

WE LOVE BECAUSE HE FIRST LOVED US

As simple as the essence of Christianity may be, for a naturally doubting and selfish human it can seem unattainable. Faith cannot express itself through love apart from God's amazing grace. Grace draws us to God, grace enables us to believe, grace causes the fruit of love to grow in our hearts, grace empowers us to serve, and grace enables us to renew our fellowship with the Father whenever we fail. Grace, for us, begins with God's love. If not for His amazing love, there would be no such thing as *amazing grace.*

The fruit of love grows in our hearts when we abide in Him. If we don't have love growing in our hearts, it indicates that we're not really connecting with God. That probably means that we don't know Him as well as we think. The apostle John—the one that Jesus loved—even went so far as to say that if we don't love our brothers, we don't really love God (1 John 4:7-12). I've known many people who profess to love God but who are filled with bitterness, disdain, and envy. According to John, that is a serious problem.

Should we feel condemned if our measure of love falls short? Absolutely not! But it should give us added incentive to seek His face. Our sovereign King doesn't expect love-starved people to mystically become loving. We can't. Love necessitates both giving and receiving, but we can't give until we first receive. We can't extend love to others if we don't first have the fruit of love growing in our hearts. Our love grows as we, by faith, begin to fathom the depths of His love for us. The fruit of love in our hearts always springs from God's love for us. As John wrote, "We love, because He first loved us" (1 John 4:19).

I am not suggesting that we seek to be superstar Christians who strive for the highest pinnacle of love, but that we capture the essence of *faith expressing itself through love.* It is through faith that we learn to plumb the depths of God's amazing love for us, and it is through a fuller realization of His love that our hearts are ignited with a genuine love for others. I can't stress the importance of this order enough. We love because He *first* loved us.

Many years ago I worked with a young man who decided to go to school to become a pastor. When I asked why, he answered, "Because I want to help people." As wonderful as his response may seem, it misses the mark. I tried to explain that effective pastoral ministry must flow from a personal, loving relationship with God—not simply a desire to do good. He would have nothing of it. I knew of the school he planned to attend and figured that he'd either quit or become a devoted Christian. When I saw the young man the following summer, I asked him how pastors' school was going. "Oh, I quit that," he replied. "They were teaching the wrong things."

In a similar vein, the increased social consciousness of many Christians is awesome—but only so long as Christ remains the foundation and the focus of our efforts. Attempting to promote the love of God without submitting to the Lordship of Christ causes us to pursue humanistic agendas rather than an eternal one. Is it okay for a Christian ministry to focus primarily on humanitarian needs? Of course. God cares about our physical needs. But wouldn't it be best for their work to complement other ministries doing the work of evangelism and discipleship?

If we expend the bulk of our energies helping to momentarily ease suffering, but never teach people to abide in grace and live in victory over sin, we give them no eternal benefit. From a biblical perspective, love and faith are not two isolated concepts. The essence of *faith expressing itself through love* serves as the foundation of our service to God. We don't define love; love defines us.

If we attempt to love others without first loving God, we become highly susceptible to the "disease" of a hardened heart. I couldn't begin to list the number of times that I have sincerely tried to help others only to be mistreated by the very people I was trying to help. Several of the circumstances—especially those involving other Christians—were rather severe and took a long time for me to work through.

My love doesn't run deep enough for me to forgive and respect those who mistreat me. I was able to forgive the offenders and maintain a tender heart only by reminding myself of the extreme price that Jesus paid for them and for me. Jesus poured out His life for me; He is worthy of all I have—and more. Apart from His love, I have nothing to draw upon other than my own shallow compassion. Only as we love others *in response* to His love for us, will we find the grace we need to navigate even the most unjust circumstances.

EXPERIENCING LOVE

I don't think that it is possible to overemphasize the importance of experientially knowing God's love for us as the foundation of our love for others. People are finite and imperfect. Even the most loving individuals will inevitably disappoint us. How much more difficult life can be when a person bites the hand—especially if that hand is yours—from which he or she is being fed!

The essence of Christianity must be *faith expressing itself through love* and not *love expressing itself through love*. Without faith, we cannot come to experientially know the love of God. Sure, we can read words on a page and memorize meaningful passages—things that I highly encourage—but we don't fully know the love of God until His reality finds a home in our hearts as we journey through the ups and downs of life in this world.

Apart from faith we rarely even recognize when His love is at work. I have been through some very dark seasons in my life—times when God felt far away and when His promises seemed to ring hollow. Only as I stood in faith on the truth of Scripture, were my eyes finally opened to see that my heavenly Father was marvelously at work through every step of my journey.

Along the way, I've met others who have had similar experiences, but who have allowed unbelief to harden their hearts. They saw only their experiences of neglect and mistreatment—only God's apparent absence rather than His presence. I am not referring to unbelievers, or even casual Christians, but to devoted individuals who made significant sacrifices in their service to others. We cannot fully love if we do not know that we are fully loved, and we cannot know that we are fully loved if we do not, in the darkest moments, believe in the One who loves us fully.

The call to love may at times feel like a heavy burden, but it is really a journey of discovery. We come to know and understand love as we seek to know God, rest in His presence, gaze into His face, and lift up His name in worship. We don't *have* to love God; we *get* to love God. We don't *have* to love God's people; we *get* to build rich and meaningful relationships. Because of the cross, we aren't bound by the need to love perfectly; we are privileged to grow in love. Love is an opportunity more than it is an obligation. The fruit of love is the desired result of *The Divine Progression of Grace*.

RELATIONSHIP TRUMPS VISION

As I've been writing this book, a very ugly scandal with a Christian organization has been publicly unfolding. I wish I could say this type of thing happens only on rare occasions. I cannot say that. Sadly, the church has been plagued by ungodly behavior almost since the day of Pentecost. Is there something wrong with Christianity, or do we fail to fully recognize the insidious and pervasive nature of human pride? What bothers me most is not that these types of scandals happen, but that the pattern continues to be repeated, without interruption, with each passing generation.

It all begins with a gifted young leader (or group of leaders), who is radically redeemed by Christ, and who sets out to change the world. Although such a person generally acknowledges the importance of godly character, his or her primary emphasis is on a *vision* to accomplish something significant. It's the vision that stirs hearts, that motivates others to action, and that brings in the resources necessary to promote a worthy cause.

In the process of pursuing that vision, a subtle transition often begins to take place. The vision begins to matter more than its methods. Things are all done in the name of Christ, of course, but the character and integrity of Christ become slowly marginalized. Image becomes all important because the vision won't sell if the celebrity status of the leader(s) is somehow marred. Inner corruption and decay begin to fester even while enviable external success is being achieved.

Eventually—and often in a public manner—some sinful act rises to the surface. Lives are severely damaged, jaded people walk away from God, and very few individuals seem to actually learn from the tragedy. This cycle is then repeated by successive generations. Sadly, the cumulative effect is a growing sense of disillusionment with the Christian faith.

One year, I visited a college on Maryland's Eastern Shore during a spring snowstorm. The world was blanketed in white as a good friend and I drove along I-97, south of Baltimore. Having lived in western Pennsylvania all of my life, I've had my share of experience with driving on snowy roads, and so the high speed of the bumper-to-bumper traffic unnerved me. Every two to three miles, a vehicle would spin out of control and slide into the guardrail or hit a highway sign. All of the drivers would momentarily lower their speed, but quickly ramp it back up a short way down the road. The same scenario would then repeat itself all over again. I don't know if I was more surprised by the craziness of it all, or by the fact that we didn't see a major accident.

For our part, as important as the mission of the church may be, it can never supersede a day-in-and-day-out walk with God. A Christian leader must *violently* resist the temptation to sacrifice his or her relationship with God on the altar of ministry. (Of course, I use "violently" in a spiritual sense; pastors are not encouraged to shoot those congregants who try to intrude upon their devotional times.) Ultimately, it is Jesus who builds His church. Our part is simply to allow Him to work in and through us as we live out an abiding relationship. We can serve God—and even accomplish many good things—apart from an abiding relationship. This type of service, however, will be somehow lacking in grace, and so the eternal fruit of our efforts will fall far short of its potential.

Based on the ambiguity of the Greek word *tekton*, we don't know if Jesus was a carpenter, stone mason, or laborer of some other sort.[42] The Son of Man worked with His hands, though, and I am sure that He knew something about building. There are times when I raise my eyes to heaven and jokingly say, "Jesus, You aren't doing a very good job of building *Your* church!" (We've become pretty good friends so I don't think He takes offense.) The truth is that God isn't overly concerned about image. He will allow all kinds of undesirable behavior in His name and do virtually nothing to intervene—except perhaps bring sin to light. But rest assured, the day *will* come when the King of the

---

42. Johannes P. Louw and Eugene Albert Nida, *Greek-English Lexicon of the New Testament: Based on Semantic Domains* (New York: United Bible Societies, 1996), 519.

Universe calls everything into account. No matter how things appear with the church universal at any given time, God knows what He is doing, and everything will come out gloriously beautiful in the end.

THE TWO CROSSES

There is another way of viewing the essence of *faith expressing itself through love* that I find helpful in living out the essence of Christianity. Each of us must reckon with *two* crosses in this life. The first is the *cross of Christ* through which forgiveness is obtained and the power of sin is broken:

> *For it was the Father's good pleasure for all the fullness to dwell in Him, and through Him to reconcile all things to Himself, having made peace through the blood of His cross; through Him, I say, whether things on earth or things in heaven.*
>
> *And although you were formerly alienated and hostile in mind, engaged in evil deeds, yet He has now reconciled you in His fleshly body through death, in order to present you before Him holy and blameless and beyond reproach—if indeed you continue in the faith firmly established and steadfast, and not moved away from the hope of the gospel that you have heard, which was proclaimed in all creation under heaven, and of which I, Paul, was made a minister.*
> *Colossians 1:19-23*

Christ's redemptive work on the cross is the foundation upon which our relationship with God rests. Without the cross of Christ, Christianity is nothing more than recycled humanism with Christian trappings. It becomes a human religion with honoring love as its ideal. Through this approach, *we* define love, and a vague concept of Jesus remains subservient to our human agendas. But we don't define love; love defines us! The cross, therefore, must be central to our ministry efforts.

Through the cross, God's life-giving grace flows freely into our hearts. Apart from the cross, we are doomed to be separated from our Creator, facilitating condemnation and death. Without His sacrificial death, there is no promise of life. Apart from the cross, religious passions vainly seek to wish away the human condition. Only through the cross can the power of sin be disarmed and the dominion of death shattered.

The second cross that each of us must deal with is a *personal cross of self-denial* through which the lustful and prideful desires of sin are crucified. Jesus bore *His cross*. We must each bear *our own cross* of self-denial in response to what He has done for us. It is not sacrilegious to say that a person's response to Christ's work on the cross is to carry his or her own cross of self-denial. This was taught by Jesus Himself:

> *And He was saying to them all, "If anyone wishes to come after Me, he must deny himself, and take up his cross daily and follow Me. For whoever wishes to save his life will lose it, but whoever loses his life for My sake, he is the one who will save it." Luke 9:23-24*

All too often, people focus on the benefits of Christ's cross while refusing to carry their own. Bad idea! Self-control—i.e. denial of selfish lusts—is another of the nine fruits of the Spirit listed in Galatians 5:22-23. *Any message of grace that neglects the importance of self-denial conflicts with the concept of grace as found in the New Testament context.*

A lot of advertisers try to hook us with flesh-tempting messages that say, "You can have it all! You deserve it!" This is the mantra of a material world—not of the Christian gospel. None of us can "have it all." And, truthfully, anyone who has tasted the bitter fruit of flesh-based living wouldn't want to have it all.

Each person's cross is unique to that individual. One person may be called to shun the limelight; another to step out of her comfort zone. One may need to humble himself by confessing a sin; another by stopping her tongue from wagging. One may be nudged to step up and lead; another to fall in behind the leader. One may be prompted to save money; another to spend. Whatever the expression of self-denial may be, we can be sure that each cross is intended to crucify the prideful and lustful desires of that person's sinful nature.

I find it fascinating that the two crosses are synonymous with the essence of *faith expressing itself through love* as it plays out in our daily lives. The cross of Christ is the focus of our *faith*; a personal cross is the vehicle of our *love*. Through faith in the cross of Christ, the *power* of sin is disarmed. Through our own cross of self-denial, the *desires* of sin are crucified.

Both crosses are covenantal in nature. Paul wrote to the Galatians of being "co-crucified" with Christ:

> *I have been crucified with Christ; and it is no longer I who live, but Christ lives in me; and the life which I now live in the flesh I live by faith in the Son of God, who loved me and gave Himself up for me. I do not nullify the grace of God, for if righteousness comes through the Law, then Christ died needlessly. Galatians 2:20-21*

Through faith, *Christ's* death on the cross as a covenant breaker has become *our* death. The curse of death was vanquished and its power nullified by Christ's blood and subsequent resurrection. In response, *our* lives become *Christ's* lives—the expressions of our grateful love in the context of the New Covenant.

BOTH CROSSES ARE NECESSARY

Both the cross of Christ and one's own personal cross are necessary for those who wish to abide in grace, live in victory over the dominion of sin, and bear the sweet fruit of the Holy Spirit. Unfortunately, Christians frequently stick to a one-dimensional emphasis—they focus either entirely on the cross of Christ or upon their own crosses of self-denial. Serious problems result.

Those who attempt to appropriate the cross of Christ by faith, but fail to carry a personal cross of self-denial will use their freedom as an *excuse* to wade back into the cesspool of sin (Galatians 5:13). In other words, their lives are characterized by a *pseudo-faith without love*. Let's face it, we're all prone toward self-determinism, and we all go down forbidden roads from time to time. Hopefully, we then taste the fruits of our sins, humble our hearts, and draw upon heaven's throne of grace.

This is the point where a one-dimensional definition of grace can become deadly as it leads to a casual attitude toward sin. Breaking free from sin can sometimes involve a lengthy process, but for the person who continues to sin *willfully*, the road ahead spells only one thing: D-A-N-G-E-R!

> *For if we go on sinning willfully after receiving the knowledge of the truth, there no longer remains a sacrifice for sins, but a terrifying expectation of judgment and THE FURY OF A FIRE WHICH*

WILL CONSUME THE ADVERSARIES. Anyone who has set aside the Law of Moses dies without mercy on the testimony of two or three witnesses. How much severer punishment do you think he will deserve who has trampled under foot the Son of God, and has regarded as unclean the blood of the covenant by which he was sanctified, and has insulted the Spirit of grace? For we know Him who said, "VENGEANCE IS MINE, I WILL REPAY." And again, "THE LORD WILL JUDGE HIS PEOPLE." It is a terrifying thing to fall into the hands of the living God. Hebrews 10:26-31

This passage clashes with our one-dimensional perspective of grace. The fact that God the Father was pleased to "crush" Jesus on the cross (Isaiah 53:10) so that we might be forgiven and redeemed does not mean that grace can be treated cheaply.

Does the heavenly Father love us? Absolutely! That's why *He* sent Jesus to die for our sins (John 5:37, 20:21). But the God of the Universe is also in covenant with the Son of Man. The heavenly Father takes it personally when people treat His Son's sacrifice lightly. Christ's cross is intended to be a means of grace to meet our deepest points of need—not an excuse to justify selfish living. These are heavy words that make sense only as we understand the covenantal nature of Christianity and empowering nature of grace. Undoubtedly, grace is available when we sin, but grace is also available to keep us from sinning. Grace helps us crucify our fleshly lusts.

Does a cross of self-denial sound painful? It should! Crucifixion was a horrid human invention, but it was the means by which the Son of God chose to give His life for us. Through our worst, God gave His best. Furthermore, the imagery of the cross brings us back to God's warning in the garden of Eden: in dying you will die (Genesis 2:17). Even with all that God has done for us, we cannot fully escape death until the kingdom of God arrives in its fullness.

As important as it is for us to carry our own crosses of self-denial, those who neglect to exercise faith in the cross of Christ will soon begin to *boast* in their self-denial as it becomes a source of righteousness—in their own eyes. *Love working without faith* is a Christian impossibility. This is where legalistic religious practice rears its ugly head as we mistakenly believe that a sacrificial lifestyle renders us acceptable to God. Self-denial should be our loving response to what God has done for us—not our means of seeking heavenly favor.

Fasting—abstaining from food for spiritual purposes—provides an excellent example of the two crosses at work. When practiced in alignment with God's design, fasting can be profoundly powerful. But if the two crosses are not properly balanced in a person's life, one of two things will happen. Fasting will either be ignored as unnecessary and irrelevant, or it will feed—rather than defeat—the power of sin.

Those who focus only on the benefits of Christ's cross will conveniently avoid fasting because of the price that it exacts. It is uncomfortable to deny human appetites; therefore, they deem fasting to be unnecessary in the light of Christ's sacrifice. They won't fast to pray for wisdom, or to see God's saving grace poured out in the lives of others.

There are also those spiritually hungry people who fully embrace fasting, but who view themselves as being *spiritually elite* because of the sacrifices they make for God. These people start to feel as though God owes them something—like a favorable answer to a specific prayer— and may even go so far as using a fast in a vain attempt to control God. Apart from faith in Christ's work on the cross, self-denial for religious reasons will always morph into self-righteousness. Sacrificial practices such as fasting are effective only as we embrace the two crosses.

If we are to abide in grace, live in victory over sin, and produce the sweet fruit of the Spirit, we must live by faith in the cross of Christ and, motivated by love, carry our own individual crosses of self-denial. The power of sin must be disarmed, *and* the desires of sin crucified. Both elements are necessary if we are to break free from the shackles of sin and fully live out *The Divine Progression of Grace*.

BLAZING A TRAIL TO FRUITFUL LIVING

If you want to break free from sin and bear the sweet fruit of the Spirit, learn to appropriate the cross of Christ by faith *and* to carry your own individual cross of sacrificial love.

CHAPTER EIGHTEEN
COVENANT FAITHFULNESS

Brethren, I speak in terms of human relations: even though it is only a man's covenant, yet when it has been ratified, no one sets it aside or adds conditions to it.

Galatians 3:15

Men invent new ideals because they dare not attempt old ideals. They look forward with enthusiasm, because they are afraid to look back.

—G. K. Chesterton

Coming to understand that *faith expressing itself through love* is the essence of Christianity can be an enlightening experience, but it can also be confusing. If grace does not give us the freedom to do whatever we want, how do we know what behavior is acceptable to God and what isn't? Some issues are black and white; others, not so much.

We can start by carefully reading several New Testament passages—Mark 7:20-23; 1 Corinthians 6:9-10; Galatians 5:19-21; Ephesians 5:5-6; and James 3:13-18—which identify the fruits and deeds of the sinful nature. These stand in contrast to the fruits of the Holy Spirit. God delights in the fruits of the Spirit, but is repulsed by the roadkill fruit of flesh. It helps to view these things not as *rules*, but as *indicators*. If our lives are characterized by the fruits of the flesh listed in the New Testament, we need to revisit our understanding of the gospel.

Ideally, as we live out the essence of *faith expressing itself through love*, we will engage the Spirit of God and disarm the power of sin. The work of the Spirit is always love-oriented while the flesh compels us toward idolatry, pride, and lust. As grace does its work in our hearts, the supernatural fruit of the Spirit begins to dominate. This is part of the process we call "sanctification." To be sanctified is to be set apart from the commonality and corruption of this world for God's purposes. Over time, selfishness will become less of an issue, and love will become more natural. However, we never completely "arrive" on this side of eternity, and so we must embrace three important truths:

1. **Sanctification incorporates the past, present, and future.** We were set apart for God at the time of salvation, and the day will eventually come when we are eternally set apart in Heaven. In the meanwhile, God is working to conform us into the image of Jesus so that we become increasingly removed from the mindsets, behavior, and fruit of this world.

2. **We never move beyond carrying our own personal crosses of self-denial.** As long as we live in fleshly bodies, we will have fleshly desires that must be crucified.

3. **We never outgrow the cross of Jesus Christ.** No matter how mature, sanctified, or transformed we become, Christ's sacrificial work on the cross alone renders us acceptable to God.

These three truths are foundational to a healthy Christian existence. Any Christian who firmly establishes these things in his or her heart will be better positioned to abide in God's grace.

THE IMPORTANCE OF OBJECTIVE TRUTH

Following the leading of the Holy Spirit is a *subjective* endeavor. Because human desires and emotions come into play, it's all too easy for us to follow selfish desires in the name of God. How many times have I heard, "God told me to . . ." as a justification for behavior that clearly conforms to the desires of the flesh? Admittedly, I've even said it myself once or twice.

Not too long after coming to Christ, I began to serve on our campus ministry leadership team. One time, our leader, Budd, wanted everyone to attend a meeting in a neighboring community that would have consumed the entire evening. What I really wanted was to spend the evening with my girlfriend (who is now my wife), but I didn't think it was smart to say that I wanted to abandon our leadership team in order to hang out with my girlfriend. Instead, I said something like, "I believe God is calling me to skip the meeting and stay in town tonight."

Budd graciously, but firmly explained to me the difference between the subjective leading of the Holy Spirit and the objective truth of Scripture. Much to my disappointment, he then pointed out a verse about "not forsaking our own assembling together" (Hebrews 10:25). Budd wasn't trying to pull the verse out of context in an effort to control my behavior. Instead, he was trying to explain that the leading of the Spirit should not conflict with a Scriptural principle or command. Unless I was absolutely certain that God was telling me to stay home, attending the meeting would be the best course of action. I realized that Budd was right and that I was simply trying to use God as a justification for doing what *I* wanted to do.

God does not limit Himself to speak only through the Bible. Still, a working knowledge of the Bible, along with a thorough understanding of biblical truth, is necessary to protect us from sinning against Heaven in the name of personal freedom. The objective truth of Scripture and the subjective leading of the Holy Spirit should always agree. If they don't, we need to take a step back, examine our motives, and yield ourselves afresh to God as we search for greater clarity.

GRAY AREAS

There are, of course, "gray" areas in which it's difficult to determine what is and what isn't sin. For example, legalism demands that drinking alcohol be off limits for all people all of the time, while a one-dimensional view of grace embraces bar-hopping as a gift from God.

When we, however, begin to view our behavior in the light of being *right* or *wrong,* are we not drawing upon the tree of the knowledge of good and evil? In this, we can easily miss a central aspect of the New Covenant—we now have liberty in Christ, but our liberty should be defined by love rather than being used as an excuse for yielding to fleshly impulses. Thus, I find it helpful to think in terms of *love and selfishness* rather than *right and wrong.* In the case of alcohol, I see some situations in which taking a drink might be acceptable and others when it wouldn't.

Drinking alcohol is not the only gray issue, of course. We can't help but encounter other areas of life that require prayerful contemplation. Through his letter to the Romans, the apostle Paul instructed the church to treat gray areas as matters of *personal conscience* (Romans 14). If we're unclear about what the Scriptures say about a particular issue, or how the Holy Spirit wants to lead us, a conscience that has been cleansed and sanctified should be our guide.

It may be easier to make rules for gray issues, but such an approach will not produce long-term fruit. As much as some of us prefer lists of rules and formulas for behavior, the Christian life is one of relationship. Certain forms of behavior that are perfectly acceptable for one person might not be for another. Our call is to grow in our walk with God, learning to submit to the leading of the Holy Spirit as we make decisions. This is all vital to the maturing process.

If you're uncertain about His leading, search the Scriptures with an honest and surrendered heart, seek wise counsel, and prayerfully choose what seems to be the appropriate path of love. Or, as we used to say when we caught a deformed fish: "When in doubt, throw it out!" (I really hated that saying because I wanted to keep—and eat—them all.)

It is with all of these things in mind that we approach an issue of considerable controversy—human sexuality. Rather than do a detailed examination of the Scriptures in defense of my arguments, I will present this topic in light of a concept that I have already emphasized—covenant. While we are free from the requirements of the Mosaic Law as a means of righteousness, God calls us to be faithful to the terms of the covenants that He has established. Two covenants are of particular importance as they directly apply to our understanding of what is and isn't sin. Thus, we will look at both the *New Covenant* and the *marriage covenant* in light of New Testament teaching.

THE JERUSALEM COUNCIL

I have already referenced the fact that Paul wrote his letter to the Gentile church in Galatia to combat the false teachings of the law-breathing Judaizers. These religious zealots professed faith in Christ but compelled Gentile converts to rely on the Mosaic Law as a means of righteousness. Galatia was not the only place in which this type of trouble erupted. In fact, the controversy became so intense that Paul and Barnabas, among others, traveled to Jerusalem to consult with the church elders and apostles. The outcome of this excursion plays a vital role in helping us navigate the world of human sexuality.

> Some men came down from Judea and began teaching the brethren, "Unless you are circumcised according to the custom of Moses, you cannot be saved." And when Paul and Barnabas had great dissension and debate with them, the brethren determined that Paul and Barnabas and some others of them should go up to Jerusalem to the apostles and elders concerning this issue. Acts 15:1-2

Paul—who so strongly emphasized Christian unity—staunchly opposed the Judaizers. The issue at the center of the debate was whether or not Gentile men who became Christians needed to be circumcised in accordance with the Abrahamic and Mosaic covenants. The Judaizers insisted that they must; Paul and Barnabas adamantly opposed the legalists. In between, were the Gentile believers, who for obvious reasons, hoped that Paul and Barnabas would win the argument.

In Jerusalem, the conflicted parties met with the apostles and elders to hash out the issue. I find it difficult to overstate the importance of this meeting. Critics of the church often consider church councils to be rife with political motives and manipulation. Such an argument would find no merit in this situation. Significant input was given by those who had spent three years walking with Jesus and processing His teachings. In addition, the council had nothing to gain politically by going against the Judaizers. In fact, almost two thousand years of religious and political tradition were at stake.

THE ESSENTIALS

When all was said and done, Gentile believers were presented not with a list of rules to be obeyed, but with a short letter which helps to highlight the central mindset of the early church:

From the apostles and the elders, your brothers,
To the brothers among the Gentiles in Antioch, Syria, and Cilicia:

Greetings.

*Because we have heard that some without our authorization went out from us and troubled you with their words and unsettled your hearts, we have unanimously decided to select men and send them to you along with our dearly loved Barnabas and Paul, who have risked their lives for the name of our Lord Jesus Christ. Therefore we have sent Judas and Silas, who will personally report the same things by word of mouth. For it was the Holy Spirit's decision—and ours—to put no greater burden on you than **these necessary things**: that you abstain from food offered to idols, from blood, from eating anything that has been strangled, and from sexual immorality. You will do well if you keep yourselves from these things.*

Farewell. Acts 15:23-29 (HCSB; emphasis added)

Due to cultural differences—we don't strangle many animals, or drink much blood these days—it's difficult for us to grasp some of what was being addressed. Most scholars believe that the four concerns listed had to deal with only two primary issues—*idolatry* and *sexual immorality*. Murder was a possible third. That was it! Gentile Christians were officially free from the need to adhere to the requirements of the Mosaic Law in order to be acceptable to God.

"Why," we must ask, "did the council address only two or three primary requirements?" As we see in Paul's letters, so much more could have been communicated about desirable and undesirable behavior. Here, however, those who had spent three years learning from the Son of God were emphasizing only those requirements that they felt were *essential* to Christian living. But why *these* requirements? How do idolatry and sexual immorality conflict with the heart of a Christian lifestyle?

Once again, the picture becomes clearer as we peer through the lens of a covenant worldview. *Both idolatry and sexual immorality were considered by the apostles to be violations of sacred covenants.* Avoiding idolatry and staying sexually pure were not merely issues of law. Instead, they were expressions of faithful and loving devotion to covenants that the Almighty God had established—and which were applicable to Christian living. A covenant established by God is considered to be unchangeable unless God Himself says differently. If and when such a change is to be made, God will clearly communicate it to His people. Such was indeed the case with the New Covenant:

1. **The coming of the New Covenant was clearly foretold by the prophets (Jeremiah 31:31-34).** The Jewish nation eagerly anticipated the advent of this New Covenant. The problem was that it didn't look how they expected it to look.

2. **Jesus spoke of the New Covenant in His blood (Luke 22:20).** This New Covenant would be unique compared to all previous covenants.

3. **Jesus didn't abolish the old covenants—He fulfilled them (Matthew 5:17).** The establishment of the New Covenant was not a denial of the covenants already put in place by God. Instead, the previous covenants formed a progression that culminated in the New Covenant.

4. **The apostle Peter—a close follower of Christ—saw a supernatural vision proclaiming all things to be clean (Acts 10:9-16).** At first, the vision seemed to relate only to various foods considered by the Mosaic Law to be unclean, but something greater was in play.

5. **God filled Gentile believers with the Holy Spirit as Peter preached the gospel to them (Acts 10:34-48).** This was it! Through the salvation of Gentiles, the full nature of God's *chesed* was finally revealed. He desired that not only the Jews, but all peoples of all nations—regardless of gender, race, nationality, or genealogy—would be fully enfolded into His covenant family (1 Timothy 2:4 and 2 Peter 3:9).

Only God has the authority to change a covenant that He has established. Thus, the essentials of the faith, as defined by the apostles and elders, were considered to be *non-negotiable*. And, of the utmost importance, there is nothing in the Scriptures to indicate that these essentials have ever changed—or that they will ever change—in the eyes of God.

I will address both idolatry and sexual immorality in light of the covenants, but before doing so, I need to make something as clear as possible. This book is titled *The Divine Progression of Grace*. From the very beginning, my goal has been to help people walk with God, to abide in His grace, and to produce the full fruit of kingdom living. In no way do I seek to condemn or belittle those who are involved with, or have been involved with, the practices of idolatry and sexual immorality as defined by the Scriptures. I remember my past far too vividly to heap condemnation on the heads of others. Redemption, reconciliation, and unity are at the top of my priority list. I, however, do not believe in unity at all costs, and so I will not deny the essentials of the Christian faith in order to accommodate those who might disagree with me. Our Christian unity is preserved by fully embracing the essentials of our faith—not denying them.

Because covenant faithfulness matters so much to God, it better matter to us. Our cultural standards mean nothing to the sovereign Creator of the Universe. We can live how we want in this world, but the clock continues to tick. New obituaries are published daily and each of us will one day draw a final breath. God's opinion will matter a lot more *then*. College professors, script writers, and talk show hosts won't be guarding Heaven's magnificent gates, nor will the opinions of learned religious leaders carry any weight. In the end, all that will matter is how we responded to what *He* expected.

IDOLATRY

I've already touched on the problem of idolatry once, so I won't go into much more detail. The fact that there is but one God is integral to both Old and New Testament teaching (Deuteronomy 6:4; Ephesians 4:6; and 1 Timothy 2:5). Therefore, the worship of man-made idols is considered to be an act of covenantal *infidelity*. When speaking through the prophets, God frequently equated idolatry with *sexual immorality* and even prostitution (Ezekiel 16 and Hosea 1-3). The emotion of these passages echoes that of a spurned husband whose trust has been selfishly betrayed. Idolatry isn't simply a matter of worshiping a different god—it amounts to worshiping *false* gods. Worse still, according to Paul, idols are not merely the products of human imagination:

> *Therefore, my beloved, flee from idolatry . . . What do I mean then? That a thing sacrificed to idols is anything, or that an idol is anything? No, but I say that the things which the Gentiles sacrifice, they sacrifice to demons and not to God; and I do not want you to become sharers in demons. You cannot drink the cup of the Lord and the cup of demons; you cannot partake of the table of the Lord and the table of demons. 1 Corinthians 10:14, 19-21*

This passage speaks for itself. Idols are not gods at all; behind every idol is a demon spirit following the age-old pattern of self-exaltation. Not only is idolatry a betrayal of one's covenant relationship with Christ, it also fuels the fires of the cosmic coup. In spite of any good intentions on the part of those who worship the gods, idolatry is nothing less than a violent assault on the throne of Heaven. We can't serve Jesus in addition to other gods; we must serve Him above, and instead of, all other gods.

"CIVILIZED" IDOLS

Those in more "civilized" cultures often view idol worship as a primitive practice. Idolatry, however, is more prevalent than we may realize. Even though people in Western cultures generally don't erect statues to worship, they do practice idolatry in a more subtle sense. An *idol* can be defined as "anything other than the one true God that a person places on the throne of his or her heart."

As recorded in Matthew 6, Jesus condemned *materialism* as a form of deadly idolatry:

> *"No one can serve two masters, for either he will hate the one and love the other, or he will be devoted to the one and despise the other. You cannot serve God and money." Matthew 6:24 (ESV)*

The Old Covenant placed an emphasis on *physical prosperity* as a sign of God's blessing. The New Covenant, however, stands radically different. God's most precious blessings are those which are *spiritual* and, therefore, eternal. The teachings of Jesus and His followers strongly emphasize this truth. God intends money to be a tool—not a goal. We either use material wealth as a resource for God's glory, or materialism rules our lives. Our "civilized" love affair with material possessions conflicts with our ability to abide in God's life-giving grace. We can have much and yet gain little at the same time.

The importance of living out the essence of *faith expressing itself through love* can be applied to money and material goods as much as any other aspect of life. Whether we lack or possess wealth has nothing to do with God's love for us, or with our acceptance before His throne. There is no condemnation in Christ for those who have wealth and no condemnation in Christ for those who don't. The real issue is whether or not wealth has us. Those who have little can be just as preoccupied with money as those who have abundance.

Love must be our guide. People with the ability to gain wealth have an opportunity to use earthly resources to advance God's eternal purposes by caring for their families, caring for the powerless, promoting the cause of the gospel, and even creating businesses that help to improve the quality of life for others. Wealth has lasting value as long as its use is motivated by love.

Keep one thing in mind, though—*wealth is deceptive*. Wealth's seductive promises of significance, security, and selfish pleasure can choke out our ability to bear spiritual fruit (Matthew 13:22 and Luke 8:14). Ignore scriptural warnings about the dangers of wealth and you will certainly regret it (Matthew 6:19-34 and 1 Timothy 6:7-12).

Furthermore, materialism is not the only form of idolatry that should concern us. Something similar can be said about romantic relationships, sports, or anything else that consumes our passions and drives our behavior. There is but one God and His name is Jesus!

BLAZING A TRAIL TO FRUITFUL LIVING

Although we are no longer bound by the requirements of the Mosaic Law, the very nature of a covenant calls us to be faithful to its terms.

CHAPTER NINETEEN
SEX IS A BIG DEAL

God saw all that He had made, and behold, it was very good. And there was evening and there was morning, the sixth day.

Genesis 1:31

Sex education may be a good idea in the schools, but I don't believe the kids should be given homework.

—Bill Cosby

Sex is a big deal for any culture. Not only were we created as sexual beings, sex plays a vital role in our continued existence. So many cultures, though, seem to be overrun by sex; in whatever direction we turn, we are inundated with sexual imagery. All of this starts at far too young of an age for our children. A person can hardly read a magazine, surf the internet, or drive past a billboard without being bombarded by sexual images. Try watching a movie—or just about anything on TV—and it becomes readily apparent that our culture is all about sex. In part, this is because of self-determinism, but it also has a lot to do with greed. Sex sells, so it is an effective means for unscrupulous people to make a lot of money.

LAYING A BIBLICAL FOUNDATION

Because so many of our cultures are steeped in sex, *sexual immorality*—our second essential issue of covenant faithfulness—warrants significant attention. Many different factors, including—but not limited to—natural desires, environmental factors, a search for significance, and greed all impact a culture's perspectives on morality.

Those in the world will do what they want, but Christians have entered into a sacred covenant with their Creator. Any person who wishes to walk with God must allow *Him* to set the terms of their morality based on what He knows is best.

Because our perspectives are heavily influenced by a multitude of desires, opinions, and other forces, we dare not trust our own natural wisdom when determining what is and what isn't acceptable to God. This is where an objective perspective of the Bible is necessary.

As the inspired, infallible, and authoritative word of God, the Bible guides us to a general understanding of God's intentions for sexual intimacy. The problem—and it's not a small one—is that the Bible is entirely out of step with our cultural practices. Actually, in the grand scope of things, it's better to claim that our cultural practices are out of step with the eternal truths of the Bible!

To gain God's perspective, we must recognize a few key principles:

1. **Breathed by the very Spirit of God, the Scriptures are *authoritative* in all matters of godly living.** Human culture may encourage—or even demand—certain behaviors, but it is God before whom we will all stand on Judgment Day.

2. **The Bible must be studied and read with honesty and objectivity.** The goal of our efforts is not to fulfill our own desires, but to honor God in all things. On multiple occasions, I have studied the issue of sexuality as presented in the Scriptures, and each time I could not help but arrive at the same conclusion. I don't see how an honest study of the Bible can reveal otherwise.

   If people want to discard the holy Scriptures—and, therefore, Christianity—that is one thing, but it is an entirely different matter to try to use the Bible to support views contrary to what it actually teaches. Let's face it—our primary struggle isn't as much with what the Bible teaches about sexuality as it is with the authoritative nature of the Scriptures. *For those who choose to embrace the Christian faith, walk with God, and abide in His grace, the Scriptures are authoritative.*

3. **There are distinct differences between the Old and New Covenants.** We cannot unilaterally apply all Old Testament commands to the Christian life. Instead, we must come to understand God's expectations in light of the New Covenant's fulfillment of the previous covenants. If this is not done properly, we end up picking and choosing commandments according to our own human thinking.

THE MARRIAGE COVENANT

The New Covenant isn't the only covenant that still matters to the human race. In the garden of Eden, God established the marriage covenant between *one man and one woman*:

> For this reason a man shall leave his father and his mother, and be joined to his wife; and they shall become one flesh. Genesis 2:24

As previously explained, any time God changes a covenant—as from the Old Covenant to the New—He makes it clear to all parties involved (Acts 10). The covenant of marriage was established in the garden of Eden, further supported by the Law (Leviticus 20:10-21) and the Prophets (Malachi 2:13-16), and then reinforced by Christ Himself (Matthew 19:3-9). Clearly, the marriage covenant transcends the garden of Eden.

Due to the influence of what is now the Hebrew Bible, Jewish culture put a strong emphasis on family and sexual purity, although some leeway—multiple wives, etc.—seemed to be tolerated. Through the direct influence of Jesus, the marriage covenant rose to an even higher prominence in the eyes of early Christians. In writing to Titus, Paul laid out the qualifications of church leaders—those who would set godly examples for others to follow:

> The reason I left you in Crete was to set right what was left undone and, as I directed you, to appoint elders in every town: one who is blameless, the husband of **one wife**, having faithful children not accused of wildness or rebellion. For an overseer, as God's administrator, must be blameless, not arrogant, not hot-tempered, not addicted to wine, not a bully, not greedy for money, but hospitable, loving what is good, sensible, righteous, holy, self-

controlled, holding to the faithful message as taught, so that he will be able both to encourage with sound teaching and to refute those who contradict it. Titus 1:5-9 (HCSB; emphasis added)

Due to the influence of Christ, Christians could never accept polygamy because it violated the essence of the marriage covenant. Church leaders could marry—and enjoy sex—but polygamy was unacceptable. This passage also emphasizes the importance of sound doctrine (teaching). Paul made it clear that cultural influences are not to determine how the church functions.

SEXUAL PURITY IN THE NEW TESTAMENT CHURCH

A careful reading of the New Testament epistles will show that the danger of sexual immorality was strongly emphasized in the letters sent to predominantly Gentile churches. Why? The Christian emphasis on marriage, fidelity, and sexual purity clashed with the pagan cultures in which those churches were birthed. The following quote provides some much-needed context to help us understand the early church mindset:

> It has been said that chastity was the one new virtue which Christianity introduced into the world. It is certainly true that the ancient world regarded sexual immorality so lightly that it was no sin at all. It was the expected thing that a man should have a mistress. In places like Corinth the great temples were staffed by hundreds of priestesses who were sacred prostitutes and whose earnings went to the upkeep of the Temple . . .

> The Greeks said that Solon was the first person to allow the introduction of prostitutes into Athens and then the building of brothels; and with the profits of the new trade a new Temple was built to Aphrodite, the goddess of love. Nothing could show the Greek point of view better than the fact that they saw nothing wrong in building a temple to the gods with the proceeds of prostitution.

> When Paul set this stress on moral purity, he was erecting a standard which the ordinary heathen had never dreamed of. That is why he pleads with them so earnestly and lays down his laws of purity with such stringency. We must remember the kind of society from which these Christian converts had come and the kind of society with

which they were encompassed. There is nothing in all history like the moral miracle which Christianity wrought.[43]

As the direct result of *Christ's* teachings, the early church believed that virtually any sexual activity that transgressed the boundary of one man and one woman in marriage was sexually immoral.[44] (This is not to say that everything is acceptable within the bounds of a marriage covenant. Love and respect should always characterize the sexual relationship between a husband and wife.) Because sexual immorality was so dominant at the time, because its effects are contrary to God's covenant design for humanity, and because the negative consequences of immorality are so far-reaching, the topic was usually approached with the utmost seriousness (see also 1 Corinthians 6:9-20, 10:8; and 1 Thessalonians 4:2-4).

Therefore be imitators of God, as beloved children; and walk in love, just as Christ also loved you and gave Himself up for us, an offering and a sacrifice to God as a fragrant aroma.

But immorality or any impurity or greed must not even be named among you, as is proper among saints; and there must be no filthiness and silly talk, or coarse jesting, which are not fitting, but rather giving of thanks. For this you know with certainty, that no immoral or impure person or covetous man, who is an idolater, has an inheritance in the kingdom of Christ and God.

Let no one deceive you with empty words, for because of these things the wrath of God comes upon the sons of disobedience. Therefore do not be partakers with them; for you were formerly darkness, but now you are Light in the Lord; walk as children of Light (for the fruit of the Light consists in all goodness and righteousness and truth), trying to learn what is pleasing to the Lord. Ephesians 5:1-10

Real love, according to Paul, leads to a sexually pure lifestyle. Our culture may make claims to the contrary and our flesh may feel passions that align with our culture, but God's word stands above it all.

43. Barclay, W. (Ed.), *The letters to the Galatians and Ephesians* (Philadelphia, PA: The Westminster John Knox Press, 1976), 161–162.
44. Gerhard Kittel, Geoffrey W. Bromiley, and Gerhard Friedrich, eds., *Theological Dictionary of the New Testament* (Grand Rapids, MI: Eerdmans, 1964–), 590–595.

All too often, people read passages like this and assume that the Bible is prudish about sex, as though Christians should think it is a terrible thing. In making such assumptions, they fail to incorporate the historical context of the New Testament. A key purpose of the epistles to the Gentile churches was to correct—and prevent—immoral behavior among Gentile believers. In addition, I remind you that sex wasn't humanity's idea—it was God's! The fact that *He* created sex to be pleasurable makes a significant statement about Him:

> *You will make known to me the path of life;*
> *In Your presence is fullness of joy;*
> *In Your right hand there are pleasures forever. Psalms 16:11*

Sex is a wonderful thing!—within the boundaries designed by God. Just as a river can be an awesome source of life and enjoyment within its boundaries, so too, sex was designed by God for life, intimacy, and pleasure. He created us as sexual beings. That's the long and short of it.

Because sexual intercourse was designed by our Creator to be immensely pleasurable, we may safely assume that its intended purposes go well beyond those of procreation. However, just as it is with everything else in this world, our human perspective of sex has been terribly tainted through the corruption of sin; too often, its life-giving beauty is overrun by human selfishness and self-determinism. When we transgress the boundaries set in place by God, that which is intended for life will soon bear destructive fruit. We may not see it today—or even tomorrow—but, one day, we will see it.

SEX CAN BE DECEPTIVE

If love is defined only as romance, then sex is the expected outcome. The guy and girl always hook up in the movies, don't they? Isn't that what we expect to happen? But we don't define love; love defines us.

Sadly, many from the younger generations view sex outside of marriage as entirely natural and innocent. "The problem," they say, "lies with religious mores. If only those prudish and uptight conservatives would let down their hair and live a little, we'd all be happier."

What the proponents of "free sex" fail to understand is that the natural act of sex has *spiritual* ramifications. When two people have sexual intercourse, they become *spiritually one* (1 Corinthians 6:12-20). The marriage covenant is meant to protect and preserve this sacred union—and the children who are born as a result.

As beautiful and enjoyable as sex may be, it can also become a deadly trap. Sex outside of the marriage covenant is always accompanied by dangerous physical, emotional, and spiritual consequences. What seems like fun and liberty today will end in shame, embarrassment, and heartbreak tomorrow.

In our attempts to remove all boundaries, we create our own shackles (Proverbs 5:22). What begins as an act of pleasure can easily become addictive. The problem of sexual addiction has never been worse for both men and women. The impact on families is painfully apparent. For the person bound by sexual addiction, few struggles seem more hopeless; few hearts feel more guilt-ridden.

I encourage all who have already compromised their sexual purity to meet Jesus at the cross. He is more than willing to forgive and to cleanse. Not only can He wash away your sins, He can also cleanse your conscience and wipe away any sense of shame that you might feel (1 Corinthians 6:9-11; Hebrews 9:11-14; and 1 John 1:9). No person's sins are so dark that the Almighty God can't—or won't—forgive.

What a person needs most is a humble heart, an honest confession, and a sincere faith to believe that the blood of Jesus is more powerful than any sin he or she could ever commit. The key to breaking free from the chains and shame of sexual immorality lies in learning how to draw upon, and abide in, God's multifaceted grace. It may take a while to work through these issues to the point of feeling a sense of dignity as God's child, but arriving at such a place of freedom is entirely possible.

If you have significant struggles with sexuality or sexual addiction, don't hesitate to find a mature leader or wise counselor to help you with this process. Thankfully, there are a growing number of Christian ministries that work hard at helping people overcome the devastating grip of sexual addiction. Now, more than ever, we need God's grace to help us break free from the whirlwind of sexual immorality. Thankfully, grace is both readily and abundantly available.

SURRENDERING YOUR SEXUALITY

Today, many single people are pressured to become sexually active; they've been made to feel as though *virginity* is a four-letter word. To violate the sanctity of sexuality as ordained by God, however, is to journey down a road of regret. God's opinion matters more than all others, and He undoubtedly has our best interests at heart. Appearances may speak otherwise, but the day will come when all other voices fade as His resounds clearly across the heavens. In his letter to Titus, Paul also wrote about the "the voice of grace" in the formative process of sanctification:

> *For the grace of God has appeared, bringing salvation to all men, instructing us to deny ungodliness and worldly desires and to live sensibly, righteously and godly in the present age, looking for the blessed hope and the appearing of the glory of our great God and Savior, Christ Jesus, who gave Himself for us to redeem us from every lawless deed, and to purify for Himself a people for His own possession, zealous for good deeds. Titus 2:11-14*

Once again, we are reminded that God's grace does not provide us with a blank check to do whatever we want. Rather, grace instructs, disciplines, and empowers us to live in a manner that honors God. Nowhere is this reality as important as it is with human sexuality. Rare is the person who doesn't experience a wide array of sexual desires. We don't need to go looking for sexual temptations—they will find us. Thankfully, God's grace gives us the ability to say, "No!"

As a whole, we have adopted a self-oriented perspective of relationships, including our relationship with our Creator. In other words, we innately believe that God exists in order to make us happy. It's as though our happiness should be the highest priority on Heaven's agenda. Such a mindset radically opposes a love-motivated New Covenant relationship with God. He is God. We are not. He does not exist for us. We exist for Him.

Did God pay a steep price for our benefit? Without question! What higher price could He have paid than sending His Son to die on the cross that we might be redeemed from sin and destruction? Further, He invests us with His presence through the Holy Spirit and promises to bless us with an eternal inheritance of all that is His (Ephesians 1:3-14). God held nothing back for our sakes. Those who enjoin Him through the New Covenant are asked to do the same in return. God thoroughly expects His betrothed to be *all in.*

> *Flee immorality. Every other sin that a man commits is outside the body, but the immoral man sins against his own body. Or do you not know that your body is a temple of the Holy Spirit who is in you, whom you have from God, and that you are not your own? For you have been bought with a price: therefore glorify God in your body. 1 Corinthians 6:18-20*

This is another passage that makes little sense apart from a covenant worldview. Like marriage, our relationship with God doesn't involve a 50/50 commitment, but a 100 percent devotion to one another. All that we have—including our sexuality—now belongs to Him. This means that we are empowered to resist sexual temptation only as we surrender our sexuality to God. And because His character is the most faithful and virtuous imaginable, we can trust that such personal sacrifice will do nothing more than benefit us (and others) in the end. By comparison, we gain much and lose little.

These ideas are especially relevant for me. At a young age, I developed an addiction to pornography, which, on top of all of my other struggles, complicated life immensely. God did a powerful work to free me from that addiction when I became a Christian, but corrupted sexual passions rarely vanish into thin air. In my mind, those desires, combined with my emotional brokenness, pointed in one direction— toward marriage. "If I could only be married," I naively reasoned, "all of my pain and struggle will vanish, and I can live happily ever after."

After thirty years of marriage—and a good marriage at that— and over twenty years of ministry, I can say with total assurance that if a person has emotional and sexual issues before marriage, they will only be intensified during marriage. Marriage isn't a fix to a problem; marriage is a covenant relationship lived out with another imperfect person. If we never fully surrender our sexuality to God, our fleshly desires will corrupt the sanctity of a marriage relationship.

One of the most difficult steps I have ever taken as a Christian was to kneel by my bed and offer a pain-filled prayer to God. "Lord, I don't know how I can possibly live this out, but I fully surrender to You my desire for a wife. If it is Your will, I will remain single and sexually celibate for the rest of my life. I only ask You to help me because this is not something that I can possibly hope to do in my own strength."

I meant that prayer with all of my heart and was determined to avoid any romantic involvement after I returned to college for my senior year. I continued to have female friends, but avoided any women not spoken for, or for whom I felt an attraction. Little did I realize that my loving Father was preparing my heart so that I could handle a romantic relationship without corrupting it. The story is too long to provide further detail, but I surrendered my desire for marriage—and sex—fully to God, and in His providence, He chose to give it back to me. I can't promise that will be the case for every person in every situation, but I can say that a fully surrendered life is something that God expects from every one of His covenant children. It's not because He wants us to be miserable—just the opposite is true. A life surrendered to God's will is a life that can handle His blessings without corrupting them.

PURITY AND IDENTITY

Human nature is extremely deceptive, so I also feel the need to share a tidbit of wisdom regarding the link between purity and identity or, more appropriately, to communicate that purity flows out of identity, not vice-versa. A person's identity is established through becoming a son or a daughter of the King of the Universe.

As important as sexual purity may be, human pride has a way of corrupting all that is good. Being sexually pure honors God, but it is not the foundation for being righteous in His eyes. Human flesh will always seek to boast—even when that flesh is modestly clothed in church-approved attire. It's all too easy for a person to feel morally superior because he or she has withstood the onslaught of immorality in our culture. This is a huge mistake! If there is one thing worse than committing sexual sin, it is developing an air of superiority because we haven't. Our acceptance with God is found only through the cross of Jesus Christ.

We may (mistakenly) think that sexual purity is the antidote for shame, but true glory can be found only through the cross. Those who have sinned at least realize their desperate need for Christ. Those who glory in their own purity may never come to realize the depths of their need. A person's significance comes from being a child of the King, not from being morally pure. Why can we lift our heads with a sense of dignity? What is it that enables us to stand against the corruption and commonality of this world? We have secure identities as the covenant children of the King. Thus, purity flows from a secure identity. A favorable identity should never be based on a sacrificial or holy lifestyle.

Conservative religious circles are often plagued by what some call a "purity culture." Purity and modesty are not problems within themselves, and God forbid that they would ever be seen as such. Law-based living, however, corrupts all that is good. At first appearance, any emphasis on purity can seem wholesome and appropriate, but when immersed in a law-based paradigm, a purity culture turns twisted and destructive. Women seem to be particularly affected.

Those steeped in a purity culture mentality can easily begin to think that all sexual desires felt by unmarried women are evil. In contrast, the sexual desires of unmarried men are seen as being natural and almost beyond male control. Accordingly, a young woman who seeks to live admirably as a Christian—as an example for others to emulate—will live a chaste life and avoid virtually all meaningful relationships with the opposite sex. Anything less represents an indelible stain on her character. Further still, if men are attracted to a female, *she* is at fault for her seductive clothing and flattering speech. Such destructive mindsets are created by a male-driven, legalistic perspective.

The problem with a purity culture is that not only does it breed a sense of pride that comes from being sexually pure, it can also create a crippling sense of shame when the woman becomes sexually active *within* the boundaries of marriage. Women are expected to "flip a switch" in a sense. One day sex is evil and she should do everything possible to avoid tempting men, the next day sex is good and she should do everything possible to please her husband. Simply said; painfully accomplished for some.

It is no secret that most men are visually oriented and so a woman who genuinely cares about others will dress modestly. Parents and leaders should also be careful not to place legalistic burdens on the shoulders of young people who are trying to discover their identities in this crazy and corrupt world. In every aspect of sexuality, love—not self-significance—should be clearly established as the primary motivation.

There is one other important area in which sexuality and identity coincide—sexual abuse. A staggering number of people in our world have been sexually violated. The strange thing about human nature is that the victims of sexual abuse often feel ashamed when, in fact, the shame belongs to the perpetrators. What is done cannot be undone, but wholeness and freedom can both be experienced through Christ's healing virtue. Rather than remaining silent and forever ashamed, a victim of sexual abuse should talk with a trusted Christian leader or counselor. Just bringing the issue into the light will help considerably. Having someone who is wise and loving as a guide will help even more. Ultimately, God is the One who brings emotional healing, but He uses people in the process.

TEACHING OUR CHILDREN

Sex was created by God and is to be freely celebrated within its intended boundaries. Young people need to understand this. They also need to know that their right standing with God comes only through the blood of Jesus and not through their personal purity. Finally, young people need to sense that they are unconditionally loved regardless of what they do. A young woman who knows the absolute and unconditional love of a father will be far less likely to crawl in the sack before marriage—or to hold onto a guy who is a poor candidate for marriage. A healthy sense of sexuality for a young woman begins with the loving and respectful manner with which her father—or father figure—treats all of the women in his household.

Our physical bodies mature long before our hearts and minds, so these issues are worth talking about if possible. (Many kids—including ours—seem to be thoroughly grossed out by the idea that their parents had sex at least once or twice.) As much as we hate to admit it, the cat's out of the bag. Pandora's Box has been opened. While silence about sex may have seemed like a reasonable option for previous generations, times have drastically changed.

Kids who grow up in sex-steeped cultures are exposed to an onslaught of information and imagery that they are not yet emotionally prepared to process. This pains me to no end, but it is what it is. Thus, it is far better for us to communicate a healthy perspective of sexuality to our kids than to remain totally silent on the issue. Such waters are challenging—but by no means impossible—to navigate.

FAITHFUL LOVE

Why do some cultures espouse the general concept of faithful love but despise the restrictive nature of the marriage covenant? Perhaps it is because they have bought into the, "You can have it all!" marketing mindset. As a result, people are led to believe that the freedom to love should mean the freedom to do whatever they want, which, in the end, isn't love at all.

A selfish and lawless spirit demands the freedom to do whatever it wants whenever it wants. On the contrary, covenant love willingly limits its expression of freedom for the sake of the one loved. Before entering any covenant, a person should be encouraged to do a "cost/benefit analysis" of sorts: "Do I value this relationship enough to willingly restrict my behavior? Is it worth surrendering the freedom to do whatever I want whenever I want?"

Whether we speak of entering into a marriage covenant with a person of the opposite sex, or into the New Covenant with the heavenly Father through Christ, it is important for us to calm our emotions and to objectively ask ourselves yet another essential question: "Do I value this relationship enough to put it above my other relationships (and opportunities) in life?" If you cannot say that you are willing to voluntarily restrict your behavior in order to enter into a covenant relationship, then you are not ready to enter that relationship.

When Debi and I married over thirty years ago, we voluntarily chose to limit the sexual expression of our love to only each other. In a very real sense, I was saying, "Debi, out of all of the women in this world I choose *you*. I choose you to be my life partner. I choose to limit my sexual intimacy to you alone. I choose to restrict, limit, and even deny my natural desires because I love you and want to be united with you in marriage."

Debi, of course, was offended when I asked her to respond in kind. Haha! Ask one hundred women about the number one attribute they would like to see in a husband, and I can assure you that sexual fidelity will be near—if not at—the very top of the list.

Is it difficult for a man or a woman to live out the devotion expected of a marriage covenant? Without question! Many aspects of marriage conflict with our natural wants. Just because a man chooses to limit his sexual love to his wife doesn't mean that all other sexual desires mysteriously vanish. Further still, it's not like a husband and wife spend all of their time in bed. A college friend once commented that he was disappointed to find out that marriage isn't a "sexathon." Sex within the boundaries of the marriage covenant can be very enriching, but let's face it, thirty, forty, or fifty years is a long time to be limited to the same person. Life has a way of changing us—our motivations and our bodies.

Forbidden fruit promises excitement, but leaves devastation in its wake. A married couple that does not work to keep their romance alive will eventually find themselves living together like "two old shoes" as the mundane responsibilities of life overrun their passion for one another. Then, one day, from seemingly out of nowhere, a cheerful and attractive co-worker will catch one of the old shoes' eyes. Vitality will return to a passion that has long been dormant. Soon, the old shoe will sneak off with a new shoe to feast upon forbidden fruit. As the two shoes tie themselves together in knots, they will leave a pain-filled trail of betrayed spouses and devastated children. Fail to invest in your marriage and your marriage will eventually fail you.

It is through a long-term marriage relationship that the glory of faithful love is revealed. Through the day-in-and-day-out mundane reality of life, two people have the opportunity to grow in their expression of faithful love for one another, that is, to grow into a deeper measure of the covenant love embodied by Jesus Himself. Our heavenly Father highly values this process of growing in Christ-like love.

Of course, our highest call is to love God first with all that we have. It is then out of this first love relationship with God that we are given the grace to overcome selfishness as we devote ourselves to another person in marriage.

WHAT ABOUT DIVORCE AND REMARRIAGE?

Of all the things I knew I would write about in this book, *remarriage* was the one that caused me the most hesitation. When addressing sexual immorality in light of the Scriptures, I knew I would be pushing against the tide of cultural trends—and against an increasing number of professing Christians. I do not see any biblical fuzziness with this issue though—God highly values a sexual relationship within the boundaries of a love-enriched marriage covenant, and He strongly disapproves of a sexual relationship outside of those boundaries. From a biblical perspective, there simply isn't much wiggle room on this issue.

The issues of divorce and remarriage are not as clear. Proponents of "progressive sexuality" will often criticize Christians for having a double standard when it comes to these issues. In part, I find it difficult to disagree with them. If conservative Christians are to take a stand against sexual activity outside of the boundaries of the marriage covenant, it seems that they should take a stronger stand on behalf of what Jesus said regarding divorce and remarriage. The problem is that this issue can be more complicated than may appear at first glance.

I don't question for a minute that we have become too lax with our practices, but various factors tend to muddy the waters, and so I find the issues of divorce—and especially remarriage—very difficult to navigate. As much as I value the ideal of a marriage made in Heaven, I've been around long enough to know that a good marriage requires deliberate effort and a lot of hard work. (Pushing my chair in after I eat just doesn't come naturally to me.) A couple can't just coast through life en route to a healthy marriage. We all have our issues, and our issues affect one another. Furthermore, those who bring baggage into a marriage will find that very same baggage sitting on their bed one morning. Emotional pain doesn't magically "vaporize" simply because two people love each other.

Further still, a man and a woman don't always enter into a marriage covenant filled with the wisdom of the ages. The decision to marry is sometimes made hastily, blindly, or under considerable pressure. Personality differences can run deep, and newly married couples don't always have the support, acumen, and tools they need to grow a healthy marriage. As much as we would like to think that every relationship will work out well, the truth is that living together can be really difficult. In addition to past issues and personality differences, people can inflict considerable pain on one another through thoughtless, selfish, and foolish choices. What begins with love, passion, and hope may end with bitterness, hatred, and a deep sense of regret.

In an ideal world, every marriage relationship is redeemable. In our real world, it takes two devoted people to make a relationship work. If one decides the marriage isn't worth the effort, or that it is somehow beyond hope, or even that he or she is no longer in love, the other may have no choice but to allow a divorce. The human will can be a terribly stubborn creature. God has never given people dominion over other people and the freedom to love will always mean the freedom to not love. This and several other factors can make it difficult to bring the issues of divorce and remarriage into theological focus.

The Mosaic Law permitted the possibility of divorce and remarriage. When, however, Jesus came on the scene, He raised the standard of marriage significantly. The only valid reason for divorce, according to Jesus, was *adultery* (Matthew 19:3-12). Paul seemed to soften things just a bit by giving additional freedom to the person who becomes a Christian but has a spouse who remains an unbeliever (1 Corinthians 7:10-16).

Most of what we find about divorce and remarriage in the New Testament comes from the two passages referenced in the previous paragraph. I'll be honest with you—the limited amount of information leaves me with a lot of questions. How do we know if a person is truly a Christian? We can't truly fathom the depths of a human heart. Then, there are legalists who profess Christ, but who bring a domineering harshness into the marriage. A revelation of grace is obviously lacking, but we don't know to what degree. Some people will give the appearance of having faith when they aren't even Christians. There are also those who present a false front as they persuade the other person to marry.

What about abusive situations? What do we do when staying together creates more grief for the children? Children are often terribly troubled when their parents split, but I've seen a few cases in which the children were relieved when the marriage broke apart; it finally meant peace within the already fractured home. We're all aware that a single parent faces multiple challenges when trying to rear children alone. Are there times when the children will be better off if the parent remarries and establishes a more stable household? All of these are reasonable questions.

FURTHER CONSIDERATIONS

Part of me wants to contend that a divorced Christian should *never* remarry, but I simply can't bring myself to establish that standard. Of course, this entire book is based on my opinions, but for much of it I feel as though I have a solid and accurate Scriptural standing. I don't have the same confidence in tackling the issue of divorce and remarriage. What I present to you in this matter has a lot more of my opinion than I care to admit.

We know that Christ's disciples were taken aback by His extreme stand on divorce and remarriage (Matthew 19:10). It is entirely possible that the apostle Paul seemed to have questions as well (1 Corinthians 7:10-12). I don't want to use my uncertainty as an excuse for not addressing this issue so I've listed several of *my* suggestions below:

1. **Any couple contemplating marriage should do several things:**

   A. Fully surrender—and continue to surrender—the relationship to God, giving Him complete freedom to shut it down if He thinks that's best.

   B. Seek honest input from parents, spiritually mature friends, and Christian leaders. They often see things that people who are blinded by passion fail to pick up. I am not saying that these people are always right, or that they should be making decisions for us, but that we should always   be open to wise, honest, and objective counsel.

C. Seek out high quality premarital counseling. Part of this will involve reading books about marriage, but it's also important to meet with someone who does premarital counseling on a regular basis. A good counselor will actually look for areas of potential conflict and help a couple work through them *before* marriage.

2. **A person—especially a woman—in an abusive situation needs to seek qualified help.** A woman should never subject herself or her children to physical abuse. An abusive husband is clearly violating the *chesed*-nature of the marriage covenant. Finding help is a huge step to take, but God can provide a way where there seems to be no way.

   While I am on this subject, I encourage a woman not to ignore some of the warning signs that may appear *before* marriage. A man who is excessively jealous or controlling will not make a good husband, nor will one who demands obedience from a girlfriend or fiancée. A man who sees a woman as a submissive subject rather than a co-heir of the kingdom will undoubtedly translate his demeaning attitude into demeaning behavior. These tendencies don't always surface before marriage, but if they do, find a way to get out of that relationship! Any sense of momentary affirmation isn't worth the long-term pain.

3. **If a married couple is struggling, a season of separation—with counseling—might prove helpful, but divorce should be seen as the very last resort.** I once talked with a young man, Matt, who had recently come to Christ, but whose wife wanted a divorce and was adamantly opposed to his new faith. Due to the conflict, they decided to separate for a season. They also had a five year-old daughter who lived with her mother. Matt deeply cared about his entire family, but was unwisely trying to "fix" his marriage through control and manipulation.

   A Christian counselor told Matt to divorce his wife and find a godly stepmother for his child. When he asked what I thought about the counselor's advice, I told him it was a bunch of bunk. "Fight for your marriage, Matt!" was my response. "If you give it all you can and it still doesn't work out, then so be it, but make every possible effort to restore this relationship." After Matt fully surrendered the relationship to God and began to pray in alignment with His will, amazing things began to happen. Within a few months, all three members of the family became active members of a church. God had brought restoration when it seemed like no such restoration was possible.

4. **If and when it becomes obvious that a divorce is inevitable, there is no condemnation for those who are in Christ.** What's past is past. We do all that we can to restore a relationship, but in the end, we cannot control another person's actions or desires.

5. **Whether a divorced person remarries or not is something that will have to be searched out in the Scriptures and decided in conjunction with wise and godly counsel.** If a divorced person does decide to remarry, I cannot emphasize enough the importance of *top notch* premarital counseling. There will always be unavoidable baggage from the previous marriage, which must be thoroughly addressed if the new relationship is to be healthy. More than once, I've seen a person remarry, only to be mired in the same issues that led to the first divorce.

6. **Those who have already divorced and remarried, regardless of the reasoning or the history behind them, should move forward with their lives together.** I believe it would be a huge mistake to try to undo what has already been done. It will only complicate things further. If they feel any guilt about the marriage, they should take it to the cross and settle things there. Bring everything under the blood of Jesus and do everything possible to shake off the chains of the past in order to move forward in a healthy marriage relationship. Even when done for the wrong reasons, divorce and remarriage are not unforgivable sins. The New Covenant alone is the highest order of covenant and so there is no condemnation for those who are in Christ (Romans 8:1).

In closing this chapter, I want to remind the reader that sex was God's invention, and the Creator of the Universe has never had a bad idea. No matter how much sin may corrupt the good things created by God, or how complicated it may make our lives, the King of Glory is able to redeem each and every situation. The key lies not in obeying a set of legalistic rules, but in learning to be faithful to the covenants that God has established.

BLAZING A TRAIL TO FRUITFUL LIVING

Sex should be celebrated as being good, virtuous, and sacred, but from a biblical perspective, our path must stay within the boundaries of a God-defined marriage covenant (Hebrews 13:4).

CHAPTER TWENTY
AMBASSADORS OF THE KING

Therefore, since we have so great a cloud of witnesses surrounding us, let us also lay aside every encumbrance and the sin which so easily entangles us, and let us run with endurance the race that is set before us, fixing our eyes on Jesus, the author and perfecter of faith, who for the joy set before Him endured the cross, despising the shame, and has sat down at the right hand of the throne of God.

Hebrews 12:1-2

From the sense of being an ambassador for Jesus Christ, hopefully, through my story and through all the improbables and the miracles that happened in my life, people are inspired or at least a little bit warmer to the idea of exploring who Jesus is.

—Jeremy Lin

As it is with grace, the love that flows from God is marked by many profound and beautiful dimensions. Our loving Father is deeply devoted to His covenant children, showering them with spiritual gifts and blessings that the unsaved sadly miss. God's desire, however, is to bring *all* people into the fold of His loving arms.

*First of all, then, I urge that entreaties and prayers, petitions and thanksgivings, be made on behalf of all men, for kings and all who are in authority, so that we may lead a tranquil and quiet life in all godliness and dignity. This is good and acceptable in the sight of God our Savior, who desires **all** men to be saved and to come to the knowledge of the truth. 1 Timothy 2:1-4 (emphasis added)*

Coming to realize God's heart for those who don't yet know Him, we cannot help but extend grace and love to the unsaved. The apostle Paul's mission to reach people was not entirely unique; our heavenly Father seeks to use *all* of His children to touch the lives of those who live under the curse of sin and death. All of this fulfills the Abrahamic Covenant; God's blessings for us are linked to our influence on others.

> *"I will bless those who bless you,*
> *I will curse those who treat you with contempt,*
> *and all the peoples on earth*
> *will be blessed through you." Genesis 12:3 (HCSB)*

God desires not that we would look down upon the world in judgment, but that He would use us to be a blessing to those who are aliens to the New Covenant. The reality is that we have no platform from which to unrighteously judge others. We are all guilty of sin and rebellion. We are all saved by grace. There's not a Christian in the world who can say that he or she stands favored in the eyes of Heaven because of superior moral character. We are who we are because He is who He is. Period.

We have been chosen by God not for selfish purposes, but to help touch the world with His love. This can be difficult for some to grasp, but God has chosen to reach people through people. In other words, God advances His kingdom on earth through His covenant children.

God's plan to work through people goes back to His very first words to the human race when He gave us dominion over the earth (Genesis 1:28). Adam and Eve surrendered that dominion to the devil, Jesus recovered it, and now we advance God's reign on earth as *ambassadors* of the King.

> *Now all these things are from God, who reconciled us to Himself through Christ and gave us the ministry of reconciliation, namely, that God was in Christ reconciling the world to Himself, not counting their trespasses against them, and He has committed to us the word of reconciliation.*
>
> *Therefore, we are ambassadors for Christ, as though God were making an appeal through us; we beg you on behalf of Christ, be reconciled to God. 2 Corinthians 5:18-20*

An ambassador serves as an authorized liaison of a government for the purposes determined by that nation's leadership. The King of Glory has chosen and appointed us as His ambassadors to help reconcile the world to Himself. Whether through prayer, sharing our faith, or practicing good works, the body of Christ is the primary means through which the love of Christ is expressed to our broken and dying world.

WIN THE BATTLE, LOSE THE WAR

A lot of criticism has been aimed toward the church over the years, and some of it is undoubtedly justified. Still, I shudder to imagine the state of our world apart from the sacrificial work of Christians all over the globe. Did missionaries enforce ridiculous cultural rules on native peoples? Yes, they did. Did they help to promote imperialist agendas? Sadly, there is little doubt. At the same time, missionary efforts have had a huge impact in helping to eliminate poverty and disease, in bringing educational systems to entire nations, and in helping to curb heinous practices such as infanticide. Opponents of Christianity usually seek to magnify the church's blemishes while virtually ignoring its massive influence for good in this world.

Christians are often called to publicly contend for moral issues—the rights of the unborn, for example—but we must take care not to lose the war for human souls in the midst of our battles. I see a desperate need for political involvement, but when Christians sacrifice the fruit of the Spirit for political expediency, everyone loses. Does it really matter whether we gain the right to post the Ten Commandments if we trample our opponents (and alienate their hearts) on our path to victory? Surely, the coming generations will pay for our errors. Christians in the United States have the freedom and the right to stand for moral causes of all sorts—and we should—but to do so in a fleshly manner will, in the long term, seriously undermine our cause. If, for example, we use controlling methods to force our ideals upon others, you can be sure that those same controlling means will one day be used against us.

Those in the world won't come to Christ simply because it's the right thing to do or because we have the best arguments. They will come to Christ because they experience the life and love of Jesus flowing through God's representatives. If Christians display the same hardness, arrogance, and bravado as some talk show hosts, they will, without question, lose the hearts of the unsaved. Fighting for moral causes may be admirable, but not if those fights somehow compromise the centrality of the gospel.

I find it interesting that the apostle Paul did little to confront the injustices of his surrounding culture. He focused, instead, on helping people receive a revelation of God's grace. It's not that God doesn't care about injustice. Through the centuries He has called many a devoted Christian to campaign against atrocities such as abortion, slavery, and sex trafficking. However, the noblest of our efforts are fundamentally flawed if we seek to bring change while failing to reconcile hearts to Christ. I can try to promote legislation to curtail the corrupt efforts of greedy bankers, for example, but if I can reconcile that greedy banker fully to Christ, he or she will no longer be greedy. *Christians should utilize every righteous means—including legislation—to protect the vulnerable, but the gospel of grace is the central message of the church, and we must guard it as the precious treasure that it is.*

ALWAYS NEEDED, NOT ALWAYS WELCOMED

The primary challenge we face is that even though people such as the greedy banker desperately need Jesus, they generally cannot—or will not—admit their need. An ambassador, then, must be wise, bold, and extremely gracious to successfully engage those mired in our world's system. This sounds like a tall order—and it certainly is—but we sometimes make things more complicated than necessary.

How will we interact with our society? Will we be pouncers who attack everything we believe is wrong, or will we be ambassadors who love the broken people of a sin-ridden world? Isn't it interesting that the sinless Son of God was a friend to tax gatherers and sinners? Jesus—the One who was full of grace and truth—so effectively served as an ambassador for the kingdom of Heaven that even those who did wrong were mysteriously drawn to Him. The love, joy, peace, patience, goodness, gentleness, and kindness of the Son of Man captured the hearts of sinners just as a sweet, colorful lollipop might grab the attention of a toddler. *The Divine Progression of Grace* enables us to walk in Jesus' footsteps.

Christ's ambassadors are called to serve in enemy territory—on the front lines of the battle between light and darkness. Our enemies are *not* people, but demonic spirits that constantly rail against Heaven's plans. All too often, though, we classify people as our enemy combatants. An ambassador of the kingdom should not be a pouncer, but rather a willing vessel through whom God can extend His gracious, unmerited favor, to those bound by the grip of death.

Without a doubt, there can be a steep price to pay in bringing God's truth and love to a world that desperately needs but doesn't always welcome them. Ours is not a nice world. Ambassadors who represent the kingdom well often come under "heavy fire" for their beliefs. None of it is fair or just. Christ, however, calls us to love even those who violently oppose His rule. The task of a kingdom ambassador is to *reconcile*—not condemn. Jesus calls His servants to love their enemies even when doing so exacts a painful personal price. This is the love that Jesus modeled as He hung dying on the cross.

All of this is especially difficult for Christians in comfortable societies to fathom. We've been accustomed to comfort and ease; our idea of persecution is often nothing more than a cold shoulder or an unkind word. We must ask ourselves if love is the law that governs our actions. Are we willing to suffer a significant price for the sake of our beloved King? Will we voluntarily reach out to others when such a move may cost us time, money, reputation, or even our physical well-being?

WHOM DO WE LOVE?

Many of us are willing to love others, but have a difficult time knowing where and with whom to focus our efforts. The widespread exposure provided by technology makes these types of decisions all the more difficult to make. None of us can ever address all of the needs in our broken world. The parable of the Good Samaritan (Luke 10:25-37) carries an important message about love, but it doesn't fully answer the question at hand. Today, my "neighbor" can be someone on the other side of the world who I read about in a social media post.

It can be overwhelming to think about all of the needs we "should" be meeting—water, food, clothing, housing, utilities, medical care, etc.—for the poor, and all of the causes we should be fighting for or against—world missions, abortion, sex trafficking, wounded veterans, environmental issues, cruelty toward animals, corporate greed, political corruption, etc. With minimal effort, I could fill almost an entire page with a list of truly worthy causes. How can one person meet so many needs? Is it even possible to educate ourselves on more than a handful of causes? I don't think so.

It is here—in the world of needs and causes—that an understanding of the *body of Christ* becomes critical. Jesus Christ is the head of His body—the church. The members of a body do not decide when and where they are to act; the head of the body chooses how to direct its members. We will always be bombarded by an overabundance of needs and expectations that we cannot possibly meet. We can, however, walk with God and seek guidance for when, where, and whom to serve:

> *For by grace you have been saved through faith; and that not of yourselves, it is the gift of God; not as a result of works, so that no one may boast. For we are His workmanship, created in Christ Jesus for good works, which God prepared beforehand so that we would walk in them. Ephesians 2:8-10*

It's not a nagging conscience—or even an occasional moment of empathy—that should guide our efforts, but rather the Holy Spirit. We are called by grace, saved by grace, and empowered by grace to do the things that God has created us to do. How do we know what those things are? We walk with Him, day in and day out, in a journey of discovery. Over time, God begins to burden our hearts for the things that He has crafted us to do. It's all very freeing—and very exciting—to know that we don't have to do everything, or attempt to meet every need, in order to please God through our service.

For His part, our heavenly Father will use all of our life experiences—both good and bad—to equip us for the work that He has called us to do. This is perhaps one of the most marvelous, mind stretching dimensions of walking with God. All of the pain, failure, and injustice that we face through the course of our lives will somehow morph into the form of beautiful and delicious fruit. The very things that we often think disqualify us from effective service can be used by our sovereign God to *increase* our ability to impact others. It really is quite breathtaking to watch the Creator of the Universe bring beauty from ashes.

Quite often, our heavenly Father will use our painful experiences to engrave ministry burdens on our hearts. My negative experiences with the Western church over the years haven't left me scarred so much as they have instilled within me a burden to help facilitate change. It's not that I don't care about the unsaved or the downtrodden, but my overriding passion is always to see the church come into its fullness. In my mind, the kingdom of God is advanced—and the human condition overcome—primarily through a fruitful and mature body of Christ. I do what I do because the Spirit of God has written these things on my heart as I have endeavored to know and obey Him.

Your vision for service will most likely differ from mine, but it will generally come by a similar means. Each person's call to service is unique to that individual. While my emphasis happens to be on spiritual formation, I fully recognize that another vital dimension of fruitfulness involves giving to those who may never bear any visible fruit. Caring for the needs of the homeless, for example may not produce many leaders, but it certainly entails a powerful expression of God's unconditional love.

SAYING YES, SAYING NO

As I've "found my way" in discovering the things that God has called me to, I've also realized that there are things that I cannot—and should not—be doing. I prefer to learn by following the Holy Spirit's leading, but admittedly, His guidance is not always crystal clear to me. When I was in my early twenties, for example, I spent eighteen months leading the (junior high) youth ministry at my church. (Isn't that what every devoted young adult Christian should be doing?) That ended up being the worst ministry experience of my entire life! It took me almost a year to recover from the frustration of my failed efforts. Through my journey of discovery, I came to realize that I am not gifted to do youth ministry. The process of elimination has helped me discover a lot of things—worship leading, plumbing, auto mechanics, etc.—besides youth ministry that I *should not* be doing with my life.

Do you want to be energized in your walk with God? Discover what God has given *you* the grace to do. Whether we serve the homeless, share the gospel with a neighbor, or work in the church nursery, we receive a supernatural impartation of life when we serve in obedience to God. When Jesus reached out to the Samaritan woman at the well, His disciples were more preoccupied with food than with souls. The Christ's response? "My food is to do the will of Him who sent Me and to accomplish His work" (John 4:34). What is God's work? It is the work that *He* calls each of us to do (John 5:19).

Recently, a number of prison ministries have begun using some of our resources to work with inmates. With a background in college ministry, prison ministry was not something I ever seriously considered. Not long ago, I attended a prison ministry conference put together by a friend. While I loved the experience and highly value what he is doing, I didn't sense God's leading to begin weekly prison visitations. I want to be better equipped to help resource their ministry efforts, but I don't feel obligated to do the work to which God has called others.

Jesus calls His ambassadors to *network* together to meet the pressing needs of this world. No one person or local congregation can possibly do all that needs to be done. This can be a bitter pill for a merciful and generous person to accept. Doing the "nice" thing isn't always the most loving course of action.

One of the keys to living freely by the Holy Spirit's leading—as opposed to being bound by one's conscience—lies in developing the courage to say "no" when asked to do things you know you shouldn't be doing. My conscience often nags at me, compelling me to meet virtually *every* need that comes my way. Making the decision not to dive into prison ministry, for example, wasn't very conscience-friendly. I am not God, however, and my shoulders are too weak to bear the weight of the entire human condition.

Not only might our consciences cry foul, so might people who expect—and sometimes even demand—us to meet their needs. Added to the vast array of human needs is the harsh reality that people often expect the benefits of the New Covenant without being willing to live according to the design of the New Covenant. For example, the idea that someone not connected with a local congregation would like a church wedding may be touching, but should a pastor be expected to expend precious time, energy, and resources for those who want nothing to do with the covenant body of Christ? Church leaders may see such an event as an outreach opportunity—which is fine—but they should feel no obligation to accommodate these types of requests. The following story helps to further explain what I am trying to communicate:

> There is an old story about a lighthouse keeper who worked on a rocky stretch of coastline. Once a month he would receive a new supply of oil to keep the light burning so that ships could safely sail near the rocky coast. One night, though, a woman from a nearby village came and begged him for some oil to keep her family warm. Another time a father asked for some to use in his lamp. Another man needed to lubricate a wheel. Since all the requests seemed legitimate, the lighthouse keeper tried to please everyone and grant the requests of all.
>
> Toward the end of the month, he noticed his supply of oil was dangerously low. Soon it was gone, and one night the light on the lighthouse went out. As a result, that evening several ships were wrecked and countless lives were lost. When the authorities investigated, the man was very apologetic. He told them he was just trying to be helpful with the oil. Their reply to his excuses, however, was simple and to the point: "You were given oil for one purpose, and one purpose only—to keep that light burning!"
>
> A church faces a similar commission. There is no end to the demands placed on a church's time and resources. As a result, the foundational purposes of a church must remain supreme.[45]

It is sometimes difficult for people to grasp the fact that I am a minister but don't do counseling. Doing what He has called me to do often means not doing what others expect me to do. It always pains me to say, "I can't help you," but I've learned to say it nonetheless. My Lord has given me a message to communicate and a manner in which to convey it. I'd better be about my Father's business.

---

45. James Emory White, *Rethinking the Church: A Challenge to Creative Redesign in an Age of Transition* (Grand Rapids, MI: Baker Books, 1997, 2003), 27-28.

I'm not suggesting that we should hyper-spiritualize everything—sometimes we just need to roll up our sleeves and help when a need presents itself. The bulk of our service, though, should be characterized by what the head of the church calls us to—not by the expectations of others, or even our own selves.

Each person's call to service is *unique*, but it is not *individualistic*. There are many parts to the body of Christ, and each plays a vital role through its connection to the other parts. For the church to function properly, we need greeters, nursery workers, teachers, ushers, worship leaders, etc. If we're all living in obedience to our leader, He will bring all of the parts together like a grand symphony. In the end, needs will be met, lives will be changed, and the kingdom of God will be advanced. The symphony, however, will be a disaster if we don't garner the courage to say *yes* and *no* at the direction of the conductor.

PREPARING OURSELVES FOR FRUITFUL SERVICE

There is no one key factor for effective service to God. A personal relationship with Him, is of course, necessary but that is only the start. Growing in the likeness of Christ—as has been emphasized in this book—should also be considered non-negotiable. Still other aspects of service are worthy of our focus.

COMPETENCY

I don't lead worship and I don't work with middle-school kids because I would be incompetent in those areas no matter how hard I tried. In the end, everyone would be frustrated. At least part of God's leading for our service should flow from the things that He has given us the ability to do. I picked up a great motto from the old television series, *Alf:* "Find out what you don't do well and don't do it." Alf's wisdom has its limits, but it does make sense as a general rule.

Those who wish to serve effectively must learn to serve *competently*. Spiritual fruit is borne out of relationship; fruitfulness is multiplied by talents, gifts, and hard work. I teach because God has called and gifted me to teach, but I also expend a lot of time and effort to develop teaching materials. If I want to serve God effectively, I must learn to serve Him competently—at least to a reasonable degree. This being said, we must be willing to obey the clear leading of the Holy Spirit even when we don't feel competent.

IDENTITY

Once again, we find ourselves face to face with the issues of ego and law-based living. A person's identity is established through a covenant relationship with God, not through ministry success. All too often, however, we marry identity and service in an unhealthy manner.

Within about a month of becoming a Christian, I knew I was called to a career in Christian ministry. In my small world, that meant one of three positions: senior pastor, youth pastor, or missionary. My experience was limited and I couldn't see it any other way. After intense prayer, I sensed I wasn't called to missions, and my experience with the church youth group confirmed that I wasn't called to be a youth pastor. I expected, by default, that I would one day become the senior pastor of a church.

My identity was so wrapped up in my idea of ministry that I was devastated when God closed the doors for me to attend seminary. It took a long time to come to grips with the situation and to fully learn that my ministry will never form the basis of my identity. Ministry is simply a matter of how my sovereign Lord chooses to use me; identity is who I am.

Not only will insecurity corrupt the work that God calls us to do, it will breed unnecessary pain and frustration by compelling us to pursue avenues of service for which we are not gifted. Only as God frees us from a quest for law-based significance can we be free to serve Him in ways that may not be popular—or even valued. How I wish every young Christian could grasp the extreme importance of securing his or her identity as a covenant child of the King of kings and Lord of lords. If you want to prepare yourself for effective service to God, ask Him to help you discover your true identity.

SIMPLICITY

It is essential for ambassadors to focus on their assigned duties. If we lack a focused vision, we become *reactionaries* who follow their emotions over God's guidance. We also increase our tendency to become entangled with the things of this world. In the end, nothing of lasting significance will be accomplished.

Those who desire to bear sweet and abundant fruit must learn the painful—and sometimes confusing—art of *pruning*. We all understand the need to remove the "dead wood"—those things that weigh us down without providing any real value—from our lives. For instance, too much emphasis on being entertained will squander valuable time.

Sometimes, however, God will call us to walk away from—or He will remove—even good, life-giving things. To illustrate, when I grow tomato plants, I commonly remove new sprouts that some people call *suckers*. The root system of a plant has limited means, so if there are too many fruit-bearing branches, the tomatoes will be small and of poor quality. Pruning helps to concentrate the life of the plant so that it can be translated into the maximum production of fruit.

Those who grow things understand both the necessity and power of pruning. As counter-productive as pruning may appear, it dramatically increases fruitfulness in the long term. Today's growth is sacrificed for the sake of even greater growth tomorrow. As is often the case, the natural process of pruning echoes a greater supernatural reality. We are finite individuals, limited by time and space. We can't have it all, and we can't do it all—a reality that we prefer not to face. If we truly want to be fruitful, we need to be willing to cut out activities, possessions, and even relationships.

Also, we must note that pruning should result from the *Holy Spirit's* leading—not from a guilt-ridden conscience. I've always enjoyed a variety of activities, but eventually realized that I was trying to do too much. Knowing the importance of ministry, I felt the pressure to drop *all* of my hobbies. That, I learned, was a bad idea. Eventually, I gave up woodworking, but I continued to garden, hunt, and fish. When these activities are kept in their proper perspective, they contribute to my emotional health and help me to be *more* productive—and, therefore, fruitful—in my ministry efforts. Like I heard an Amish farmer once say in a bait store, "I go fishing because it helps me work better."

MONEY

How often have you wanted to give to a worthy cause, but lacked the finances to do so? More than once, I've encountered a person who desperately wanted to step out in service to God, but, due to considerable debt, was unable to do so. Putting our finances in order is another practical way that we can prepare ourselves for God's service.

Several years before I made the jump into Christian ministry as a career, Debi and I began to give more serious attention to our finances. Sensing that we would be sacrificing a considerable amount of income, we sought to prepare our household for the challenges ahead. Although already budgeting, we began to take extra steps to pay off our debts. Looking back, I can see it was one of the smartest things we could have done. There is no way that we would have been able to continue on our ministry journey had we not paid down our debts and learned how to live more frugally.

Debi and I also made the decision to put giving at the top of our budget. We want our lives to be characterized by giving and not consuming. Even when our financial situation seems daunting, we continue to prayerfully give to our church and to other ministries. We can't give what we don't have, though, so none of this happens without deliberate, prayerful effort and long-term attention to self-discipline.

For spiritual people who seek to advance God's kingdom, dealing with finances can seem like a frustrating waste of effort. Such is definitely not the case! I discovered years ago that the very same virtues—self-control, faith, generosity, prayerful decision making, etc.—that enable us to manage money well also affect our ability to advance God's kingdom purposes. Show me a person who handles money in a godly manner, and I will show you a person who can be an effective ambassador in serving God's government. Taking the time and effort to set your financial house in order will pay off in multiple ways over the long term.

CAN I REALLY MAKE A DIFFERENCE?

Fruitful service to God, as you can see, requires a great deal of patience (another essential fruit of the Holy Spirit). Perhaps, like me, you have been plagued with doubts about your ability to make a difference in this world. Perhaps you are too broken, too judgmental, too fat, or too whatever. Perhaps your focus has been on highly-gifted, perfect-looking televangelists who seem like they have it all together. Deep down, you might feel that Heaven smiled on them at birth, while you were forgotten in a dark corner. Let's settle something—not one of us is sufficient within ourselves to do *anything* to advance God's purposes. Not one!

Moses, one of the greatest heroes of the faith, felt like he was an abject failure. Abraham was a liar, David a murderous adulterer, and the "great" apostle Paul a violent persecutor of God's people. Don't you see it? The failures of these men became seedbeds for humility, which then led to amazingly fruitful lives.

Your calling is not really *your* calling. It's *God's* calling upon your life. If you are a covenant child of God who has been purchased with the blood of Christ, you don't really have a right to refuse Him. All you can do is keep moving forward, step by step, from faith to faith. If you are willing, He will meet you with each faltering step. It may take years for the fruit of your life to fully mature, but it will. If not in this generation, then in the next.

The beauty of grace is that being used by God is not so much about us as it is about Him. Our part is to yield, to trust, to learn to abide, and to position ourselves for Him to use us. It's never a perfect process. But, somehow, out of the twisted chaos of our broken, imperfect lives, God is able to accomplish unimaginable things (1 Corinthians 2:9 and Ephesians 3:14-21). This is *The Divine Progression of Grace*. And, we will soon see, even those with little or no natural ability can learn to draw upon the supernatural empowerment of God's amazing grace.

BLAZING A TRAIL TO FRUITFUL LIVING

The blessing of spiritual fruitfulness comes to those who, by God's leading, serve to bless others. Let us deliberately prepare ourselves so that we may be useful in our Master's hands.

CHAPTER TWENTY-ONE
EMPOWERED TO SERVE

In the days of those kings the God of heaven will set up a kingdom which will never be destroyed, and that kingdom will not be left for another people; it will crush and put an end to all these kingdoms, but it will itself endure forever.

Daniel 2:44

If the Holy Spirit was withdrawn from the church today, 95 percent of what we do would go on and no one would know the difference. If the Holy Spirit had been withdrawn from the New Testament church, 95 percent of what they did would stop, and everybody would know the difference.

—A.W. Tozer

The atmosphere of the room was electric—even though electricity had not yet been discovered![46] At the Lord's command, Peter and the other disciples had gathered for a meeting. The past three years—and especially the past few weeks had been a roller coaster (not invented yet either) ride of emotions. Being with Jesus had taken them to the highest of heights and into the lowest of depths.

Heart pounding, Peter unconsciously crept toward the edge of his seat. A quick glance around the room confirmed that the other disciples were anticipating the same announcement. For the past forty days, Jesus had proclaimed the glories of His eternal kingdom. Surely, this would be the day for the Messiah to finally reveal His strategy for throwing off

---

46. I've taken a few artistic liberties to describe how Peter may have felt during some of the experiences recorded in Acts 1-2.

the yoke of Roman oppression. Surely, this would be the day in which God's long awaited kingdom would be established in Israel.

Peter's sense of anticipation was further heightened by a twinge of nervousness. One thing was certain—with Jesus, the unexpected was to be expected. What Jesus said next, though, seemed like a major letdown.

> *Gathering them together, He commanded them not to leave Jerusalem, but to wait for what the Father had promised, "Which,"He said, "you heard of from Me; for John baptized with water, but you will be baptized with the Holy Spirit not many days from now." Acts 1:4-5*

Really? The long awaited answer was to wait even longer? Almost simultaneously, several of the disciples blurted out, "Lord, is it at *this time* You are restoring the kingdom to Israel?" The Messiah's response?

> *"It is not for you to know times or epochs which the Father has fixed by His own authority; but you will receive **power** when the Holy Spirit has come upon you; and you shall be My witnesses both in Jerusalem, and in all Judea and Samaria, and even to the remotest part of the earth" Acts 1:6-8 (emphasis added).*

As Peter racked His brain to process the Teacher's words, Jesus suddenly began to rise into the air. The Son of Man didn't merely stand to His feet; He literally rose into the sky. Then, in an instant, He was gone! Three years together through thick and thin and now, without warning, the upsetter of money tables had mysteriously ascended into the clouds. Now what?

The rest of the day remained a blur in Peter's memory as he again found his comprehension stretched beyond its limits. Were those two men—the ones with the ultra-white robes who had mysteriously appeared—really angels? Perhaps that was the plan. Jesus would send back the Holy Spirit along with a few thousand angels to overthrow the dreadful Romans.

Peter couldn't be sure, but one thing was certain—they needed to do what the Master commanded. Time after time, Jesus had proven Himself true to His word. Peter, for his part, would not fail his Savior again.

THE DAY OF PENTECOST

Several weeks after the Messiah's crucifixion and subsequent resurrection, Jerusalem remained unsettled. The Father's plans were still a mystery so the best course of action would be to stay together and pray while maintaining a low profile. Sooner or later, Jesus would make a move, and they wanted to be ready when it happened.

On the day of Pentecost, Peter finished breakfast and gathered the group to pray. Without notice, the entire room began to vibrate. As a wry smile formed on his lips, Peter glanced over at his brother Andrew. Suddenly, a violent, rushing wind came out of nowhere. Peter's smile vanished and his eyes widened as strange tongues of fire appeared above all of their heads. Peter closed and reopened his disbelieving eyes. No, it wasn't his vivid imagination. Perhaps this would be his "Moses experience"—fire without heat or pain!

Just as Peter struggled to grasp the meaning of the flames, a tingling warmth began to pour over his head and down through his body. It was like being immersed in liquid love and joy at the same time. Peter began to joyously praise God, but He couldn't believe the mysterious words flowing seamlessly from His mouth; they certainly weren't his native Aramaic—or even the common Greek.

Suddenly, in the midst of the most intense spiritual experience of his life, the Christ's teachings about the kingdom began to flood Peter's mind. Then he got it—Peter finally understood! The reality that he had struggled to grasp over the past three years had, in an instant, become crystal clear. The kingdom had nothing to do with armies and governments. God was going to advance His reign on earth through *the anointing of the Holy Spirit*. Boldly, Peter rose to his feet to address the large crowd of onlookers that had begun to gather . . .

Christians traditionally celebrate the experience recorded in Acts 2 as the birth of the church. It was then, through the Holy Spirit of grace, that God began to empower His people to advance His kingdom on this earth. Filled with, and empowered by, the very presence of God, the nascent church began to liberate countless souls who had been bound by darkness. It was all very chaotic at times because evil forces do no yield easily to good, nor does broken and sinful flesh always respond calmly to the work of the Holy Spirit.

GOD'S PLAN

I have already gone to significant lengths to emphasize the importance of abiding in God's transformational grace—of learning to disengage the flesh and facilitate the growth of spiritual fruit in our hearts. There remains, however, another dimension of grace that plays a significant role in fruitful living—God's *empowering grace* as poured out upon His people.

A change of covenant took place between the Old and the New, but there has been no change since—at least not on God's part. If anything has changed, it is that God's own people have limited the scope of the work that the eternal King wants to do in and through them.

Christ did not return as quickly as was expected and, once again, God had thrown His followers a curve ball of sorts by failing to do what was expected. Though the church remained vibrant for many years, the fervor of God's people eventually began to fade. Kingdom leadership became corrupted by political maneuvering, vibrant prayer was replaced with endless wrangling, and spiritual gifts were passively forgotten in favor of natural talents and abilities. God continued to work in spite of the missing vitality, but clearly, something had been lost.

When I am struggling, I often find it helpful to go back to the time when I was doing well and to follow the track to my "derailment." Generally, I acted selfishly or with unbelief as I failed to respond to a particular difficulty in a way that honors God. Regardless of the exact nature of my circumstances, the same general principles always seem to apply.

When it comes to the vitality of the church, we can study the teachings and experiences of Christ and His disciples in an effort to understand how God intends to work through people. By recognizing where our forefathers erred, we can make changes in an effort to renew the vitality of our faith and the fruitfulness of our service. Picking up where the early church left off, so to speak, we can see the dynamic work of God take place *in our day*.

Be forewarned, however! God's empowerment is a kingdom issue, and so it will always involve conflict and controversy as the powers of darkness seek to maintain their iron-like death grip upon this world.

THE GOD OF THE UNEXPECTED

A first step to understanding God's empowerment of His people involves looking at how our Lord began His New Covenant work—and through whom. In bringing Heaven's life to earth, the Almighty either bypassed the "elite"—as with Jewish and Roman leaders—or humbled them—as with Paul. Law-based pride has always been humanity's downfall and so God chose to work in humble ways and through humble people. With the Creator of the Universe, the unexpected is to be expected.

The coming of God's kingdom was announced by John the Baptist—a loner of sorts with no significant pedigree—to common people in the Judean wilderness. The announcement "should" have been made in the Jewish temple or, at the very least, in Jerusalem.

Jesus then came into this world under questionable circumstances—was the Messiah born out of wedlock? His father was a laborer, not a priest or government official, and His birth took place in a stable of all places. Sure, angels proclaimed His birth, but to whom? Common shepherds. Jesus then grew up in the nowhere town of Nazareth. With God, expect the unexpected.

Jesus followed the Jewish pattern of training disciples, yet He chose *ordinary* men; Christ's disciples were neither educated nor spiritually elite. Even the greatest of Israel's spiritual leaders couldn't grasp why the Messiah allowed Himself to be beaten and crucified in His quest to vanquish the power of evil. Subsequently, Jesus rose from the grave and conquered the power of death. Finally, instead of staying around to set up an earthly kingdom, the Son of God mysteriously ascended to the heavens. Rather than triumphantly returning with a host of angels, Jesus followed through with the Father's promises by *baptizing* His disciples with the Holy Spirit. The experience created quite the spectacle as Christ's followers were filled with a divine unction to speak in languages that they had not learned. Did anyone see that coming? The ways of the expected One were unexpected.

THREE PRINCIPLES; THREE MYTHS

In light of our current topic, as we look at the manner in which God worked in New Testament times, three key universal principles emerge:

1. **The kingdom of God is spiritual in nature.**

2. **Our wise and loving Creator will go to great lengths to avoid human elitism, choosing instead to work through humble people.**

3. **The sovereign King of Heaven will not be controlled by human expectations.**

By understanding the foundational manner in which God has always operated, currently operates, and will continue to operate, we can catch a glimpse of how He chooses to work in our day and time. What emerges is the realization that we have made three significant errors as we have sought to advance the cause of the gospel. The unfortunate result is three ministry myths:

1. **Christ's disciples were of a special caliber, handpicked because of their unique potential.**

2. **God no longer uses the Holy Spirit to empower people in the same manner that He did the early church.**

3. **A person's spirituality serves as a badge of honor by which that individual is validated.**

There is not an exact correlation between our three universal principles and our three myths; instead, they are inherently intertwined. Rather than proceed point by point, I will touch on each issue by examining the progressive work of the Spirit in the early church and then showing how the Spirit's work integrates into our current times.

THE HOLY SPIRIT'S PROGRESSIVE WORK

The advent of God's kingdom on earth begins with the life of one man— Jesus Christ. It is essential to note that the Messiah—i.e. the anointed one—ministered not as the Almighty Son of God, but rather as the *Son of Man* filled with an unlimited measure of God's Spirit. This is not to say that Jesus wasn't the Son of God, but that the Messiah was *functioning* as the Son of Man. Christ's nature was divine, but in taking finite human form, He laid aside many of His divine abilities. Jesus, for example, was not all-knowing (Matthew 24:36). Because He was sinless, however, the Son of Man had an *unimpeded* connection to the Father and was filled with the presence of the Holy Spirit without measure.

The Scriptures provide us with no evidence that Jesus Christ ever performed a miracle before His water baptism—when the Holy Spirit alighted on Him as a dove—at the age of thirty. Then, after forty-days of fasting, testing, and temptation, Jesus began His ministry in earnest.

> *"You know of Jesus of Nazareth, how God anointed Him with the Holy Spirit and with power, and how He went about doing good and healing all who were oppressed by the devil, for God was with Him." Acts 10:38*

Do you see it? Jesus was the Messiah—the Anointed One—who initiated the advancement of God's kingdom on earth. There are probably many reasons that Jesus chose to minister in the manner that He did, but near the top of the list had to be the issues of *dominion* and *pride*. God had given dominion of the earth to mankind (Genesis 1:28 and Psalms 115:16), and through a man He would reclaim it. Furthermore, it was pride that derailed Lucifer, a third of the angels, and the human race. As the Son of Man, Jesus overcame every prideful temptation and lived in perfect humility. The One who deserved the most *willingly* became the least.

The kingdom of God on earth began with *one* individual who, empowered by the Holy Spirit, healed the sick and cast out demons:

> *Jesus was going throughout all Galilee, teaching in their synagogues and proclaiming the gospel of the kingdom, and healing every kind of disease and every kind of sickness among the people. Matthew 4:23*

Interestingly, Jesus could have gone to the cross as a sacrifice for our sins at any time. Instead, He chose to minister among the people for about three years. This was partly to announce the coming of the kingdom, but something else was in play. *Twelve* disciples were chosen and trained to serve through the anointing of the very same Spirit that was upon the Christ:

> *And He called the* **twelve** *together, and gave them power and authority over all the demons and to heal diseases. And He sent them out to proclaim the kingdom of God and to perform healing. Luke 9:1-2 (emphasis added)*

What began with one soon involved twelve, but the progression did not stop there:

> *Now after this the Lord appointed* **seventy** *others, and sent them in pairs ahead of Him to every city and place where He Himself was going to come. And He was saying to them, "The harvest is plentiful, but the laborers are few; therefore beseech the Lord of the harvest to send out laborers into His harvest. Go; behold, I send you out as lambs in the midst of wolves." Luke 10:1-3 (emphasis added)*

> *"Whatever city you enter and they receive you, eat what is set before you; and* **heal those in it who are sick, and say to them, 'The kingdom of God has come near to you.'"** *Luke 10:8-9 (emphasis added)*

Here, Jesus used *seventy* "nameless" individuals to advance His kingdom according to His pre-established pattern. Do you see it? Our human tendency is to elevate Christ's disciples as though they were an elite breed of spiritual human never to be duplicated, but such a mindset completely conflicts with how God works. The magnificent thing about the disciples is not that they were a group of elite individuals, but that *they weren't*. God's glory was revealed through the anointing of the Holy Spirit as He used ordinary men in extraordinary ways.

> *The seventy returned with joy, saying, "Lord, even the demons are subject to us in Your name." And He said to them, "I was watching Satan fall from heaven like lightning. Behold, I have given you authority to tread on serpents and scorpions, and over all the power of the enemy, and nothing will injure you. Nevertheless do not rejoice in this, that the spirits are subject to you, but rejoice that your names are recorded in heaven."*

At that very time He rejoiced greatly in the Holy Spirit, and said, "I praise You, O Father, Lord of heaven and earth, that You have hidden these things from the wise and intelligent and have revealed them to infants. Yes, Father, for this way was well-pleasing in Your sight. All things have been handed over to Me by My Father . . ."
Luke 10:17-22a

The progression is clear—the heavenly Father handed power and authority over to Jesus. Jesus then did the same with His followers— and not just the original twelve disciples. Afterwards, He sent out seventy others to strike down darkness and advance the kingdom of light so that people could be delivered, healed, and set free. The "wise and intelligent" were the elite. These people were commoners—the very ones despised by the high-minded.

It's been said that our Lord's one prayer request can be found in Luke 10:2:

And He was saying to them, "The harvest is plentiful, but the laborers are few; therefore beseech the Lord of the harvest to send out laborers into His harvest."

How often do we quote this passage out of context in our efforts to motivate Christians to reach those outside of the New Covenant? God does indeed want us to reach out to others, not in our own strength, but through the empowerment of His Holy Spirit. The arrival of Pentecost brought the fulfillment of the progression that God had sought all along.

Through the cross of Christ, sinful men and women can be cleansed of their sins and born from above. Not only will the Holy Spirit then dwell in our hearts, He wants to empower us with His supernatural presence and power. When Peter arose to address the growing crowd on the day of Pentecost, this is how he started:

"Men of Judea and all you who live in Jerusalem, let this be known to you and give heed to my words. For these men are not drunk, as you suppose, for it is only the third hour of the day; but this is what was spoken of through the prophet Joel:

'AND IT SHALL BE IN THE LAST DAYS,' God says, 'THAT I WILL POUR FORTH OF MY SPIRIT ON ALL MANKIND; AND YOUR

SONS AND YOUR DAUGHTERS SHALL PROPHESY, AND YOUR YOUNG MEN SHALL SEE VISIONS, AND YOUR OLD MEN SHALL DREAM DREAMS; EVEN ON MY BONDSLAVES, BOTH MEN AND WOMEN, I WILL IN THOSE DAYS POUR FORTH OF MY SPIRIT and they shall prophesy.'" Acts 2:14b-18

Peter went on to explain that the empowerment of the Holy Spirit was intended for *all* of God's people and not simply for an elite few:

*Now when they heard this, they were pierced to the heart, and said to Peter and the rest of the apostles, "Brethren, what shall we do?" Peter said to them, "Repent, and each of you be baptized in the name of Jesus Christ for the forgiveness of your sins; and you will receive the gift of the Holy Spirit. **For the promise is for you and your children and for all who are far off, as many as the Lord our God will call to Himself.**" Acts 2:37-39 (emphasis added)*

The work of the Holy Spirit is progressive in the sense that He seeks to fill and use men and women of every race, nationality, and background. I am not suggesting that every Christian will be endued with a vast array of "superpowers" but that the Holy Spirit will supernaturally empower those who believe as He chooses to empower them (1 Corinthians 12:11).

Sadly, many Christians treat the presence of the Holy Spirit as they do communion juice—a tiny amount is doled out because a *representation* of Christ is all that is wanted. This mindset effectively closes the door to the ministry of the Holy Spirit.

GRACE GIFTS

While the New Testament employs the word *charis* for grace, a similar word, *charisma*, is most often translated as "gift." In a few contexts, charisma refers to the free gift of salvation (Romans 5:15-16 and 6:23). More often, charisma refers to *a supernatural impartation of spiritual* (Romans 12:6; 1 Corinthians 12:4, 9, 28, 30, 31; 1 Timothy 4:14; 2 Timothy 1:6).

The recognition that God's grace is intended to empower ordinary people brings us back to the multifaceted nature of grace:

As each one has received a special gift [charisma], employ it in serving one another as good stewards of the manifold grace of God.
1 Peter 4:10

This wasn't a message from an elite apostle to an elite group of leaders. This is a message from a former fisherman—who experienced an extraordinary empowerment by the Holy Spirit—to a group of commoners.

By the personal and intimate work of the Holy Spirit of grace, ordinary people can be used by God in extraordinary ways. Without that anointing, however, "effective" ministry becomes the work of an elite few who speak with golden tongues and sing like angels. All that remains, then, is for the rest of us to applaud—and finance—the efforts of ministry superstars.

Spiritual gifts are *grace gifts* from God intended to empower and equip ordinary people to effectively advance His kingdom on earth. The kingdom of God is spiritual in nature, and so it must be advanced primarily by spiritual means. We make a huge mistake—and depart from God's design—when we rely solely on natural and creative measures to advance the cause of the gospel. Worse still, we limit effective ministry only to those who are educated and/or possess certain natural abilities.

Sadly, the church has adopted the world's definition of *charisma*; it no longer embodies a supernatural impartation of empowering grace, but rather a *natural* ability to speak and relate to people in dynamic ways. These abilities may be both God-given and impressive, even while the supernatural empowerment of grace remains absent.

MODERN CONTROVERSY

Today, controversy swirls in the church between two opposing evangelical camps—both of which have valid points, and both of which make painful errors. The first camp involves a group of Christians who are often called "cessationists," meaning that they believe the Holy Spirit has ceased giving "miracle" gifts to His people. Those from the second group are generally identified as "continuationists" because they believe that God continues to empower His people with spiritual gifts just as He did on the day of Pentecost.

The fact that I belong to the continuationist camp does not mean that I don't have any criticism of its practices. Through their focus on the empowerment of the Holy Spirit, many continualists have virtually ignored the transformational dimension of grace. In other words, they've sought for power while neglecting to emphasize the huge importance of godly character.

It is my opinion that cessationists have a very weak scriptural argument for their position. Nowhere does the Bible teach that spiritual gifts were intended only for the early church. Various arguments are proposed, but all involve either speculation or an incomplete reading of the Scriptures. I'll respond to four of the more common arguments:

1. **"Miraculous spiritual gifts were given only to help 'jump start' the early church."** While spiritual gifts certainly did help get the early church off of the ground, the advancement of God's kingdom still remains a spiritual matter.

    In addition, grace gifts are to be employed as a means to more effectively love others. Jesus didn't simply heal people in order to announce that He was the Messiah—Jesus healed people because He loves people (Matthew 9:36, 14:14). And while we may have difficulty accessing His healing virtue—at least partly due to unbelief as the result of teaching against healing—our God continues to care about our physical and emotional well-being.

2. **"We cannot use our personal experiences as the basis for our theology."** This argument is often used to refute someone who might say, "I am a Christian and I speak with other tongues. What do you do with that?" Interestingly, cessationists will often argue from their *lack* of experience. Someone may well reason, "I am a devoted Christian and God answers my prayers, but I have never spoken in tongues. Tongues, therefore, must not be for today."

    Spiritual gifts are released and received through faith. In my experience, most people who speak in tongues pursued the gift because they believed what they read in the New Testament. If faith is lacking, a person will not receive the empowerment that comes through any of the spiritual gifts. If we teach that God no longer gives miraculous gifts, should we be surprised when He fails to move miraculously in our midst?

3. **"The Bible, in 1 Corinthians 13:8-12, teaches that certain spiritual gifts will cease."** To arrive at this conclusion, a person must take Scripture out of context and make an erroneous assumption.

Love never fails; but if there are gifts of prophecy, they will be done away; if there are tongues, they will cease; if there is knowledge, it will be done away. For we know in part and we prophesy in part; but when the perfect comes, the partial will be done away. When I was a child, I used to speak like a child, think like a child, reason like a child; when I became a man, I did away with childish things. For now we see in a mirror dimly, but then face to face; now I know in part, but then I will know fully just as I also have been fully known. 1 Corinthians 13:8-12

I appreciate the fact that cessationists usually put a strong emphasis on objectively interpreting the Bible. Their interpretation of this passage, therefore, baffles me. The "perfect" they say, "refers to the *canonization of the Bible*. When the Bible, as we know it, was completed and officially recognized as the word of God, some of the spiritual gifts became unnecessary and so God ceased giving them." I'm not exacltly sure who gets to choose which gifts are still valid and which ones are not.

Notice, however, that the context of this passage refers to *the return of Christ and the full consummation of His kingdom.* Unless someone claims to have surpassed the relationship Moses had with God, we still, even with the Bible, "see in a mirror dimly." Nor will we look upon Him "face to face" until the kingdom of God arrives in its fullness (Exodus 33:20 and John 1:18). Only then will any of the spiritual gifts become obsolete.

4. **"The apostle Paul's letter to the Ephesians states that there is only one baptism."** Again, context becomes the primary issue.

Therefore I, the prisoner of the Lord, implore you to walk in a manner worthy of the calling with which you have been called, with all humility and gentleness, with patience, showing tolerance for one another in love, being diligent to preserve the unity of the Spirit in the bond of peace. There is one body and one Spirit, just as also you were called in one hope of your calling; one Lord, one faith, one baptism, one God and Father of all who is over all and through all and in all. Ephesians 4:1-6

The context of this passage deals with the unity of the Christian faith. As recorded in Acts 1:5, Jesus Himself stated that baptism takes two forms: baptism in water and baptism in the Holy Spirit. Further, this pattern is clearly established throughout the book of Acts.

Confusing the *indwelling* of the Holy Spirit with the *baptism* of the Holy Spirit is a huge mistake. After His resurrection, Jesus breathed on His disciples that they might receive the Holy Spirit (John 20:22), but He still told them to wait and pray for further empowerment (Luke 24:49; Acts 1:4-5). Every believer is a temple of the Holy Spirit, meaning that He dwells in his or her heart. Not every Christian, however, experiences the full immersion in the Spirit which leads to further empowerment. Sadly, many fail to pursue a greater anointing because they are taught that they've already received all that they need.

I could continue along these lines and address other arguments, but that is not the primary purpose of this book. Instead, I am trying to explain *The Divine Progression of Grace*. Through His amazing grace, God saves those who are undeserving and transforms their hearts into the likeness of Christ. As glorious as our salvation may be, the Sovereign Lord of the Universe deeply desires for others to be saved by using His ambassadors to supernaturally advance His kingdom on earth.

To severely limit—on weak theological grounds—the empowering work of God's grace is to play into the hands of the devil. The human condition will continue to characterize our human experience unless God's supernatural power is brought to bear on its sad state. The miraculous gifts of the Holy Spirit exponentially increase the ability of God's people to bring hope, freedom, and wholeness to our dying world.

GRACE GIFTS ARE UNMERITED

The argument that cessationists seem to use most often against continuationism focuses not on the Scriptures, but on the *lack of character* often displayed by those who embrace spiritual gifts. This argument has significant merit and is worthy of our attention.

To begin, spiritual gifts are *grace* gifts—meaning that they are given without merit. Just as a person need not be of mature character to receive God's free gift of salvation, neither must he or she be of mature character to receive a divine empowerment of grace. This reality presents a significant source of confusion for people from both camps.

Imagine a guy named Bill who has a prophetic gift. God speaks to Bill in mysterious ways, and he often knows things that others don't. As Bill shares prophetic words of comfort, exhortation, and encouragement, people are genuinely blessed. (I have seen this type of thing happen almost more times than I can count.) While attending a church meeting, Jim receives a prophetic word from Bill and is especially touched. It's as though Bill were reading Jim's journal as he shares God's encouragement for a situation that has created heartbreak in the man's household. Later in the evening, Jim runs to the store for milk and notices Bill shoplifting a candy bar. Bewilderment immediately sets in. "How can Bill be a thief and still hear from God? Was the experience real? Maybe Bill made it all up or—even worse—perhaps he has hidden a camera somewhere in my house!" Both confused and concerned, Jim looks for a new church where prophetic ministry is not welcome.

A grace gift is exactly what it sounds like—a *grace gift*; it does not serve as a mark of validation or super-spirituality. Anyone who believes that supernatural gifts are marks of elite spirituality needs to do some serious searching of the Scriptures and of his or her own heart.

Spiritual gifts are received by faith. A person does not have to abide in God's transformational grace—i.e. grow in godly character—in order to receive spiritual empowerment. Furthermore—and this can be especially confusing—God will not withdraw His grace gifts just because a person sinks into a sinful lifestyle (Romans 11:29). Therefore, it falls to us to ensure that we give at least as much attention to the nine fruits of the Spirit as we do to the nine gifts of the Spirit.

WHERE "CESSATION" IS NECESSARY

A Christian can be empowered by grace for ministry, but still live by law in pursuit of social righteousness. Wasn't this one of the primary mistakes made by the Corinthian church? Lacking in a secure identity, the Corinthians began to use spiritual gifts, among other things, as a means of self-validation. Paul's first letter to the Corinthians addressed this problem on several fronts.

Paul chastised the church for its petty identity squabbles and encouraged them to recognize God's blessing on those with little earthly significance. He also emphasized the foundational importance of love as the only godly motivation for seeking and using spiritual gifts. Many of us cherish 1 Corinthians 13 as the "love chapter," but we often fail to incorporate the greater context of this profoundly beautiful passage. Paul was challenging the motives of those who used spiritual gifts for selfish means.

I don't know if the Corinthians ever truly understood what Paul was trying to communicate, but I can say with confidence that many in the continuationist camp do not grasp Paul's intent. Instead, law-based living has created a spiritual circus of sorts. Christian celebrities parade themselves around as though they are God's gift to the church. We are often encouraged to believe that their feet rarely touch the ground through the course of a day. With the ordinary person in awe, these "charismatic" men and women of God embrace high-sounding titles and accumulate great wealth. Obviously, we are led to believe, this is the way that God's blessing always looks.

I can't help but wonder how many sincere and godly cessationists have been alienated from more effective ministry because they've been repulsed by self-absorbed behavior in the continuationist camp. It's nearly impossible to convince celebrity leaders to lay down their pursuit of fame, so it falls upon God's people to exercise the wisdom— and courage—to identify rotten fruit and to stop following and funding those who try to use spiritual gifts to feed their egos. All who wish to see God multiply the fruitfulness of their lives would do well to embrace both the transformational *and* empowering elements of God's grace.

I've seen more than I've wanted to in my thirty-plus years as a Christian. The behavior of some Pentecostals has so disappointed me that I have at times been tempted to turn my back on spiritual gifts. To do so, however, would be to severely limit the advance of God's kingdom. After a lot of searching, I decided to align myself with a group of people who understand the importance of *both* spiritual gifts and spiritual fruit. We are far from perfect, but we at least serve from a solid, hope-filled foundation.

Over time, I've come to realize that character breakdowns on the part of some continuationists make a poor excuse for rejecting spiritual gifts. If we won't accept hypocrisy in the lives of professing Christians as justification for rejecting Christ, neither should we allow corrupt behavior on the part of some people to be a valid excuse for rejecting the full ministry of the Holy Spirit.

THE ESSENCE FOR EMPOWERMENT

I'm not sure that many of us grasp just how good the good news is. Not only can sinful and broken people be cleansed and freed from the dominion of sin, those who are virtual nobodies in the eyes of the world can be used powerfully by their Creator. Think about it: a person with a sordid moral background, no education, social status, or financial wealth, and no innate talents or abilities can be supernaturally empowered by grace to touch the lives of others. God's empowering grace is anti-elitist at its very core!

Several years ago, a few friends of mine took a mission trip to Asia. As they walked near the edge of a forest, they noticed a young man sitting under a tree reading a comic book. God gave one of the guys, Paul, a supernatural *word of knowledge* (1 Corinthians 12:8) about that young man's broken relationship with his father. Stepping out in faith and love, Paul said something like, "Excuse me, my friends and I are Christians, and we've learned that God sometimes speaks to His children. I believe He's telling me that you and your father are at odds."

If the young man had not been sitting on the ground, he probably would have fallen to it. That very morning, he and his father did have a huge argument. Because of that simple word of knowledge, combined with an obedient step of faith, that young man and eight members of His family were transferred from the oppressive domain of darkness into the kingdom of light! This is what spiritual gifts are all about. God still moves miraculously because He still loves people.

All over the world, in places like Africa, Asia, and South America, the church of Jesus Christ is growing rapidly—and not because of short messages and well-equipped creative teams. No, the church is growing rapidly because God's people are being empowered by grace to supernaturally touch the spheres in which they live. However, it's an often messy process that can violate a person's sense of religious order.

Herein lies our challenge—and it's not a small one. Pursuing the freedom of the Spirit does not mean that leaders should allow aggressive people—even if they mean well—to control their meetings, or that they should abandon all sensitivity toward those who lack an understanding of spiritual gifts. Through faith, love, and wisdom, we must surrender control and learn how to govern our ministries in a way that blesses people and advances God's eternal kingdom.

When it comes to being empowered by grace, the essence of *faith expressing itself through love* continues to stand supreme. By faith, we objectively study the Scriptures and conclude that God still gives spiritual grace gifts to His people. Motivated by love, we then actively seek those gifts, receiving them by faith.

By faith, we surrender control to God, accepting whatever good gifts *He* chooses to impart. By love, we gather the courage to value biblical truth over the criticisms of those who disapprove. By faith, we are all made equal in the eyes of God. By love, we each play our part to build up the body of Christ. By faith and love, we step out in obedience as ambassadors of the King to exercise the grace gifts He gives us.

BLAZING A TRAIL TO FRUITFUL LIVING

Our ability to bear sweet and abundant spiritual fruit is multiplied when we place *equal* emphasis on the fruit of the Spirit *and* the grace gifts freely given by God.

CONCLUSION

Men of low degree are only vanity and men of rank are a lie; in the balances they go up; they are together lighter than breath.

Psalms 62:9

A man there was, though some did count him mad, the more he cast away the more he had.

—John Bunyan

Recently, I attended an event in which an employee of NASA talked about the magnificence of the Universe while showing images from the Hubble telescope. It didn't take long for the nerve endings in my brain to begin overheating as he talked about planets, stars, and galaxies.

Some scientists estimate our Milky Way galaxy to be 100,000 light years—about 6,000,000,000,000 miles—in diameter. It's even more mind stretching to realize that the Universe may contain upwards of *7,500 billion* galaxies with more than 100 billion stars in each.

When compared to the magnitude of the Universe, a human life is virtually meaningless, and human pride nothing short of foolish. Thankfully, the story doesn't end with a meaningless existence! The God who created the Universe—and holds it in His hand—also fashioned us in His very own image. Even though Adam and Eve violated their sacred bond with their Creator, He never gave up on the human race.

Through a series of covenants, God drew ever-nearer to sinful humanity. Each new step—like the giving of the Mosaic Law—was intended to move things toward a desired goal. The fateful day came when Jesus, the Son of God, lowered Himself to become the Son of Man. In the process, He paid a horrific price to redeem us from our treasonous pride.

Today, God seeks to dwell in the hearts of people from every nation, tribe, and tongue. He desires to fill each of us with the overflowing life that produces sweet spiritual fruit. In the midst of this earthly chaos, through the rubble of the human condition, God will raise up a truly righteous generation of covenant children who live by faith, abide in grace, and are compelled by love to sacrifice what amounts to nothing for what will one day be realized as everything.

Is it unrealistic to think that the God who spoke the entire Universe into existence is able to establish for Himself a people who are re-created in His image, who worship in Spirit and truth, and who bear a rich harvest of spiritual fruit as the full expression of grace at work in their hearts? Evidently, God seems to think that He is able to accomplish such a feat. Jesus said that He would build His church upon this earth and that the gates of Hades would not prevail against it (Matthew 16:17-19). His life will be released not in church buildings, but in the spiritual temple that is the church—the unified body of Christ.

Our eyes open wide when we see what the King of Glory is able to accomplish—even through our failures. The seeds of this book were planted over twenty years ago when I cried out to God because of my inability to live out my Christian faith. Now, looking back, I can see my heavenly Father's guiding hand at work as I blazed a trail from frustration to fruitfulness.

Though my journey is unique with regard to the details, it is like that of any other Christian in that it follows the same pattern God established with Abraham. He calls each of us out of familiar territory— our comfort zones, if you will—and into the unknown to live by faith. In the process, we each blaze a trail from sinful to godly living. Perhaps the most amazing part of the journey is that, along the way, God uses us to touch our own unique spheres of humanity. It's not about us trying to do great things for God; it's about His amazing grace working in and through us.

In this life, we'll always have the potential to fail. No one ever truly "arrives" as long as we are on this side of Heaven. Failure, though, no longer defines those who become children of God. We are now new creations in Christ. Somehow, through our struggles, the Master Gardener will increase the harvest of spiritual fruit in our hearts, and multiply that fruit in the lives of others.

What a profound opportunity God's grace gives us to participate in His grand design! May He grant us the wisdom to be wise master builders as we seek to live by faith rather than self-sufficiency. May our lives be established, transformed, and empowered by His multifaceted grace as we serve, through one Spirit, to bring life to our dying world. May *The Divine Progression of Grace* run its full course so that we bear a rich harvest of sweet and abundant fruit for God's glory. And finally, may our fruit remain for all eternity!

BLAZING A TRAIL TO FRUITFUL LIVING

Through the progressive work of grace, we are accepted, transformed, and empowered to become agents of change for God's eternal kingdom.

RESOURCES FROM SFME MINISTRIES

Additional copies of *The Divine Progression of Grace* can be purchased through our SfMe Media website (www.sfme.org) and at major online retailers. Volume discounts are also available.

Each of the fifty-two devotional readings in **Champions in the Wilderness** draws from a deep well of truth to help encourage, strengthen, and instruct those who desire to walk with God but are struggling in the face of adversity. The format of *Champions* lends itself well to group discussion.

The Search for Me: A Journey Toward a Rock Solid Identity is a 12-part DVD study that boldly but lovingly touches many of the core issues that influence human behavior. This excellent small group resource does not make for casual interaction as it interweaves the gospel with the issue of personal identity. The effects are multifaceted as participants grow together in faith, renew their love for God, and break free from sin. The audio files of the series are free for streaming from our website for those who would like to review the study before purchasing.

GIVING TO SEARCH FOR ME MINISTRIES

SfMe Ministries burns with a vision to impact our world for Christ, but we need help doing so. We are a faith ministry, meaning that we seek to put our focus on God as our provider and do not aggressively solicit contributions. "Opportunity without pressure" is our motto when it comes to raising the necessary funds to fulfill our vision of forming and equipping a generation of world changers for Christ.

Those whose hearts move them to give financially are more than welcome to join us in advancing God's kingdom. The resources will be put to good use. Also, we do not distribute contact information, nor do we badger our financial partners to give. More information about financial partnership can be found on our ministry website (searchforme.info). SfMe Ministries is an IRS recognized 501(c)(3) non-profit organization. Regardless of whether you feel led to give or not, your prayers for our ministry efforts are always appreciated!